Conversations in the Raw

Books by Rex Reed

Do You Sleep in the Nude?
Conversations in the Raw

Rex Reed

Conversations in the Raw

Dialogues, Monologues, and Selected Short Subjects

THE WORLD PUBLISHING COMPANY
New York and Cleveland

For
Floy Dean,
who knows why

Acknowledgments

The author wishes to thank the editors of *The New York Times, Holiday, Women's Wear Daily, Cosmopolitan, Playbill,* and *This Week* for permission to reprint most of the material in this book the way it was originally written instead of, in some cases, the way it was later published.

Contents

Conversations in the Raw

Bette Davis

"HELLO!"

On an Arctic iceberg or in the middle of Macy's, the voice on the phone could have belonged to only one person. Part Fanny Skeffington and part Margo Channing, but *all* Bette Davis.

"Come on Tuesday. I should have the papers signed by then. What? You're not calling about the mortgage? Oh, the *interview!* Well, I'm a basket case before noon. For years I had to be on the set at dawn, now when I don't work my greatest luxury is sleeping late. So come for lunch. My dear, I'm terribly sorry, I thought you were from the *bank.* My address—now don't laugh—is One Crooked Mile. Just ask anybody. They all know the house."

They did, too. One Westport resident told me it is impossible to go for Sunday drives without seeing the cars lined up to get a peek at her behind the curtains. And I don't blame them. There never has been—and never will be—anyone quite like her. In a business where stars are killed off as fast as Indian extras, she is one of the few genuine legends still left to the imagination. To people like my father, who never go to movies ("Why go, when you can see Bogart and Davis on the late show?") she is one of the only names left on a marquee that doesn't have to be explained. And to legions of kids, discovering the magic of her films all over again, she is zero cool. The whole banana. They go away raving (At her best, she is

11

devastating) or they go away laughing (At her worst, she is merely the best Bette Davis caricature out of all the other stars who've built careers doing Bette Davis caricatures), but they never go away bored. Because Davis is an original in an industry full of stand-ins. Froggy-eyed, lipstick-slashed or glowing like a Tiffany lamp, she is exciting enough, even when photographed through gauze, to make the nubile youth cultists about as interesting as a withered logarithm.

There she stands, in the door of her Connecticut farmhouse, waving her by-now practically petrified cigarette, saying, "Call me Bette or we'll never be friends." Swamp fevers, gunshot wounds, bubonic plague, the deaths of countless lovers, the brain tumor to end all brain tumors, car accidents, shipwrecks, beatings at the hands of the syndicate and suicide on the Chicago train tracks —she has survived them all and, most amazing, the wear doesn't show. "Nobody knows what I look like because I never looked the same way twice." Today, it can be said with all immodesty, she looks sensational. She was wearing tight black-and-white checked wool slacks, loafers, a boy's button-down shirt with the sleeves rolled up and a little gold doggie pinned to her lapel. Her hair is finally back to its natural soft walnut color after Tennessee Williams made her dye it Popsicle orange a few years ago for her Broadway appearance in *Night of the Iguana,* and she wears it exactly as she did when she played twins in *A Stolen Life.* Unlike most star ladies her age, she has never had a face lift, yet she looks younger than any of them. "I could've been lying in bed with maribou feathers, but I decided what the hell, might as well see me exactly as I am. I'll be 61 years old the first week in April of '69 —but don't send flowers—I'll be in bed all day. I only look as old as I feel, and I'm having a ball."

Lunch was ready. Yankee stew with grits, artichokes (and a lecture on how to cook them), fresh fruit with

kirsch and cornbread sticks "courtesy of Aunt Jemima—
everything else I cooked myself." We ate from old pewter
plates on a big wooden country kitchen table with a revolving lazy susan filled with spices and flowers and the
two things that are never far from wherever she happens
to be, her ashtrays and cigarettes ("If there is any truth
to that cancer rumor, my dear, I've got it already!"). She
talked a blue streak about her children (B.D., 21, who
lives with her husband in nearby Weston; Margo, 18,
a retarded daughter who has been in a special school in
Geneva, New York, since she was three; and Michael, 17,
in his senior year at Loomis, near Hartford), Hollywood
("I was always a Yankee girl at heart—it was never a
cozy town anyway, unless you did the social thing, which
I never did—even at the height of my career, I always
came back East between pictures.") and, most important,
her latest film for Twentieth Century Fox, *The Anniversary*, made in London, in which she makes a real Davis
entrance from the top of a staircase with a scarlet patch
over one eye to the tune of "Anniversary Waltz," celebrates
her husband's death with firecrackers, blackmails one son,
exposes the second as a transvestite, drives the third son's
girl into hysterics by placing a glass eye under her pil-
low, and threatens the life of her daughter-in-law by paying her off each time she has a baby, knowing secretly
she has a heart condition. If you think she's something
with both eyes, wait until you see that one Davis eye
doing the work for two.

"Well," says Bette, "it may not be the greatest movie
ever made, but it's a good old-fashioned Bette Davis movie
and I *do* get the best of everybody in the end. And it was
a challenge. She's a completely non-sequitur woman who
never listens to anything anyone says, like playing a prose-
cuting attorney. The eye patch was absolute torture. I
couldn't get my balance for a month. Then I got all the
light in one eye. The only time I took the damn thing off

was at lunch and it blistered the skin around my eye. But it is most definitely *not* a horror film. I waited two years for a part like this. Let's face it. Nobody is writing scripts for older women. Everything is youth-oriented now. When I was 15 or 20 years younger, I got all of Miss Bankhead's or Miss Barrymore's parts from the stage, but if you want to stay with your profession, you have to stay up with the times. This is the age of horror films. The world is pretty horrible. So I did four or five stinking pieces of crap in a row, like that thing where I played Susan Hayward's mother. I don't even remember the name, but it paid for my daughter's wedding. And I did some Westerns on TV, even though I can't stand all the shooting, but I kept up with the times, which is more than I can say for most of the other dames—and let's face it, there weren't many in our class to begin with. I never did care terribly about my appearance. If my career was different from the other ladies, that had a lot to do with it from the beginning. I could always make myself look different. It was expected of me, and that's why I was offered a lot of smashing parts, because they knew I could do them. Hollywood always wanted me to be pretty, but I fought for realism. Even in *The Catered Affair*, one of the best films I ever made, I made myself look blown-up and flabby by *thinking* fat and covering my arms with white powder. It takes courage to do that in our industry. That's why I went on a p.a. tour after *Baby Jane*—people were so amazed to see I wasn't falling down. I used to hate my face when I was young, but now I'm glad. It's been a blessing. But I never kidded myself into thinking the crap I made was really art in disguise. And I've never seen any of those films. *Whatever Happened to Baby Jane* was a challenge and fun. *Anniversary* was fun. *Hush, Hush, Sweet Charlotte* was fun up to a point, then it became ridiculous. But I always hated the crap, and I was always right. Every now and then it turns up on TV to remind me I didn't fight hard enough. But all that is over now. I'm not rich, but I don't need money as much now as I used to, so I no longer need to make crap. I could've made literally half a million in the last six months just doing vignettes. I won't play vignettes for small salaries. I tried that and they ended up putting my name above the marquee anyway, so I learned my lesson. You want to know what's ruined this business? Actors. They'll walk across the screen for anything, but I'm the only one of those dames who kept her price. My price for putting my name on that marquee is $200,000 and ten percent of the gross and I won't even talk to anybody for anything less because when they see me on the screen they're seeing 37 years of sweat. They pay for my experience and if that loses its importance I might as well get lost. I was offered the lead in *Oh Dad, Poor Dad* and I said if Bette Davis goes Off-Broadway that means the value of everyone else my age goes down. I was offered the mother in *Cool Hand Luke*. Another vignette. Jo Van Fleet played both of those parts, but I wouldn't. I was offered the touring company of *Killing of Sister George,* but I would've been stuck with somebody else's interpretation and staging with no time to make it mine. I was offered the madam in *Everything in the Garden*. Did you see it? If Edward Albee's name hadn't been on it, I wouldn't have believed he had anything to do with it. The biggest disappointment was not getting the film of *Virginia Woolf* or my part in the film of *Iguana*. Those heartbreaks nearly killed me. And I don't really like the stage. The actors you have to work with. Don't get me started on the Actors Studio. There was one actor in *Iguana* who took an entire day to figure out the motivation for taking off his shoe. I finally stood up onstage and yelled, 'Why don't you just take the goddam shoe off? It's just a shoe!' So. I do roles that are star roles in films I can still do for my price, and to do that I have to sometimes do crap, but I'll tell you one thing—

I still know the crap when I see it. I've fought like a bull deer to keep that image flying."

Anyone going to a Bette Davis interview expecting a shocking fan-magazine revelation of the true-life behind-the-scenes scandals during the days when Hollywood movies were the Great American Pastime will be disappointed. She is tough, but she is too much of a lady to be a tattle-tale. Later, after a few Scotches, she may tear loose with a few unprintable sizzlers about everyone from Susan Hayward to Alec Guinness, but she never rats on her friends for publication. "That was the biggest problem writing my book, *The Lonely Life*. It was absolute torture, like going to an analyst. But I wrote it. I disapprove of autobiographies—they mustn't be too modest, mustn't be too conceited, and then there are lots of other people involved too, and you have to know when to name names and when to protect people's reputations. Oh, the things I could've printed about Errol Flynn! But I've always believed in looking ahead, not back, so there were many incidents in my life I had forgotten and I had to haul them out again. But I felt obligated to tell people things they didn't know, not just put together a lot of newspaper and magazine clippings written by someone else, and I felt another obligation to tell people today what it's like going into the fame area. Also, I didn't want to tell so much that my children would have to go into class and have all the other kids say, 'So *that's* what your mother did!' But I must admit I came off worse in that book than anyone else.

"I care more about what my children think than anyone else, and I've always done my best to shield them from being Bette Davis' children. I never had any problems with B.D. She was always much taller and more mature than the other children her age. But Margo, who was a perfectly beautiful, normal baby until she was three, developed a brain defect and I had to place her in an in-

stitution. If you don't think I don't sit around here in this
house crying my eyes out night after night about the
fact that my child is a vegetable, you are out of your
mind. The worst part of it is that she is only half a vegetable. She looks beautiful and acts like a young lady,
but then suddenly something will happen and she will
digress back into the world of a child again. On her last
birthday I took her to New York and really pulled out the
stops—nightclubs, the works—and everybody wanted my
autograph everywhere we went, and then in the car going
home she turned to me and said, 'Mama, can I have your
autograph too?' And you have to laugh and cry at the
same time. That play *Joe Egg* was right. You laugh or
you won't survive the tears in life. She wants a baby and
she talks about nothing but getting married, and it will
never happen. You think that doesn't tear a mother's
heart out? And now the thing that is eating me up inside
is what I'm going to do when I die to protect my children
from taking on that responsibility. I'll never do it to them.
So don't go around thinking Bette Davis lives the life of a
glamorous movie star. My life is anything but roses."

She refilled her glass and led the way through rooms
with fireplaces and antiques and friendly flowers nodding
happily in pots and vases, walls of books, plaques, cita-
tions and awards, lighting her cigarettes by striking big
kitchen matches under the tables and chairs of whatever
room she's in with enough gusto to start another Chicago
Fire. She's not a scrapbook collector ("They only gather
dust"), but there were her two Oscars, primly guarding
the mantel, sharing the smell of nutmeg and cloves with
an orange tree, a Volpi cup sent by her biggest fan, Musso-
lini, the first magazine silver cup ever awarded to a Hollywood movie star ("What does it say? Oh yes, *Redbook*
—oh God, what they started!"), her Emmy award, cita-
tions from the Mexican government for her work in the
illiteracy campaign, a silver cigarette case from Frank

Sinatra, some John F. Kennedy buttons, stuffed ladybugs the child next door rides on, golf clubs ("I played for years until I broke my back"), lamps made out of old milk cans, Sarah Bernhardt ashtrays, a plaque from the Hollywood Canteen ("Not many things I'm proud of in my life—that was one of them").

We curled up in overstuffed easy chairs in front of the fire in a glass room overlooking the snow melting in the Saugatuck River, and she talked some more. "You asked me about success. There's a theatre in Greenwich Village where every time they show *All About Eve* you can't hear one word I say because of this cult that says all my dialogue aloud from memory. Edward Albee told me that. Isn't that spooky? I'd like to go the next time and see that. But that's not success. I wouldn't faint if all the best tables at Sardi's were taken when I got there and I had to take the worst. This was never one of my goals in getting there. Success is something you don't think about until it happens. I was fresh from the stage and I just wanted to work. It took many years of work and sweat to get the other. But during all the getting-there years there was a challenge which young people today don't seem to have. I had to eat, earn a living. That was a reason. I had a five-year plan. I was all prepared to become the best secretary in the world if Hollywood didn't work out in five years. I learned there is no short cut to anything. Now I know my favorite years have been as a mother, and I'm still learning. You should hear them on politics—it's fascinating. At 16, I never knew such a thing existed. I raised my children to condition themselves to accepting my career as part of them. They visited all my sets, knew it was hard work. My home was never an actress' home, I never considered myself special. And now neither of them has any desire to act and I could not be more grateful. B.D. was in *Payment on Demand* as a child and she had a small part in *Baby Jane* because I thought it would be fun for her. She got it out of her system. Any woman is most fortunate if she isn't driven by something she has to prove. To some, it'll be a shock to discover Bette Davis is no longer driven, that she likes living in the country. Puccini! I went to his farm outside Pisa. It was a funny, simple little house. That's the way most of us want to live.

"Today all the fun is gone in making movies. In the old days, we had time to be individuals. You don't even get to know the men on the crews any more and I always knew my crews. How do you think I got all those great camera angles? I was right there behind the camera lining up the shots! In *Anniversary* I was the only American on the set, so when the Fourth of July came I had a jacket of stars and stripes and a top hat made out of the American flag for a big joke and I remember feeling guilty because I was afraid I was taking up 15 minutes of everyone's valuable time. In the old days at Warners we were like a football team—everyone felt important but we still had fun and some of that came through on film. We all had a style. I've tried to answer to myself many times how things changed. I think it's more gimmicky now. If you make a film in Budapest, for God's sake let's see Budapest. Performances used to count for more, films were photographed more in detail. Nobody traveled. I never went on a location in my life except once or twice for a day or two at a time. Everything was created right there on the set and there was a dedication among performers to sell their product. Now those films like *Dark Victory* are considered old-fashioned, but they are still the ones audiences love because they got to know the people onscreen. Today they *cast* films, they don't *write* films. They never say, 'We'll write this for Suzy Glutz,' they buy it and then ask Suzy Glutz if she'll be in it.

"Scripts were developed for stars in my time. Bogey and I made our first one together—an awful little thing called *Bad Sister*—I played the *good* sister, my dear. (Enormous roar.) I always wanted to do a real film with him but in those days one star really had to carry it alone and they were not eager to waste us on each other's properties. So I never worked with Cooper, Gable, Grant—any of the real kings of the screen. They had their films and I had mine. Sometimes we were treated badly and then we'd walk out. Do you know they never recorded 'They're Either Too Young or Too Old,' which I introduced in *Thank Your Lucky Stars*? And I put that song on the top of the Hit Parade. The damn fools. Once I walked out on suspension for nine months and I remember in the last conversation I had with Jack Warner he said, 'Please don't go, Bette, we've got this new book for you called *Gone with the Wind* and I turned around, leaned across his desk, and said, 'Yeah, and I'll just bet it's a *pip!*' I had lunch one day recently in the old Warner's commissary with Olivia de Havilland and I said, 'Oh Livvie, what ghosts there are in this room!' and she said, 'Yeah, and wouldn't you just know we'd outlive them all?' "

I had already missed the early train, so she phoned the market and sat cross-legged on the floor, cooking lamb chops in the open fireplace while her two Oscars frowned down, remembering swankier evenings. "You asked me about mistakes. If I had to do it all over again the only thing I'd change is that I would never get married. But then I wouldn't have my kids and without them I would die. But my biggest problem all my life was men. I never met one yet who could compete with the image the public made out of Bette Davis. You think being a well-bred Yankee girl brought up with a moral sense of right and wrong, it doesn't kill me to admit I was married five times? I am a woman meant for a man. I get very lonely sometimes at night in this big house—there's nothing glamorous about that. But I never found a man who could compete. I sat here two nights ago in my living room all alone and watched a film I made with Gary Merrill while we were married. Same billing, everything. At the end the announcer said, 'Ladies and gentlemen, you've been watching *Phone Call from a Stranger* starring Bette Davis, Shelley Winters and Gary *Davis!!* So help me God. And that's what men had to put up with. And I don't blame the men. I was a good wife. But I don't know any other lady in my category who kept a husband either, unless she married for money or married a secretary-manager type where there was no competition. That's a price I've paid for success, and I've had a lot of it.

"What am I going to do next? I'm going to get into my Mustang and drive to Yale and ask them if they'll hire me as a teacher, because I'm bored and that's the only thing I haven't done yet, and if they will, I'm going to teach those kids how to act without all this Actors Studio crap and all this self-indulgence actors have today. I'll be rough as a cat, but they'll learn discipline, because that's the only way to survive. I survived because I was tougher than everybody else. Joe Mankiewicz always told me, 'Bette, when you die they oughta put only one sentence on your tombstone—*She did it the hard way!* And he was right. And you know something else? It's the only way."

She waved goodbye in the farmhouse door and I could see her silhouette in the moonlight, like the end of *Now Voyager*, lit by the stars and the torch on the tip of her inextinguishable cigarette. Seconds later, on the way to the station in the taxi, the world seemed duller already.

Ruth Gordon

There are a lot of fabulous people in show business, and then there is Ruth Gordon, who is all of them put together. Although it is not possible to write seriously about her in less than 50,000 words (half to describe her properly, half to quote her accurately, and if there's anything left over she'll write it herself), it is as much fun as an old Marx Brothers movie to try. They were trying back in 1915, when she made her stage debut with Maude Adams in *Peter Pan* at the Empire and they've been trying ever since. Whole Ruth Gordon cults were formed by men like Charles Laughton, Thornton Wilder and Alexander Woollcott long before anyone ever heard of jitterbugs or cellophane or dial phones or Adolf Hitler, and today, after 50 years as one of the most fascinating actresses in the English-speaking language, new generations of kids are culting all over again after seeing her play a swinging jet-age witch in *Rosemary's Baby*. "It's a mean, stinkin' thing to say—but all you have to do to become a hit in show business is just hang on, just outlast the others!" Her words, not mine. She ought to know.

Nothing about Ruth Gordon is ordinary. Even her suite at the Algonquin looks like something out of an old Ina Claire movie, crammed with steamer trunks, bulletin boards full of invitations to every major A-list party and opening night in town, typewriters (She's also, in case anyone needs reminding, one of the best writers around), coffee pots and freshly washed cups, the smell of lilacs and fresh rain pouring on the double windows (which are wide open in spite of the air-conditioner, which is turned on full blast and whirring away to beat the band). Flowers abound in every corner as though she tried to bring Santa Monica to Manhattan: peonies, sweet william, two dozen roses, creeping ivy and ten pots of geraniums. And sprinting through the petals and confusion is the lady herself. She'll be 73 in October, 1969. Hell, she doesn't even look 39. Five feet, 103 pounds of laser beam, she cuts through the room like she cuts through her plays and movies. You can't take your eyes off her. She bolts, she darts, she shuffles like they do on the Mississippi levee, in a dainty little-girl Chanel suit with a pleated skirt, white stockings, Mary Jane shoes, a black velvet bow ribbon in her hair, and around her neck some Indian sandalwood hippie beads Mia Farrow brought her from visiting the Maharishi. 73? "*Liss*-en," she says in that legendary voice that sounds like ten baby mouths eating Crackerjacks, "I wanna be in *Hair.* Didja see it? It's terrr-*if*-ic! I was right in there swingin'. Nobody's asked me to be in *Hair* but I bet I could do *some*thin' if I got in there. The theatre is as different today from the way it was when I arrived on the train from Wollaston, Massachusetts, in 1914, as American theatre is from Chinese theatre, but my greatest triumph is that I'm still part of the scene. Whether I have a dollar or whether I'm in debt up to here, you'll never get *me* in no old-folks home!"

She runs around with the cool Ferrari crowd, has a membership at The Factory and does all the hip new rock dances to electric guitar music, and the world of Ruth Gordon's legendary Broadway blends like angel-food icing with the world of Ruth Gordon's swinging Hollywood. After 25 years of being away from the cameras (She was once Mary Todd in *Abe Lincoln in Illinois* and Greta Garbo's secretary in *Two-Faced Woman*) Lotus Land has rediscovered her genius for lighting up movie screens as well as Broadway stages. *"Liss*-en," she says, waddling her bantam rooster walk with one hand on her hip and the other going in and out like a treadmill, "I been an actress, see, since 1915, and damn it, I never got a Tony. What does it mean, I say—what does this mean, what does that mean—but the fact remains I guess I'd like to *have* one. I remember once Armina Marshall called me and asked me to give a Tony to Tyrone Guthrie for directing me in *The Matchmaker* and I said, '*Liss*-en, go screw yourself!' I did that play for 68 weeks and if those damn Tonys are any good at all, *I shoulda had one!* So now maybe I'll win an Oscar, who knows? Edith Evans never won anything either, so I told her, '*Liss*-en, OK. Maybe I don't feel so bad after all.' I never made it in the movies. I dunno, a cog went wrong someplace. You gotta have talent, but you also gotta have *talent* for having talent. Orson Welles never won an Oscar either. Can you believe that? Talent is such a terrific thing—like an octopus grabbin' ya—ya gotta be a spring breeze at four o'clock and a hurricane at five. I don't know which is worse. Failure dims ya down and success kills ya. You'd like to open the door with your drawers on and say thank you, don't bother me, butcha never can."

She thinks *Rosemary's Baby* is the best film she's ever made. "I was in *Dr. Ehrlich's Magic Bullet* in 1940. You weren't even born then. Then after 25 years, I did *Inside Daisy Clover* and *Lord Love a Duck*. They didn't work out right. But now *this* one! I wanted to meet Roman Polanski anyway, because he was young and with it, so when Paramount called, I went to his office and he said, 'Have you heard the Beatles' "Lonely Hearts Club Band" and I said yes and he said, 'Let's listen.' I said, 'But I *own* it,' and he put it on anyway. Well, we had not even met or shook hands, we're sittin' there, see, listenin' to Sergeant Culpepper and I'm thinkin', 'Well, Ruth, here you

are out this time with a real crazy buncha *nuts!*' Then I
thought, '*Aha!* He wants to see how good I *liss*-en!' so I
lissened real good and then Bill Castle, the producer, took
us to lunch and Roman, he is very impatient, see, so he
turns to Castle and says, 'Well, we gonna hire her or
aren't we?' and Castle clears his throat and says, 'Now,
Miss Gordon, did you follow that with *The Three Sisters*
or Nora in *Doll's House?*' Roman had never heard of me
and at the next table were Gene Saks and Walter Matthau
and they kept coming over and throwing their arms around
me and hugging me and I could see Roman had never heard
of *them,* either, but he and I hit if off right away. There
was somethin' there, boy. The name Ruth Gordon meant
nothing to him, but he kept saying, 'Well, we gonna hire
her or aren't we?' So I took him aside and I said, 'Now
look, Roman, you and I obviously love each other, but you
don't know me and you're in a tough spot. You should
see the other people for this part and then make a fair
decision and let me know later.' So three or four weeks
passed and I got the job. What a picture. Usually the
Hollywood slogan is 'I don't want it good, I want it Tues
day.' Not on this one. Every time I looked around someone was shooting over my ear. Roman wanted total realism.
He even brought us to New York for three days after the
film was over to get Tiffany's window in the snow. They
rebuilt a whole replica of the Dakota on an entire sound
stage at Paramount. It brought back memories. The first
time I went there Pauline Heifetz was going with George
Gershwin and there was old Mr. Heifetz and old Mama
Heifetz and Jascha and all that and we all had dinner
and it was like a museum, where all the Heifetzes lived.
The next time I went to a tea party at Mrs. Somerset
Maugham's. I was getting $75 a week then and living
across the street from the Booth on 45th Street in Martin's
theatrical boardinghouse and every night after dinner
everybody sat on the steps and watched folks arrive at the

theatre. I always sat on the top step because on the bottom step whenever a star would arrive you'd get kicked to death in the stampede."

She had arrived in New York against her father's protests, with his New England sea spyglass, which she hocked for $40. That, plus the nickels she swiped from the hairpin trays of the other girls in the boarding house, kept her going on a budget of ten cents a day for food. By 1918, she was a star, playing Lola Pratt in Booth Tarkington's *Seventeen.* In 1921, she had her bow legs broken by a Chicago doctor to straighten them and make her more of a leading lady, but she's been an ingenue ever since. Mia Farrow calls her "my only real hippie friend." "Look at my charm bracelet. Mia gave' it to me." It was a gold baby devil with two ruby eyes, a forked tail and horns. Rosemary's baby born at Tiffany's. "Sayyy, you didn't ask me about Mia. *Liss*-en, I betcha a year from now she'll be the biggest star there is. Mia's 19 going on 90. Deep, really deep. Garson and I took her to this very chic luncheon in Hollywood and after it was over she asked us if we wanted to see her secret oasis. We all changed to sneakers and then drove out to the desert and got lost and finally Mia found the dirt turnoff and we came to this old house with a dirt floor and walls made out of totem poles and this little old man played the piano with every other key missing, but Mia said it was all right, we'd hear the missing notes anyway, and we did. It was really some experience, and when we left we got lost again in the middle of the desert and I wondered were we lost at the fashionable luncheon earlier in the day or were we lost in the peaceful reality of the country? Mia started me thinking about things. I'm getting a button that says 'Stamp Out Reality.' Mia is like Garbo. They are both individuals. People laugh at Garbo, but she's a unique person and there's nothing you can do about it. Cecil Beaton brought her to dinner a year ago and I said to him on the phone, 'Bring her on Thursday' and he called back and said, 'She said how do I know on Monday what I'll want to do on Thursday?' I understood that, so I just said, 'OK, if she comes, we'll just throw on an extra potato.' So on Thursday the door opened and there she was. She looked dazzling and spent most of the evening in the kitchen having a long chat with the cook. Hell, I never heard of French pastry till I got to upper Broadway. My mother used to read all the society columns in Wollaston. The other day Gloria Vanderbilt told me she thought I was a real lady. If my mother ever heard one of the Vanderbilts callin' Ruth Gordon Jones a lady, she'd die."

In Hollywood, Ruth and her husband, director-writer Garson Kanin, live in a cluster of citrus groves and marble statues and sculptured lawns better known to the Beverly Hills social set that can't get past the iron gate as "Merle Oberon's estate." Forget everything else you ever read in *Town and Country*. The most sophisticatedly swinging "in" dinner parties in California take place at the Kanins, where on any given night Ruth's cook might be serving hot boysenberry pie to Kate Hepburn, George Cukor, the Jack Lemmons, the Billy Wilders, Vincente and Denise Minnelli, Natalie Wood, Gregory Peck, Bill and Edie Goetz and Jean Renoir. When they are in New York, they usually hold court at the Algonquin because their own lovely home in Turtle Bay is rented. "We were in California so much and the staff was just sittin' there eating its head off, so we rented it for three years and now we have to live in hotels when we come to town. I love the Algonquin, though. I was here before the famous Round Table got famous. In 1921, I was married to a darling actor named Gregory Kelly and we lived in one room in the back of the hotel so people would see our address and think we were doin' all right. I never had tea with any of that Round Table bunch. I had other fish to fry than sitting around with Wolcott Gibbs and Dorothy Parker. They were people

I could see any time. Kate Hepburn talked us into buying our house with her Connecticut Yankee smartness. We were going to buy somewhere else and she said, 'You can't afford it,' and I said, 'How the hell do *you* know what we can afford?' She talked her next-door neighbors into selling out and we moved in. She was right, the property value has gone sky-high since we moved in. But I really wanted to live right in the middle of Times Square. It was so elegant when I was young, and look at it now. I remember everything and never throw anything away."

She produced a batch of yellowed letters a friend had just sent her from her home town—letters she had written home from 1912 to 1917—"the most awful lies, written during 39 weeks of one-night stands trying to impress everyone"—letters written in parlor cars and hotel rooms in places like Wabash and Osage. Her handwriting hadn't changed a bit in all the intervening years. "*Liss*-en, I went on the stage to meet a lotta swell people and make money. The first swingin' show I ever sneaked off to in Boston was *The Pink Lady* with Hazel Dawn as a wicked siren from Paris with spangles on and pink Bird of Paradise feathers in her hair. All I wanted out of a career was to look like Hazel Dawn and wear pink feathers. Somewhere along the route, I learned that doing the work was more important than the money. When you learn the performance is the party, and not the party after, that's when you make the first major step toward becoming an actress. Sayy, *liss*-en, I gotta *go* somewhere, so if there's anything else, you gotta ask it *now!*" Hand on hip, bantam rooster walk, edging toward door.

"I just wanted to ask one thing—why, at your age, are you still so passionately career-conscious?"

The eyes looked bathed in the glow of a thousand Christmas mornings. "Well *liss*-en, why dintcha ask that three hours ago, 'cause it's gonna take three days to answer *that* one, I mean, *liss*-en, you hafta come back again

some time. Sayyy, I didn't even offer you a drink or anything. You want a beer or anything? I mean I gave a
lecture at the American Academy to the graduating class
and I don't have a lotta pictures of me in frames around
the house, but here's the picture they took. The text of
the sermon was 'Don't give up!' and Garson said, 'That's
silly, you're talking to kids who are not even started yet
and you're telling them don't give up,' and I said, 'Sure,
that's when they *do* give up, when they're just getting
started.' I had a lotta success and everything's swingin'
and look at me in the picture, I look just like I did when
I was in school. You can see I'm doin' OK 'cause all the
other people in the picture are standing up and clapping
for me. So *liss*-en, I'm determined to have a film career
and I'm gonna do a Broadway musical—Hal Prince offered
me the Lotte Lenya role in *Cabaret* but I told him I'd
rather play the Joel Grey role and I still think I was right
—and right now I'm the valet to Garson Kanin and I'm
finishing the screenplay to Thornton Wilder's book *Heav-
en's My Destination* which is gonna be the greatest thing
ever hit the movies and" . . . the door was closing on the
smell of lilacs and the sound of rain . . . "*I* haven't even
started yet . . ."

It was the last thing I got squeezed into the note-
book before the pencil point broke.

Jane Wyman

Joan Crawford sells Pepsi, Veronica Lake waits on tables, June Allyson married a barber, Merle Oberon moved to Mexico, and when last heard from, Hedy Lamarr was still trying to get a new Diner's Club card. In Hollywood, the only thing you hear more than "Let's have lunch someday" is "Whatever happened to . . . ?" New faces and short memories is what it's all about. For the star ladies over 40, it can be rough. The smart ones save their money, the lucky ones end up on TV battling out the ratings with the new faces, and the ones who are desperate either make horror movies or play the new faces' mothers. Well, don't worry about Jane Wyman.

At 55, the gal who started out as Sarah Jane Fulks from St. Joseph, Missouri, is smart ("She's loaded," says a friend who knew her when and still knows her now), lucky (Along with Loretta Young, she pioneered the movement into TV, starred in her own TV series which ran for three years at a time when most of the declining glamour queens were still being photographed through gauze), and she's *never* been desperate. "I dropped out for a while because all they offered me was ax-murderers and Lesbians. I won't play Lesbians, honey, not *this* kid."

Now she's back, starring in her first movie in six years, looking keen and peachy in her old Jane Wyman bangs (it's a wig), and giving the Paramount lot a run for its money. She sits in the commissary, full of ginger and jazz, behind a big Paramount menu that reads "Keep the Ten Commandments Says Cecil B. DeMille" and says, "OK, C.B., I'll begin by declining the Dorothy Lamour salad. What in the hell is a Dorothy Lamour salad, anyway?" It's fresh pineapple, sliced bananas and strawberries with cream cheese and bar-le-duc. No thanks. She decides instead on a steak with french fries, a package of Kents, which she chain-smokes with the energy of a lady riveter, and a slice of watermelon. "This is where it all started, honey," she says, spitting out watermelon seeds. "I came out here from Missouri and became one of the Leroy Prinz dancers. They made a test of me at Universal for a Carole Lombard movie, then I got cut out of that and signed a contract at Warners in 1936 and became the Torchy Blaine of the B's, following right along in Glenda Farrell's footsteps. I thought I was the greatest thing since Seven-Up. I even remember my first line. Bill Powell played a producer and I was in the chorus line. 'What is your name?' he asked. And my line was, 'My name is Bessie Fuffnik; I swim, ride, dive, imitate wild birds and play the trombone.'" She hoots so loud she nearly falls into the watermelon juice. "It was one of the *Golddiggers,* honey, but I forgot the year. Years later, on the night I won the Oscar for *Johnny Belinda,* I got this wire from Ray Heindorf: 'Dear Bessie Fuffnik—I swim, ride, dive, imitate wild birds, play the trombone, and win Academy Awards.' I've never forgotten it. Anyway, for ten years I was the wisecracking lady reporter who stormed the city desk snapping, 'Stop the presses, I've got a story that will break this town wide open!'" Another hoot. "But you know, honey, I was one brassy blonde who tried to learn something about both the camera and my craft. The turning point came in a big dramatic scene in a Chinese restaurant in *Princess O'Rourke.* I went to New York to do some publicity and while I was there this book called *The Lost Weekend* came out and it was all anybody talked about. I got a call saying come home, Billy Wilder wants you for the girl opposite Ray Milland. He'd seen *O'Rourke* and wanted me for this serious role and I got it and we made it right here at Paramount and it changed my whole professional life. Now I'm back."

The new film is called *How to Commit Marriage*. It's her 74th (count 'em) film and she's teamed with Bob Hope and Jackie Gleason. Plot: Jane and Bob are getting a divorce but decide to wait until after their daughter's wedding to break the news. Gleason, the groom's father, is the president of a rock 'n roll company who is anti-marriage, anti-Establishment, anti-anti. When he meets the in-laws he recognizes Bob as a realtor who once sold him a house that got demolished in a mud slide. Everybody fights. At the wedding, Gleason announces the divorce plans and the disillusioned kids end up unmarried hippies expecting a baby. Bob and Jane get remarried, Bob dresses up like the Maharishi to reunite the kids, and everything ends happily in a rock 'n roll theme song. The End. OK, so it's not *Johnny Belinda*, but if it gets Jane Wyman back on the screen, nobody's asking questions, least of all the lady herself.

"The studios are afraid to hire the old stars because they're afraid we might bomb. Then they bring in people who bomb anyway because they have no experience. This way, they figure the combination of three old pros like us plus the kids and the music of today gives them something to sell. I haven't worked in so many years and I just wanted to get back in front of the cameras and see if I could do it. It's not a return. What do you call it? A re-entrance? Anyway, it's a lot of fun, and comedy is harder to play than drama. I was going to do a nightclub act with Donald O'Connor in Tahoe. I had the white furs and the Spanish guitars and I was going to make a very glamorous movie-star entrance on a white staircase, but I got peritonitis of the pancreas and nearly died, so that was off. This is the first movie I've been offered that I figured I could have a good time with, and working with Bob and Gleason is a ball. I'm not complaining."

We saunter over to the sound stage where Bob Hope is shooting. Everyone lights up like the Accutron sign on Times Square when they see her coming. Hope blows her a kiss from across the set. "I'm not in this scene, so let's go over to my dressing room. I don't like to stand in Bob's line of vision when he's working. It throws him off." We cross the lot where Alan Ladd rode the Orient Express with Veronica Lake and it stirs memories. "We used to have such a ball on the set," she reminisces. "Over at Warners we were like a family. Every room had a bar and we used to yell at each other from one room to another. Even when we weren't working, we'd have lunch together every day in the studio commissary. We turned out 52 pictures a year from one studio alone, so we had to get along. I remember when Bette Davis went back to New York—she always hated Hollywood—she had the biggest trailer this town has ever seen and she said, 'I want Janie to have it.' I tried to bring it to Paramount and it was so big we couldn't get it through the DeMille gate. I finally had to give it away and now some real estate man uses it for an office out in the San Fernando Valley. We all got along and we helped each other. We were trained by pros. Kay Francis helped me the most when I got started. And we weren't afraid to get out there and get our feet wet. These kids now can't learn. There's nobody around to help them. It's like baking a cake for the first time. You gotta get the oven right. There's TV, but you turn out a show in three days, the writers keep changing and the directors don't know what they're doing. They're learning on the job, too. It's ticker-tape entertainment. TV hasn't got its diapers wet yet."

There's no bitterness in the dialogue. She has somehow managed to survive the toughness and the harshness that happens to most women who have made 74 pictures. "What happened to me was part of a cycle. We had the gangster cycle with Jimmy Cagney and Bogart, then the war cycle, then the John Wayne movies where all the men got the best parts, then the *Ben Hurs* and the Charlton Heston spectaculars, then the 'method' came in and they lost me right there. Somewhere along the line the kind of pictures I used to make—*Belinda, So Big, Blue Veil, Magnificent Obsession*—the women's pictures—went out of style. The year I won the Oscar for *Belinda* I was up against Irene Dunne for *I Remember Mama*, Olivia de Havilland in *Snake Pit*, Barbara Stanwyck in *Sorry, Wrong Number* and Ingrid Bergman in *Joan of Arc*. Now they're old-fashioned and we're going back to musicals. There's not much imagination around. The screen is not building women for women's pictures. TV has ruined everything. People talk and eat while everything's going on on the screen. It's taken a big bite out of the industry. Also, after the war the studios lost their theatres and the double bills went out, so they stopped making A and B pictures. Everyone went independent. I made two pictures, but I had bad luck because they both came at the end of cycles. *Stage Fright*, which I did for Hitchcock, came at the end of the suspense drama movies. We had to re-dub everything because Michael Wilding mumbled all the way through it and you couldn't understand a word he said. By the time it came out, that kind of movie was dead. Then I did *Miracle in the Rain*. I hate to bring up my own work, honey, but what a wonderful movie! But by the time we got that one out, Van Johnson and I weren't so big and Warners was already spending all its money promoting *Giant*, so it never got any attention."

The conversation was interrupted by three Belgian priests visiting the lot. They passed up Richard Harris and Sean Connery. The only person they wanted to meet was Jane Wyman. "Isn't that sweet? They remembered *The Yearling*. You can't fault that one; it's a classic. Spencer Tracy and Anne Revere had started it and the deer got too big and they had to shelve it and Gregory Peck and I came in late on it. I always did what I wanted to do, so I don't have a favorite. *The Blue Veil* was the hardest, but *Belinda* was the most creative. I studied for six months in a school for the deaf and did the whole movie with my ears sealed in wax to blot out every noise except percussion sounds. I still remember the sign language. That film was almost never released. We filmed up on the California coast and Jack Warner hated it because when he saw the footage he yelled, 'It's just a simple story and they're up on the coast shooting a bunch of damned sea gulls!' After the first preview, he hated it so much he stuck it in cans and nobody knew what happened to it. Everyone was fired at the end of the picture and Jean Negulesco wasn't even allowed to do his own editing. He has never to this day set foot in the Warner Brothers studio again. One day somebody was rummaging around in a lot of dusty cans of film in the New York office and found some reels of the picture and ran them and it finally got shown and you know the rest. I made Jack Warner take out an ad and apologize to everyone connected with the film, from the grips to the water boy and he named every person by name. It just proves it's all timing. You can't be a smart ass in this business.

"Then I lost a baby and was sick for a while and I went into television and my eyes went to pot reading 5000 scripts a month, just to get 38 shows. Loretta and I used to trade. I'd say, 'This part's too pretty for me, you do it— that one's too ugly for you, let *me* do it.' We used to trade leading men, too. One of my best shows came from a garage mechanic who handed us two pages of paper while he was filling the car with gas. I gave him $100 for it and the damned thing won an Emmy nomination. It was very grueling work for three years. I had to cast, produce, do the office work. I used to go down to the airport and hand the film to the pilot myself to get it to New York by Tuesday night so it could go on the air. Things are more sophisticated now—bigger budgets, shorter working hours. But the reason I got out of it was because of a cycle again. The anthology show went out of style overnight and the series with regular characters came in. But I learned one thing— you can always get quality if you *are* quality. Some of these new shows are lousy even with their big budgets because they don't have the quality to begin with. I learn every sequence of a film in its exact place before the picture ever begins. Now they just learn each day's take and the hell with it. I have no patience with that. If an actor says, 'I can't do that because I don't feel it,' I just get my hat on and go home or have a beer someplace."

The one subject she does not discuss is ex-husbands who become governors of California. Namely Ronald Reagan, whom she divorced in 1948. "It's not because I'm bitter or because I disagree with him politically. I've always been a registered Republican. But it's bad taste to talk about ex-husbands and ex-wives, that's all. Also, I don't know a damn thing about politics. I don't care who does what to who and anyway, now that I've moved into a new apartment, I live in a different district and I forgot to register, so I can't vote anyway."

Both of her children by Reagan are grown. Maureen, 28, makes records in Nashville, and Michael, 24, is a boat racer. ("You can only mother them up to a point, then if there's anything they need to know they can ask somebody.") Her third marriage, to composer Fred Karger, ended in 1965 and her house in Beverly Hills was robbed ("three times, honey, once by a Mexican who was in the house while I was undressing for bed—they found him in a church in Tijuana with *my* pearls in his pocket"), so she now lives alone in a modern apartment building at a spot in Century City which used to be the Twentieth Century Fox back lot. Living alone has now increased her enthusiasm for returning to the cameras. "I'm perfectly willing to make more pictures as long as I can find good ones, but I won't play monsters or women who are terrorized by hoodlums on LSD or any of that stuff. Somehow along the way, I got a nice-lady image and it got in the way. I'm ready to work, but they just haven't gotten around to me yet."

As for the future, she's trying to write a book of anecdotes called *Whatever's Fair* but "I can't write, honey. I'm the kind of gal who spells cat K-A-T. There was some talk about me doing *Mame* on Broadway, but I sang a few songs for them—it was the first time in my life I ever auditioned for *anything*—and they were willing to give me only a week's rehearsal. I need a lot longer than that. I would like to do a play." They were calling her back to the set to shoot a new scene with Bob Hope and there was a new batch of autographs to sign outside the door. She grabbed a fresh pack of Kents, waved merrily and, bangs bobbing in the afternoon sunshine, bounced across the parking lot, still chattering. "If you need a closer, just write 'The End' at the bottom of the page. Like I said, I'd like to do a Broadway show, I'd like to do a lotta things. But if they want me for a Broadway show, let 'em build one. I got no place to go in a hurry."

Ingrid Bergman

"I owe my entire career to an elevator boy."

With that, she begins. Ingrid Bergman backstage on a windy November evening, waiting for the curtain to rise. Sitting on the bony edge of an uncomfortable chair in a lime Jello-colored shift and soft mauve boots up to her still-pretty knees, with her soft brown hair pulled back in a girlish pony tail, streaked now with silver strands too real and unphony to lose in a bottle of rinse, smoking cigarettes and smashing them out in a tiny ashtray no bigger than a cameo in her tiny snuffbox dressing room that smells of rouge and powder and greasepaint and stale smoke. I don't know what people expect movie stars to be like, but surely this Bergman would be a disappointment. No prize for the moon-faced and starry-eyed, she drinks her Scotches and laughs her curly giggle and doesn't give a damn what people think. Behind her are the klieg lights and the countless Hollywood movies ("I don't remember how many; I didn't count") and the Rossellini scandal and the Academy Awards and the bloody headlines and the pain. But people love to forgive, and now she's back on Broadway, for the first time in 21 years, acting on the stage in a marathon role in Eugene O'Neill's *More Stately Mansions,* a play the critics didn't care much for and she's mad as hell. "Yes, mad. Really mad." But the anger comes later. After she's gotten down to the nitty-gritty.

"I will tell you about how I decided to come back to

Broadway, but first let me start at the beginning. I was studying in a dramatic school in Stockholm. It was my first year and in the summer vacation I went to the Swedish film industry and did a test and got a job. Just like that. I was 18, and I felt that if I went back to school I'd be an old woman before I got out, so I stayed in films. But all the while I knew I had to learn something. I didn't want to be one of those girls who get discovered in drug stores and become movie stars. So I kept up my theatre training on the side while I made Swedish movies. Two years later, I made my first stage appearance in a little French comedy called *The Hour Age*. Then I got my first lead in a play, written by a Hungarian, called *Jean*. Hollywood was all over Europe then, looking for talent, and I had barely begun my stage career when I was asked to come to America. Every studio was signing girls to seven-year contracts and then they'd come back after a year and their chances at home were ruined, because if you're no good in Hollywood who wants to see you at home? Many girls ruined their careers that way, jumping into films. Anyway, I played it cagey and waited for the right role and the right man who would only sign me to one film. I had done *Intermezzo* in Swedish, but I don't think anyone in Hollywood noticed. However, there was an elevator boy of Swedish descent in David Selznick's office building in New York who went to every little Swedish movie he could find. One day Selznick's story editor, Kathryn Brown, rode up in his elevator and he told her, 'You're always looking for new faces, why don't you go down to such-and-such a cinema on so-and-so avenue and look at this picture, *Intermezzo*?' She saw it, sent a copy of the print to California, and Selznick wrote to me with one of those seven-year offers and I said no. So he sent Miss Brown to Sweden to see what was wrong with me. I guess they thought I was crazy. But when I learned they wanted to do a remake of *Intermezzo* in English I agreed to come to America and I loved it. I did that one film

and by that time the war had broken out and I stayed.
"Then there was a period when everything stood still.
I had made some fine films, but all the leading men and
all the directors were at war and they were not making
as many films. So one day I was sent a script of *Liliom,*
which Burgess Meredith wanted to do on the stage. There
was the part of Julie, which was the lead, and the part
of her friend, a comedy role, not very big. I said, 'It's too
funny and my English is not good enough to play comedy,'
and I sent back the play. They said, 'Funny? We wanted
you for Julie.' I met Burgess Meredith at a Thanksgiving
party for the first time in 20 years and he's still laughing
about that story.

"But you know, I could not get the theatre out of
my blood. I think they thought I was crazy in Hollywood.
I would make a film and on the side I would try to talk
people into doing a play. Not many other stars were interested in the theatre, so they couldn't understand it.
But I have to be active. I have to work to be happy. So I
talked David Selznick into letting me do *Anna Christie,*
and I played it in three places—Santa Barbara, San Francisco and Maplewood, New Jersey. You couldn't buy a
ticket in any of those towns. Then, when I left Hollywood,
I did *Hedda Gabler* in Paris, then *Tea and Sympathy,*
which was a great success. Robert Anderson was a bit
shocked at first, I think, because the sets were different
and I was not like Deborah Kerr, but it was a happy time.
And two years ago I did *A Month in the Country* with
Michael Redgrave in London. But I hadn't been on the
New York stage since I played Maxwell Anderson's *Joan
of Lorraine,* 21 years ago at the Alvin Theatre. We ran
for 11 months to standing room only every performance
and every night a group of kids would gather at the stage
door and bring me flowers and write me letters. I called
them 'The Alvin Gang.' I left the country for 10 years
and when I came back for one day to accept the New

York Film Critics award for *Anastasia* I stepped off the plane and there they all were at the airport with a big sign: 'The Alvin Gang—We Love You!' It felt wonderful. They are all grown-up people now, with their own families, but for 20 years they have written to me and sent presents to my kids on their birthdays. When I opened this time in *More Stately Mansions,* there they were outside the theatre, the same kids who once stood every night in the snow. I have the same fans through the years. I have to hold on to a lot of wood"—she knocks her large Swedish knuckles on the bottom of her dainty chair, then spreads her arms and raps the wall—"I'm afraid to say it, but I've been fortunate. People *do* come to see me."

Indeed they do. There are so many Bergman fans, in fact, that the lineup for tickets began the morning after the critics thumbed their noses at *More Stately Mansions* and the influx has been so great ever since that the "This Performance Sold Out" sign never leaves the entrance to the Broadhurst Theatre. But why this play? Why O'Neill? Why a vehicle she knew would never be a commercial success? She tilts her regal head toward the dressing-room mirror, framed in the glass by cold-cream jars and silver-rimmed photo cases containing portraits of her husband, Swedish theatrical producer Lars Schmidt, and warms the room with a smile, talking over the roar of a vacuum cleaner in the early evening stillness. "Because," she begins, "I had to do it. If I just wanted to do any old play, I could do that in Europe, closer to home, where it's easier on my husband and children. It had to be something I would regret all my life if I didn't do. And *More Stately Mansions* is that play. Usually I have had to fight in films because they made me play either the villain or the good, good girl. This character is both. Also, in this play I play my own age for the very first time." (She's 52.)

"I am the only member of the company who ever met O'Neill personally. The Swedes have always loved his work, you know, that's why he always gave us his plays to produce first. He was very influenced by our own Strindberg, just as Edward Albee is today, and we loved him for that. We understood him. So when I was playing *Anna Christie* in San Francisco, I was flattered and excited when his wife Carlotta came backstage and asked me to come home and meet her husband. He lived in a great house on a cliff over the ocean several miles from the city, it was called Tao House, and we drove there for Sunday lunch. He took me up into his study and there were all these plays lying around, plays here and there and everywhere. He told me about his plans to write this saga of an American family, beginning in the 1800's and ending up in modern times, tracing their ups and downs, their greeds, nastiness, triumphs, everything. He wanted the same group of actors to sign up for all the plays so that he could have the same faces in the same roles. I was fascinated. 'How many plays?' I asked. 'Nine,' he said. 'And how long would you want me to sign up for?' 'Six years,' he said. Well, I was under contract to Selznick and I just didn't have time, so I never did the plays.

"Years later, when the offer came to me in Europe to do this play, it seemed like O'Neill was calling me again. I felt I owed it to him. The Swedish version lasted four hours and forty-five minutes and in its full play form it reads between five and six hours. When José Quintero came to Europe, I told him I simply did not think we could get Americans to sit still that long. The Swedes will sit through anything as long as it's O'Neill, but Americans come to the theatre with a couple of martinis under their belts and they just want to be entertained. So he agreed and we got it down to two hours and forty minutes, and every word is still O'Neill's. It is a difficult play. You must study it as well as I have to realize how much depth it has, but audiences don't listen to the words so they don't learn anything. We worked very hard, trying to present to the public something important, and then what do I do but pick up Mr. Clive Barnes in *The New York Times* and read, in the first phrase of his review, that of all the playwrights in the world, Mr. O'Neill is the most banal. And I nearly dropped dead!"

And here the anger starts, turning her high Swedish cheekbones into raspberry tarts. "I cannot believe that a man who calls himself a critic could think so little about the greatest playwright America has ever produced, and a winner of the Nobel Prize. I'm mad because it's so unfair. I'm mad because *The New York Times* is the only critical opinion that matters in New York and now Mr. Barnes has ruined this play all over Europe, because who will produce it now? I'm mad that just because a sick man says we have not done a finished play, it's *Out! Out* Quintero! *Out* Bergman! *Out* O'Neill! I am a serious person. I like to be stimulated by theatre, then go home remembering what I've seen, not just have a few laughs. I mean, you may have more fun at *There's a Girl in My Soup*. I haven't seen it and I only use that as an example because I think the title is so funny. But I know I wouldn't have returned to Broadway in a play like that. I would rather return in O'Neill. Isn't it more interesting to see what a man like O'Neill had in his head, even if it is not one of his best plays? I have no respect for a theatre which ceases to be a forum for the ideas of great men. I would like to see all of O'Neill's plays performed, whether he wished them performed or not. Now when some critic says we should not have done this play I say that is ridiculous. I would be very unhappy if this play had stayed in a drawer and I think it's a horrible crime that they burned the others. I am only happy that there was a little angel looking over this one."

And now that she's back, are there any regrets? Any backward glances toward more commerical times? "Absolutely not. I do what I want to do. I wouldn't have lived my life the way I did if I was going to worry about what people like critics were going to say. I have been facing critics of one sort or another all my life. I have a reputation for being a woman of great courage. You can't be anything without courage. You can't even be good without the courage to be good."

She laughs again, waving her hands, and the flash of anger vanishes in a trail of pale-purple cigarette smoke. The standing-room-only crowd is filing into the theatre and she smiles at the sound. Proving, of course, that she still has what it takes at the box office. And proving, also, that Thomas Wolfe was wrong when he wrote *You Can't Go Home Again*. Home, they say, is where the hatrack is and, long after the roses wilt and the cameras stop turning and the glitter is packed up and locked away in studio wardrobe, there will always be a hatrack in the theatre with Ingrid Bergman's name on it.

Myrna Loy

There's a wan little smile in Myrna Loy's voice, no louder than a twig crackling in the autumn wind. From the window of her penthouse overlooking the East River, a soft breeze licks against that famous red Nora Charles hair which has never turned gray, and even now, on a violent big-city afternoon, she brings back the quiet aura of a time when kids fell in love to Dinah Shore records and nice women never took their aprons off until 5 P.M. A portrait of Eleanor Roosevelt, inscribed "To Myrna Loy, with my warmest good wishes," is on a table nearby ("*You* want *my* autograph?" Mrs. Roosevelt had asked when Miss Loy made her request). Sitting down in her smart little brown dress, the actress straightens her skirt over her sensible round knees and sips plain club soda over cracked ice. Myrna Loy is a lady. Not one of those phony-elegant "I'm being interviewed" ladies who try not to crack their Touch-and-Glow when reminded of the past, but a "here and now" lady, poised and cool, laughing about yesterday and eager for tomorrow.

There's a reason for the visit—a new movie called *The April Fools,* to open in May. It's her first film since she played Doris Day's addled aunt in *Midnight Lace* in 1960, and she gets it out of the way first. "I did it because it is the only thing I've been offered lately where I didn't have to play an alcoholic or an ax murderess. I love comedy, but when you're not young enough to play glamour girls any more the comedies are hard to find. So I jumped at the chance to do something gay. I play sort of a modern-day fairy godmother. It's a strange part, with a sense of magic to it. Jack Lemmon is this successful businessman, married to a woman who is more interested in her house than in him. He's the typical Thurber man, the Westport commuter. Catherine Deneuve is married to Peter Lawford, an ex-used car salesman who throws parties for the jet set and lives at the UN Plaza. She's only part of his collection of people. She and Jack meet and go out on the town together one night and run into me in a Greenwich Village discothèque. I'm married to Charles Boyer and we live in this castle in Conneticut and only go out at night because we hate daylight. We stand for the exact opposite of most married people today. We shut out all the destructive elements, all the material values. We're quite mad, but quite wise.

"Anway, these two young people see the way we live and they fall in love. It's very romantic. I have no idea whether it will be any good or not, but at least it's not a horror film. I hate to see what's happened to Bette Davis."

The new biography of Irving Thalberg by Bob Thomas lies on the coffee table with a bookmark in it. She keeps eyeing it as if she'd love to get back to it. "Have you read it? Oh, everyone's in it. I'm in it. Thalberg brought me to MGM, but I didn't know that until years later. He had seen me in one of my Chinese temptress roles, I guess. I played a lot of those, first in silent films and later when sound came in. I didn't always play perfect wives and mothers, you know. For years I played nothing but wretched women with knives in their teeth." The smile in her voice is touched with sage. It seems queer, the thought of Teresa Wright's mother in *The Best Years of Our Lives* with a knife in her teeth. She puts her forefingers to her eyes and slants the eyelids. *Shazam!* Instant Anna May Wong. "See? It wasn't hard. I must have some Mongolian ancestry. Something sneaked in there."

Not really. She was born Myrna Williams 64 years ago on a cattle ranch in the Crow Creek Valley of Montana. Real pioneer stock. Her grandfather was a Welsh boy who came to America and started a pony express. Her father was a rancher who served in the Montana legislature. "That's where I got my interest in politics. He was quite a gourmet for Montana. He used to import cracked crab on ice from Chicago." Her mother wanted to name her Annabelle, but from a train window her father had once seen a sign with "Myrna" written on it, so she was named after a railroad whistle stop. After her father died in the flu epidemic of 1918, her mother moved her to California where she attended Venice High School. Venice is a slum now, but on the cracked and brown lawn of its old high school a statue still stands of the young Myrna Loy. "One of my teachers made a sculpture of me to represent 'Aspiration.' I went back to see it once. My arm had been knocked off. I had been mutilated. Every time the football team came from Santa Monica they'd hang a rubber tire around my neck. It's a wonder I survived, but I'm still there."

She studied dancing and landed in the chorus line at Grauman's Chinese Theater when she was 17. Rudolph Valentino saw her photo and invited her to test for the lead in something called *Cobra*. "I went to the studio and met him and his wife Natacha. They were wonderful to me, but I was just a skinny kid with no experience. I didn't get the part, but I did play some bits in girlie movies. I tested for the Virgin Mary in *Ben Hur*, but ended up playing an exotic. There were fashions in leading ladies. Mary Pickford was the rage and nobody thought of me as the virgin, I guess. I had these slinky eyes and a sense of humor." So they changed her name to Loy because it sounded Oriental and for seven years she played nothing but Chinese, Japanese, Javanese, Malayan and Hindu sirens, with an occasional quadroon thrown in for luck.

When sound came in, she had to talk pidgin English

to go with the slanty eyes. "Many of the stars fell by the wayside because of their voices. There was no reason for throwing John Gilbert away the way they did. But it was a matter of life and death; either you made it or you didn't. I finally got fired because they ran out of hussies for me to play. I see the same thing happening today. Young people get miscast and they're stuck with the wrong images, playing the wrong roles. People are so blind. That girl in *Baby Doll*, Carroll Baker. She's a marvelous comedienne, but they never give her a chance."

She finally played a Caucasian with Jeanette MacDonald and Maurice Chevalier in *Love Me Tonight* and MGM began to throw her a few sophisticated bones. In 1934 a low-budget "B" flick was organized in 14 days for William Powell. She was to play his wife. It was called *The Thin Man* and the rest, as they say in the Polo Lounge, is history. "We made that one on a small budget and 21 days of shooting, but it was such a hit we went on for ten years and made five sequels. There isn't a day of my life that someone doesn't ask me about the roles of Nick and Nora Charles, about Bill Powell, or about that dog, Asta. He was a wire-haired terrier, and they were not popular at all at the time. His name was really Skippy and he was highly trained to do all of his tricks for a little squeaky mouse and a biscuit. He'd do anything for that reward. But the minute his scenes were over, it was definitely verboten to hug him or have any further contact with him off the set. I don't see Bill Powell any more. He retired and moved to Palm Springs and you can't get him out of that air-conditioned house. But we're great friends and we talk on the telephone.

"It was really Clark Gable and I who were the 'King and Queen of the Movies.' I still have the crown they gave me somewhere. We all had nicknames on the set. Clark called me Queenie, Spencer Tracy was the Iron Duke, and Victor Fleming, who directed all three of us in *Test Pilot*, was the Monk. We never had a name for Jean Harlow, but she was a very dear friend of mine. I seldom get angry, but that book about her life was a pack of lies. The part about her alcoholic trip to San Francisco was a complete lie; she was with *me* the whole time. She and Bill Powell were very much in love and when Bill and I went on location to make one of the *Thin Man* pictures, Jean went along with us. Everyone in America thought Bill and I were married anyway, and when we arrived at the St. Francis Hotel in San Francisco they had reserved the bridal suite for us. Jean and I moved in there, but there was a convention in town and Bill had to sleep in a pantry. Jean was very tragic and very, *very* ill, but she was none of the things in that book! I remember she looked very ill in San Francisco. I didn't like her color and I told Bill. She promised to see a doctor, but she never did. Then when she really became ill with that kidney infection, I told Bill I thought we should get her to a hospital, but by the time she finally got there it was too late."

In *Myra Breckinridge*, Gore Vidal describes Myrna Loy's Hollywood image as "the good-sex wife," but when she tired of the image after all those years, she got into politics. "One morning in 1948 I picked up the paper and read that a vice-president of the American Federation of Labor was calling me a Communist! I sued for a million dollars and he had to retract it all. I hadn't done anything. I hadn't even left my car parked in front of the wrong person's house! All I did was have my picture taken with red roses in my arms reading the preamble to the United Nations Charter at a Slav meeting at Carnegie Hall. You could do the most innocent thing and get ruined in those days. So a group of us joined together and fought to abolish the House Committee on Un-American Activities."

With her name cleared, she moved to Washington and worked actively for UNESCO for five years. She campaigned with Eleanor Roosevelt for Adlai Stevenson and, recently, for Senator Eugene McCarthy. She is a member of the National Committee Against Discrimination in Housing, a loud voice in the fight for civil rights, and, all told, a well-adjusted law-abiding Democrat. The only time she gets testy is when she is asked about her four marriages (one to Mr. Hertz of the rent-a-car world). *"Yes,"* she mocks, like a child playing Red Rover, then blushes, as though sensing she has bordered on rudeness. Then she adds quietly, "I don't talk about that." Perfect wife on screen. Four childless marriages ending in divorce in real life. I can't blame her.

She has given up California ("You never see a poppy out there any more. They used to grow wild on the MGM lot. Now all you see is this damned *ivy!*"). She likes New York and wants to do stage work, but the roles are slim. "I always wanted to do a play but, with no training or technique, I was reluctant. You can't learn to act unless you do it, so I toured for two years in *Barefoot in the Park* with Richard Benjamin and learned to hold for laughs and move in on the end of applause—in short, I learned my way around. I even won the Sarah Siddons award in Chicago. I'm ready for a play now, but with the way things are going in the theater, I don't know if there is any place for the kind of sophisticated comedies I like."

She still likes movies, but she's not exactly in love with the direction *they're* heading in, either. "I admire some of the people on the screen today, but most of them look like everybody else. I will say one thing for the old days—we had individuality. There was none of that business of telling us we had to look like someone else. And we were protected. These poor kids today are totally exposed. They step off a plane without any sleep, looking terrible, and the flashbulbs start popping. I came along before the candid camera. Now the worse they can make you look, the better. Glamour is dead. Some of the rules we had *were* silly. In the *Thin Man* pictures, Bill Powell and I even had to have twin beds. But pictures were more sophisticated. Young actresses are always telling me they can't go to an audition any more without undressing. The boys have to take their clothes off, too.

"It's too excessive, and it's getting very boring, all this nudity. It'll be a shame if it upsets people so much that it brings on the need for censorship. I hate censorship. But I'm afraid we're heading in that direction. There's no mystery! No privacy. And frankly, no sex, either. Most of the sex I've seen on the screen looks like an expression of hostility toward sex. I know mystery is a dirty word to the young people of today, but a suggestion of sex is much more interesting than actually showing it, don't you think?"

Don't get the idea Myrna Loy is a prude. At one point in Lotus Land history, she caused a bit of a scandal herself by playing so many sexpots her navel was banned in movies. "Listen. Last week Roddy McDowall called me up and got me over to his apartment on the pretense of showing *Wuthering Heights*. But when the lights went out, the big surprise was *The Mask of Fu Manchu,* a terrible movie in which I played Boris Karloff's evil daughter. I carried around a pet python and whipped a young man tied to a rack and all sorts of dreadful things. Now I had been reading a little Freud around that time, so I called the director over one day and said, 'Say, this is obscene. This woman is a sadistic nymphomaniac!' And he said, 'What does *that* mean?' I mean, we did it *all* before these kids today ever thought of it, and we didn't even know what we were *doing!*" The sound in the voice stops being a smile. It's a full-grown laugh now. Pure Myrna Loy. And wicked enough to make Dracula cry uncle.

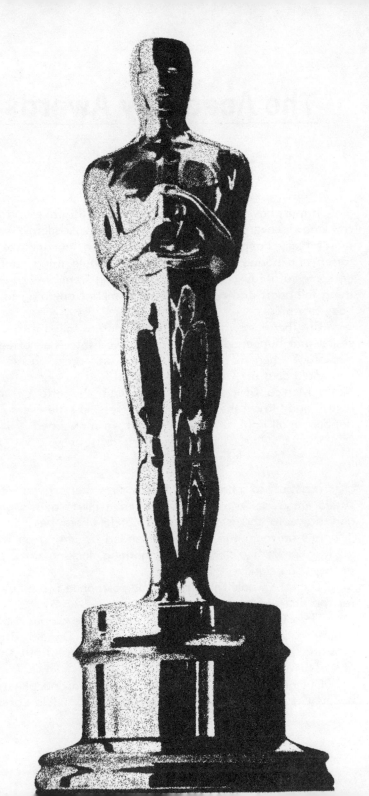

The Academy Awards

April, 1968

It must have been a bad joke. Maybe I'll wake up tomorrow and discover, hopefully, that the 40th Academy Awards didn't really happen. Maybe it was just a rehearsal of how rotten and boring and humorless the whole thing could be on some future Oscar night if everything went wrong, everything fell apart and nothing about it meant anything to anybody any more.

But then I see this tacky little program soiled with coffee stains that happened when I got shoved into the coffee urn backstage when more photographers and press agents than you could beat off with a stick chased Rod Steiger out of the Santa Monica Civic Auditorium yelling, "I gotta get outta here," and I know the whole sad, depressing little event really happened, all right, and I can't say I wasn't warned.

• • •

It got off to a bad start. Bosley Crowther arrived with no studio limousine to meet him, rented a Hertz at the airport and drove to the Beverly Hills Hotel, where he was told, "There's no room for you," and ended up sitting on top of his luggage at 3 o'clock in the morning, looking for a place to stay. Bad sign.

Then the whole thing had to be postponed two more days for the first time in history.

Then Denise Minnelli leaned across the dinner table at columnist Joyce Haber's house and told Donald Brooks: "Darling, may I tell you something? Nobody goes to that thing unless they are nominated for something."

Out at the beach Christopher Isherwood and playwright Robert E. Lee announced to Patty Duke and Angela Lansbury

54

that there were only two things in California they wouldn't be caught dead at: The Rose Parade and the Academy Awards.

Finally Truman Capote, outraged at the nominations, told the *L. A. Times:* "It's outrageous! It simply proves that it's all politics and sentiment and nothing to do with merit."

• • •

He's absolutely right, but I went to see it anyway, and the first thing I saw was 300 limousines locked in a lethal traffic jam so tangled people were deserting their drivers and walking.

The next thing I saw was the sun, beaming down from a cobalt blue sky on what looked like several thousand screaming teenie-boppers being led cheerleader-style by a local cretin called Army Archerd, who conducted some kind of local TV broadcast from a platform on which he interviewed (if that's the word) the arriving stars with the aplomb of a third-rate sideshow barker in one of those cheap circuses that always play cow pastures. "And here she is, folks, stepping up to the stand, a nominee for *Barefoot in the Park*, Miss Natalie Chadwick!" Mildred Natwick promptly looked sick, but she was too much of a lady to punch him in the nose. "It's Mildred Natwick," she sniffed coolly. "And how many Oscars does this make for you?" "Well, none actually . . ." "Thank you very much, Miss Mildred Catwick . . ."

They were coming fast and furious. Natalie Wood. ("I know why I won't see you up there getting an Oscar, Natalie, it's because you didn't make a picture this year, har har . . .")

Edith Head.

Ed Begley.

Danny Kaye.

Sonny, in a sequin taffeta cossack suit, and Cher, looking like an Egyptian slave girl in an old Maria Montez movie.

Phyllis Diller in red ostrich plumes sticking out of a chinchilla dress ("It's a Brillo pad, stretched.").

The teenagers yelled their little heads off.

George Cukor and Stanley Kramer, get them out of the way quick, no glamour, folks, to make way for, yes, it was she, in person . . . Annette Funicello! Baby Annette! Wearing the ugliest gown of the evening, a banana-split nightmare by Mr. Blackwell, if you'll excuse the expression.

• • •

By 6:30 there were more stars stepping on one another and shoving their way into the auditorium to avoid teenie-boppers in Bermuda shorts than the dog show (held in the same building) had fleas.

Greer Garson, Ann Miller, Angie Dickinson, (in a Ray Aghayan backless with her navel peeking out through pie-crust lace), Mrs. Gregory Peck in a lime sherbet Yves St. Laurent ("Yessir, he's really great, that Yves," hollered Army), Rosalind Russell in a black-beaded Galanos, Dustin Hoffman with Senator McCarthy's daughter, Ellen, Anne Baxter, Katharine Ross with some guy in a cowboy hat, Audrey Hepburn, men in Don Loper turtlenecks and hippie beads, Martha Raye in monkey fur. And on and on, all being insulted by this Army Archerd character, because that's the way the Academy sets it up, see.

And all the time, the sun is shining!

By the time Dame Edith Evans, 80, practically got pushed off the stand into the arms of a gang of Lotus Land's hungriest paparazzi ("You wanna snap her?" "Who is she?" "Dame somebody."), I had had enough outside.

• • •

Inside stars and fans alike were pushing and shoving and sweating their way into an illuminated grotto surrounded by eight color monitors and decorated with three Spanish panels on each side of the auditorium holding lighted chandeliers. At 7:05, 153 klieg lights were turned on the audience with a blast of heat that made you feel like you were being slowly fried to death. The curtain rose, in a roar of applause, revealing chandeliers, potted palms and plastic Sears, Roebuck flower arrangements, with more gold paint on the walls than on the Oscars, which only cost $60 apiece. (Actors used to hock them, now it's forbidden by law. The Academy buys them back for $10.) They make good doorstops.

At 7:20 Gregory Peck gave a boring speech about electronics. (What happened to the Martin Luther King speech the Academy got so much publicity out of announcing? Do I detect phony liberalism?)

• • •

The motto used to be "When in doubt, get Bob Hope onstage." This year he was definitely off in timing, delivery and sharpness. Most of his quips with the stars had been either changed at the last minute out of hokey Academy genuflecting to the Negro cause and fear of stirring people up, or cut altogether, a fact which became apparent when his planned routine with Carol Channing left her looking yummy in the dress of the evening—a beaded rhinestone turtleneck covered with a sunshine yellow jumper coat by Ray Aghayan—with nothing to say. Instead, Hope left everyone yawning with last-minute lines like, "The women are all beautiful but Dame Edith Evans in a micro mini is too much." (Closeup of Dame Edith, regal enough to bring tears to the eyes, looking thoroughly puzzled. She didn't even wear a mini, which shows how much thought went into everything.)

By 7:30 George Kennedy got the Best Supporting Actor Award, the first upset in an evening filled with weird and totally absurd developments.

At 7:50 Dustin Hoffman and Katharine Ross gave the Cinematography award to *Bonnie and Clyde* with the animation of paraplegics. They were either scared to death or no-vocained.

• • •

About this time I began to understand the value of watching the whole thing on television. The awards are geared for the control room. In its mausoleum-like in-person atmosphere you can't see anything, hear anything (Louis Armstrong did a stupid song with a stuffed elephant in total silence, which was just as well) and you burn up from the heat.

Technically, the show was a mess. At one point the lectern got stuck in the floor and the mikes went dead, leaving Hope and Diahann Carroll to ad-lib their way through the Live-Action Short awards. Rescued momentarily by a hand mike provided by a stagehand, they had to walk across the stage to reach the cord, which wasn't long enough, then kneel down onstage to be heard, since the mikes were still in the stuck lectern in the floor. Then they were down too low to see the cue cards.

Martha Raye tripped on her monkey fur, then read a boring letter from General Westmoreland about entertaining the troops that had nothing to do with Oscars.

The Kodak commercials were often shown off the backdrop because the stagehands missed their cues to lower the movie screen.

•   •   •

Elke Sommer (a real live-wire and all-around great actress who added glamour and excitement to the show when they could have gotten people who don't mean anything, like Bette Davis and Joan Crawford) gave the Sound Effects award to *The Dirty Dozen*, an unbearably inept film which made a big impression on the Academy because it had a lot of guns going off.

For the "best explosions, fires, earthquakes or hurricanes" Natalie Wood gave the Special Visual Effects award to *Doctor Dolittle*, a film with no explosions, fires, earthquakes or hurricanes.

Between awards, Bob Hope fenced with the sound men in the wings; men nailed down the stage and knocked on walls.

Art Direction and Set Decoration awards went to Camelot. Pretty amazing for a movie in which you never knew what season it was supposed to be, except when they sprayed detergent across the screen for snow. Also pretty amazing is the fact that the same film got the Costume award, when *Bonnie and Clyde*, which only started a fashion revolution, got nothing.

The Editing award to *In the Heat of the Night* floored me, since *In Cold Blood, Bonnie and Clyde* and *Two for the Road* were all masterpieces of editing not even nominated. (This category, I learned, is nominated and voted for by film editors only and none of them like directors who edit their own films, such as Richard Brooks, Arthur Penn and Stanley Donen—consequently, no nominations or awards. Small wonder, then, that the best films of 1967 were ignored.)

· · ·

By 9 P.M. people were already walking out, and although I didn't blame them, they missed the spectacle of Barbra Streisand stepping all over Eva Marie Saint's toes trying to get up the aisle to give out the Best Song. She walked on, giving everybody a drop-dead look with the personality of a frozen zesto, costumed in frizzy peroxided hair and black mascara like a Toulouse-Lautrec poster, and gave one of the most ludicrous awards of the night to "Talk to the Animals," which had just been murdered by Sammy Davis, Jr., in a performance that could only be described with great generosity as lackluster. This whole category with the exception of Burt Bacharach's song, "The Look of Love," was painfully embarrassing. Lainie Kazan was forced to sing a song nobody ever heard of from *Banning*, a movie nobody ever heard of; Louis Armstrong sang some hideous song about monkeys from *The Jungle Book;* and that left only "The Look of Love," the Dolittle song and the cute but hardly provocative "Thoroughly Modern Millie," which oddly enough, in the magic hands of Angela Lansbury, provided the show with its only showstopper. You could hear the "Oh, nos" loudly in the theatre when the Dolittle song won, but I don't know if they carried over the airwaves or not.

· · ·

Leslie Caron, whom everybody was trying desperately to keep on the opposite side of the auditorium from Warren Beatty, gave Mike Nichols a "Please forgive us for not giving it to you when you really deserved it for *Virginia Woolf* instead" award for Best Director; Audrey Hepburn gave Rod Steiger a Please forgive us for not, etc. . . . for *Pawnbroker*" Best Actor award; and Sidney Poitier gave Katharine Hepburn a sentimental "Please accept our love for your devotion to Spencer Tracy and forgive us for being so stupid when you didn't win for *Long Day's Journey into Night*" Best Actress award for *Guess Who's Coming to Dinner*, a film which looked like it had been made 20 years ago. (It also got an award for Original Screenplay, although it also sounded like it had been written 20 years ago too.) The least Miss Hepburn could have done, embarrassing as it must have been to get nominated for a film this pretentious, was be there. Other actors took salary cuts, left Broadway plays, cut shooting schedules and disrupted routines to fly out for the awards. Why couldn't she? The final thrust was *In the Heat of the Night* as Best Film instead of *Bonnie and Clyde* or far superior, overlooked films like *Two for the Road*, *In Cold Blood* and *Ulysses*. (Of the 2,980 Academy members who vote for best film, 883 are from such non-craft branches as "public relations," "executives," "administration" and "members-at-large" and 175 are producers. Richard Brooks never takes a producer credit on his films and is not a member of the Screen Producers Guild. This alienates the other unions, so that explains why *In Cold Blood*, perhaps the best American film of 1967, wasn't even nominated.)

By this time, so many furious people were walking up the aisles like buffalo herds nobody had time to ask one serious question: How can the Best Director of the year not have directed the Best Film?

• • •

In this whole night of back-stabbing and utter stupidity, only one award made any sense at all: Estelle Parsons, radiant and real as a newborn flower, totally deserved her Best Supporting Actress award for *Bonnie and Clyde* and accepted it with tears of genuine emotion and gratitude and no phony best-friend speeches.

And there was only one major ovation: for Angela Lansbury, whose "Millie" number was four-and-a-half minutes of glittering, dazzling entertainment. She put the whole corny show in her little fur pocket and walked away with the entire evening. The audience gave her a screaming ovation that could only be stopped by changing the scenery. Even after it was over, it was all the audience could talk about. Mame came back to Hollywood and rubbed their noses in it.

When it was all over, utter chaos reigned backstage. A mad, strangled attempt was made to get the stars herded through the press lines like cattle. They were shuttled through five rooms, laid out like a funeral parlor—rooms for deadline stills, non-deadline stills, press interviews (where everybody crowded in and shouted at each other), newsreels, tape-recorded interviews—then back through a patio and out into the screaming mob of teenie-boppers, cops, photographers who couldn't get press passes, fan-mag reporters, autograph hounds and the great unwashed public.

Press agents rushed about trying to sell clients who didn't get nominated for anything, writers got separated from angry photographers who couldn't get into the writers' arena. "How does it feel to win?" they yelled at Rod Steiger, who tried to run. "I gotta go to work at 8:30 tomorrow morning," Steiger yelled back. Mike Nichols' press agent frantically clutched the Best Director Oscar. Nichols had disappeared. Somebody asked Estelle Parsons—the only movie star who didn't deliberately try to look like a movie star—who designed her gown. "I bought it four years ago in a store."

• • •

There was more speculation about who was going to what party than there was about the Oscars. The most exclusive party in town was the one the Billy Wilders threw at the Bistro, where the Vincente Minnellis, Rosalind Russell, Cyd Charisse, Audrey Hepburn, the Irving Lazars, the Sam Goldwyns, Ruth Gordon and Garson Kanin, Joe Mankiewicz, Irwin Shaw and Claudette Colbert were just *some* of the selected guests.

The *Bonnie and Clyde* people all went off to the Kenneth Hymans and got drunk. The rest of the action ended up at The Factory, where Raquel Welch, Tony Curtis, Peter Lawford, Kevin McCarthy and Elke Sommer were all eclipsed by Angela Lansbury in a bra-less floor-length white satin Harlow dress, getting a standing ovation when she swept in. Carol Channing ate organic peaches from a Mason jar and grinned widely, "I can't dance, because my dress weighs 36 pounds and I fall down when I stand up."

• • •

It was all about over at 3 A.M. when model Donyale Luna (who has got to be seen by the human eye to be believed) did the Hokey Pokey Broadway in a filthy-looking two-piece nude fishnet bikini as Dame Edith Evans threw down her menu after two sips of Los Angeles water (it tastes like Geritol), stuck her fingers in her ears to drown out the noise, marched grandly toward the elevator, fed up with Oscar and his kingdom, and went home for a bowl of cornflakes.

I don't blame her. Now I've met Oscar myself in person, and if I ever see him again it'll be on television.

Uta Hagen

TAKE 1: Uta Hagen, actress, appearing onstage for the first time in six years in Eva LeGallienne's APA revival of *The Cherry Orchard*. Reclining on a chaise longue that has seen happier days, smoking a sad brown cigarette, laughing a throaty croak in a voice somewhere south of Marjorie Main's, and draping her beige chiffon gown about her legs with one last ounce of aristocratic dignity before the ax falls on Madame Ranevskaya's cherry trees. Trying to blend into the production without standing out like a star, but standing out anyway, unable to harness the energy and magic that have made her one of the theatre's most exciting monoliths. She could have been a movie star, too, if she wanted to. She didn't. She could be rich if she wanted to. She doesn't. She long ago turned her back on money, stardom, on working for the sake of working, and yet she remains a legend without a marquee to announce itself. Except for rare occasions, like *The Cherry Orchard*.

"It's the first thing since *Virginia Woolf* I've wanted to do. The part has always fascinated me. Chekhov is difficult to play because what is seemingly true on the surface is never a direct line to the character. I won't get to the heart of this character for months to come, and we're only doing it for some 40-odd performances. I won't get bored. Another reason I'm doing it is Eva LeGallienne. She gave me my first chance and I hadn't worked with her in 31 years, so I was anxious to be a part of her production."

The voice is low-pitched, enthusiastic and always close to the verge of laughter as she tells the story: "When I was 17, I wrote her a passionate letter from Wisconsin, where my father was a professor. I was full of ideals and I told her I wanted to be a serious artist and only play Shakespeare and Ibsen. I was coming to New York with my parents for two weeks and could I meet her? Well, I met her and read for her and then I went back home and enrolled for college and the day I got home from enrolling I had a letter from her asking me to play Ophelia to her Hamlet in a company she was forming in Massachusetts. That was a wonderful summer, but the company disbanded in the fall and although I was only 18, it was the end of the American theatre for me. My heart broke. I went back home and squawked so much my family let me return to New York, where I lived on $6.50 a week for months, doing the rounds from 9 to 6 every day. The following January I got an audition with the Lunts and made my Broadway debut as Nina in *The Sea Gull*. Going to the opening of *Cherry Orchard* the other night in a taxi, it suddenly occurred to me that I was opening once again on Broadway exactly 30 years to the month I made my debut. And in all those years I never played a small part. Maybe I *should* have."

Instead, the critics made her celebrated before she was old enough to know the meaning of the word. From *The Sea Gull* in 1938 she went directly to a play in summer stock in which she had to flatten her leading man, José Ferrer, with a pair of boxing gloves. A few months later, in December, she married him. The marriage lasted ten turbulent years; their daughter, Leticia, is now 27 and married to an actor named Brandwell Teuscher ("The wedding sounded like a scene from a Brontë novel—'I Leticia take thee Brandwell,'" jokes Uta with typical Hagen humor). It was also the period when she came as close as she ever got to being a movie star. "People always ask why I never made movies. I was very snobby about it. I never wanted to do commercial trash even in the beginning, and I went around saying 'I'm an *artiste,* I don't do commercial things' and so on. Now I'd like to try it, but it's too late. Just as it is too late to go back and play Saint Joan again. I played her before I was ready, I think. I once told Dame Sybil Thorndike I thought I was too old to play the part again and she said, 'Oh *no,* my deah, you can *never* be too old to play Saint Joan, you can only be too *young.'*

"Anyway, in 1939 Joe Ferrer and I were both swept off to Hollywood, where for about three months a great to-do was made over us and we were tested by all the studios. We hated Hollywood. One studio would make a fuss over me and not want Joe and the next one would want him and not me. It nearly wrecked our marriage. So we fled in the middle of the night and all the way back to New York we got telegrams begging us to come back. At every filling station the price would go up. I never went back and I have no regrets."

So she concentrated on the theatre, playing Desdemona to Paul Robeson's famous Othello, Blanche to a host of Stanleys in *A Streetcar Named Desire,* and a brassy blond film star in a quick flop called *In Any Language,* which she did because "I was flat broke and I thought it would be a hit since it was written by two Bob Hope writers and directed by George Abbott. I took it for all the wrong reasons so I deserved what I got. That's when I decided never to appear in anything again I didn't believe in. And I haven't."

She began teaching with Herbert Berghof in 1947 and married him in 1951, spicing her classroom schedule and her efforts to raise money for their school with fewer roles but greater triumphs, like *The Country Girl* and *Who's Afraid of Virginia Woolf?* "People get mad at me and say it's a scandal. 'You should be working every season,' they tell me. Then I ask, 'What did you see this season you think I should have been in?' This is always followed by dead silence. Ninety-five percent of the things I turn down either never open or they close in one week. I'm bored and dis-illusioned by the commercial theater. By the time a play opens so many people, from the angels to the producers, have speculated on how much money it will bring in that you no longer get the real McCoy. We've overpriced our-selves right out of business, from the real estate owner who gets a third of the cut right down to the carpenters' union and the scenic shops. Every time a union scale goes up, somebody is out of a job. Then the English come in and undercut us and the critics become Anglophiles and decide the English are better actors. It all comes back down to an economic problem. It's grotesque and cockeyed, so I stay out of it. But just because I'm not working on Broadway doesn't mean I'm sitting around on my laurels doing noth-ing. I teach four classes a week and act in projects at my studio, where the work counts. You *must* function. Other actors don't have a studio, so they must express themselves by doing commercial trash. I don't have to do that."

So Uta Hagen takes home her weekly paycheck as a teacher ("one-tenth of what I could get on Broadway if I did all the junk I'm offered") and repairs the toilet in the studio. "Acting is my work," she says, "but the studio is my life." Not that she doesn't give equal concentration to both. Once, while playing opposite Anthony Quinn in a tour of *Street-car*, the lights did not go out in the scene where Stanley is supposed to attack Blanche. Quinn dragged her to the bed, where he remained stupefied, not knowing what to do next. Uta knew. "Rape me, you idiot," she gasped, *"rape me!"*

TAKE 2: Uta Hagen, teacher, property owner, and dedi-cated idealist, dealing stacked decks of theatrical knowledge to 900 eager students a week in a renovated stable on Bank Street called the HB Studio. The Russian grande dame of *The Cherry Orchard* is nowhere around. She has been replaced by a rumpled, rusty-haired lady wielding a ham-mer, wearing pants and a railroad conductor's cap, sipping coffee from a paper cup, and waiting patiently to be photographed under a bulletin board where a note by one of her students reads: "Dear Mommie: Will you please leave me in peace, Mommie? I'm not coming home, for God's sake. Break a leg (and I mean it.) José."

She leads the way past admiring students ("When are you coming back to class? We miss you."), showing off her school like a proud mama. In a neighboring building, she points out a 75-seat theatre, where plays by aspiring playwrights are staged by the studio. "We're expanding. This building belonged to someone we called the Cat Woman. A character right out of Tennessee Williams. It cost more to fumigate than it did to buy the building. With all the building permits and zoning laws, it was two years before we could move inside." The three buildings which now make up the HB Studio still need work and, more important, money, since almost everybody works there out of love. "We never have enough money. But we have a dream. Herbert started out when he was a refugee, with a language problem, and he saw all the actors, sitting around in Walgreen's with no place to talk or work or develop their craft. Now we hope to do more than just teach acting. We want our own theatre. The American theatre is underrated, undersold, underdeveloped, unexplored and unappreciated. I hope that out of this studio will explode an acting company of the finest quality guided by first-rate directors and playwrights with an aim. Then perhaps we will make a real contribution to the theatre. In my Broadway and other commercial work I become periodically disillusioned, but this is the only place where I have known real fulfillment."

TAKE 3: Uta Hagen, the woman. Forbiddingly experienced in life as she is onstage. Deriving as much pleasure from making a flower bloom as playing Saint Joan. Opinionated, articulate, brainy and charming. Sitting in her living room looking down on Washington Square in an old building which, on the day of the interview, is out of both heat and hot water, and where someone with a dirty mind has scrawled a four-letter word in the elevator. "This is where I loaf. I'm a slob, really. In my supermarket in the Village one day I heard one of the checkers tell a customer, 'See that woman over there—she goes around pretending she's a Broadway star,' and I looked around to see whom she was talking about and I realized it was *me!*"

She falls back on the sofa, slapping her knee at the lunacy in such a notion. With her schedule, she never has time to put on the tiaras and the false eyelashes and the star-face. "The only real vacation I ever had was in 1961 when Herbert was in *Cleopatra*. We cashed in his first-class ticket to Rome and bought two tourist fares and I had a glorious time. We were in Rome from September to June and in all that time he only worked eight days! We lived on his daily expense money and saved his salary to buy our second building for the studio. We also have a house in Montauk where we go for three months every summer and I do nothing but garden. I grow all my own daisies and zinnias and do all my own canning and bake my own bread. I love flowers and sometimes I even go out and water them at 4 A.M. by flashlight. Then in the fall I spray everything with dried blood and cover it with salt hay and manure to keep the wild deer from eating my bulbs in the winter. I never go to the theatre and seldom go to the movies. Herbert goes, but I don't. I look at acting all day long, so I don't want to go out in the evening and look at it some more. Between the studio and Montauk and my own schedule, I don't have time. In my spare time, I cook. You can criticize anything in my acting, but don't attack my cooking. Come see my Christmas present."

She beckons me past walls of paintings and awards and bookcases crowded with Kafka and Freud and Willa Cather to her favorite room, the kitchen. "I have my own noodle machine and an ancient six-burner stove where I can keep a lot of pots going at once. This," she points proudly, "is my prize possession. It's called a Ronson automatic food preparation center. It is equipped with all-electric meat grinders, blenders, ice crushers, the works. You should see the meals I cook up on this thing. I grow all my own herbs, and organically grown vegetables." She snaps out a photo of Uta Hagen, not looking like anybody's idea of a great actress of the serious theatre, holding two home-grown zucchinis bigger than bowling pins. "This is what life is all about."

She means it. And as long as she is talking about the things that move her, she is a happy, headstrong, radiant broth of a lady, involved to her fingertips with the business of not getting trapped in the suffocatingly small world of show business. But mention acting and she stiffens, begins to actually shake visibly. "A man from CBS called me and asked me to go on TV to explain my acting technique last week, and I think he was quite insulted when I said no. I do not talk about my technique or how I teach it. I am bored to *death* by TV programs, discussions and newspaper interviews about how to act. You never see musicians discuss how they hold their bows, or painters telling how they hold their brushes. I was asked to write a book about acting in 1955 and I stupidly signed a contract and spent the advance. I never finished it and I never will, because there are no blanket statements to solve the riddle of acting. It's a technique by which a person discovers within himself certain behavior patterns, then brings them to life onstage. Every actor is different, with a whole new endless cycle of problems to solve. In addition, every individual has a certain radiance or quality to communicate which has nothing to do with acting. Talent is cheap, star quality is something entirely different. I don't know if I have that or not. Who's a star and who isn't? If making a million dollars means you're a star, then I'm not a star. Girls on TV panel shows can outdraw me, but I know I'm a better actress. Yet when I

leave the stage door nobody recognizes me. Whenever people asked me for an autograph, they used to look at it and
then say, 'Yewta Haygen, who's that?' Now I ask them
whose autograph they want before I sign, because I know
they can swap ten Uta Hagens for one Paul Newman."

You can't be a star in Montauk. And today, at 48, the
problem does not cross her mind. "Oh once, when I was
young—before I was even 20—I was in *Key Largo* at the
Ethel Barrymore Theatre with Paul Muni and Joe Ferrer
and I had just gotten notices like you wouldn't believe and
I got pretty drunk on my own perfume and thought I was
terribly important. So I got into a cab one day and said very
haughtily to the driver, 'Take me to the Ethel Barrymore
Theatre, puh-leeze,' and the cabbie turned around and said,
'The *what* theatre? Lissen, lady, I been a hack for 20 years
and I ain't never heard of no Ethel Barrymore.' It taught me
a lesson for the rest of my life."

Simone Signoret

The interview with Simone Signoret is set for two o'clock. She is thirty minutes late and nowhere in sight. Her suite at the Plaza doesn't answer, and trying to get through to the publicity department at Warner Brothers-Seven Arts to find out what's going wrong is like trying to put through a person-to-person call to the Apollo 8. For reasons never clear to the people who have to interview actors on press junkets, but best understood by the kind of people who schedule such circuses, it seems that someone has brought most of the stars of *The Sea Gull* over from Europe at the same time. Now they are all scattered throughout the city missing appointments and losing their schedules—in varying degrees of undisciplined temperament—like high-school kids on a Beta Club convention. I walk through the candy-box lobby of the Plaza and phone again. "Try the Edwardian Room—I saw some of them go in there a little while ago," says the operator with a slight trace of hysteria in the voice.

There she is. I don't know what people expect her to be like from the roles she plays, but she's no fading Colette heroine. Nowhere is there a trace of the ripened older woman from *Room at the Top,* inspiring passions in younger men. She's no femme fatale, either. The tender qualities she showed in her early films like *Casque d'Or*—which the slick magazines used to describe as "lyricism in a country bed"— are only youthful memories now. Her manner is tough. There's a rough, fruit-peel texture to her skin. A hard smile braces the edges of her mouth. She has broad, fullback shoulders and short, masculine hands—scruffy, with broken nails, like a scrubwoman's—which punctuate the air with brisk, expressive karate chops. She wears little makeup, her hair—once described by *Time* magazine as "chablis-colored"—is now rinsed into an unstylish mop with a mind of its own, and maybe it's my imagination, but the air around her table seems slightly blue, possibly from being sprayed with so many four-letter words.

"Don't tell me your name," she says, "because I am French and we never hear names. It will just go right in one ear and out the other. I will just call you Mr. New York Times. This is David Warner." Warner, who starred in *Morgan* and now plays the very British-sounding Russian son of the very French-sounding Signoret in *The Sea Gull*, extends a limp hand. "I hate this room. They didn't want to let me in without a tie," he says, shaking his hair, which is long enough to braid, and blinking his eyes nervously behind oblong glasses thick enough to see the moon through. Signoret then introduces Mrs. Warner, a round-faced young Swedish morsel who looks like a stand-in for *Candy*, and Moura Budberg, an elderly Russian dowager who translated and adapted the film version of Chekhov's play. Miss Budberg stares coldly at the intruder from a hooded cape, looking very much like an old photo of Isak Dinesen. "The old hag claims to be a baroness," says Signoret, "but we all suspect her of being an old Russian phony." Miss Budberg cackles, enjoying the insult. They've all been drinking several bottles of white wine and they're all a bit smashed.

"We should all drink nothing but champagne and eat nothing but caviar," says Mr. Warner, "and charge it all to Warner Brothers. They expect it, you know. They charge it all to taxes anyway."

"I hate these publicity trips," adds Signoret. "We only came so we could all be together again. I know you always hear actors on publicity trips say, 'I love my co-stars' and 'Oh, God, what an experience!' and it's all bull crap, but this time it's true. We all loved each other in *The Sea Gull*, didn't we, David?"

"Oh, yes," says Warner, picking up the cue, "we all loved each other."

There is a telephone call from James Mason, another co-star. "Well, bring it to the table," scolds Signoret. "I refuse to walk across the room. Don't you have any of those little white phones like they have at the Beverly Hills Hotel?" Somebody finds a phone and plugs it in. "Hello, this is Miss Signoret. No, I do not wish to make a call. *You* are calling *me!* No, no, I had a call from Mr. James Mason. Mason! M-A-S-O-N . . . My God, what kind of place is this? They never heard of James Mason!" She slams down the receiver. "I hate this hotel. I tried to get the Algonquin, but the people at Warners are all such idiots, they can't do anything right. I've been here two days and they still have not given me any spending money. I never carry my own money on publicity trips."

"I never do publicity," says Warner. "James and Simone and Vanessa are all deluged with interviews on this trip, but I told them before I came over from London I would not waste my time being interviewed. I think interviews are boring."

"Well, the people at Warner Brothers are such idiots," says Signoret, "they have my entire schedule all mixed up. I don't know where I'm supposed to be right now, but now that Mr. New York Times is here, I suppose I might as well do the goddam interview. Let's all go up to my room."

"I don't do interviews," says Warner, "so you go up alone and I'll join you later." Already it's turning into a day to be grateful for small favors.

Inside the room, Signoret throws the keys on the desk and kicks off her shoes. "So what is America coming to? I guess we're going back to the McCarthy witch-hunts under

Mr. Nixon. This is the first time I've never been allowed on TV in this country. Two years ago I won an Emmy and now they won't let me work because I refused to answer their stupid questions in order to get a visa. I have what they call a 'B-2 visitor's permit,' but I have been refused an 'H-1 work permit.' Most Americans have no idea of the insulting questions you have to answer to work in this country. 'Are you a homosexual?' 'Do you take drugs?' 'Are you planning to kill the President?' My dear, if I was planning to kill the President, would I say yes? It's *The Crucible* all over again. They have always suspected me of being a Communist here, anyway, because during the war I worked as a typist for a pro-German newspaper in Paris. I could have become a collaborationist, I suppose. I had no conscience in those days. But I didn't. I was never a Nazi, but many of my friends were Nazis. I was never a Communist, either, but I was thrown in with people who were rightish, leftish, *everything* —and we were always signing peace appeals and taking stands against things the American government didn't like. So they make me sign all sorts of insulting papers now in order to work in America. I will not do it. It's a question of pride. I choose not to be insulted. If they want me to work here, it's their problem. All it means to me is that now I won't have to go on TV and talk to Mr. Merv What's-His-Name. Now that I know I don't do TV I don't have to look good, so I think I'll booze it up."

She calls room service and orders a bottle of vodka, a bottle of gin, a bottle of whiskey, two bottles of Scotch, a bottle of brandy, and lots of ice. "Let's have a drink while we wait," she says, pouring a Scotch into a bathroom glass. It tastes like toothpaste. "Now what do you want to ask me?"

"Well, about *The Sea Gull* . . ."

"It all started when I made *The Deadly Affair* in London for Sidney Lumet. James Mason, David Warner, Harry Andrews, Sidney and I all got along so well that we said, 'Let's do a Chekhov one day.' People are always saying that.

but Sidney is the first director who ever lived up to his word. One year later he called me in the South of France and said we'd do it and this past summer we all went to Stockholm and did it. We accomplished it all through a horrible selfishness and an enormous bath of love. The twelve people in the cast had the most incestuous love affair I've ever seen. Everyone was in love, from David Warner, who is 27, right up to that phony old baroness, who is 73—all laughing together, crying together, moved by the same things. We didn't just go to work and then go home to the hotel at night. We lived together in each other's rooms, ate together . . . suddenly *The Sea Gull* became *Hamlet* and I was Gertrude, David was Hamlet, Mason was Claudius, Vanessa was Ophelia . . . we were like children playing a game and we played it that way in the movie. Why do people take LSD? To travel, see colors. Well, to us, playing Chekhov was a trip. I don't sleep with women, but I loved Vanessa Redgrave so much that I took her home with me to Paris and she stayed a week at my house in the country. We couldn't bear to be separated. It all sounds like crap, but for once it's all true."

Is she satisfied with the final result? "This woman I play, this Arkadina—she's a bitch, the kind of woman I detest. But bitchery is something I know about. I'm no saint. I also know how to play older women. I *am* one. And I've lived, my friend. I never look at anybody but myself in my films. All actors are like this. The others, who say they don't look only at themselves, they are liars. But this is the first time I ever looked at the other actors. That sounds like crap too, no? You will write it and it will sound like crap. That's why I hate interviews. Let's have another drink."

She lights up a Marlboro and flicks the ashes all over the Plaza's imitation Versailles rug. "I started out playing whores. I'd rather have played a pharmaceutical student, but it was all I was offered. The minute I felt the label, I quit. Then after I won the Oscar playing that Mrs. What's-

Her-Name in *Room at the Top* all I was offered was middle-aged women who seduce young men. I don't go to bed with boys young enough to be my sons and I won't play them. So I didn't work much after that. But I enjoyed doing it that one time. It wasn't the greatest book ever written, but it was a damn good story. I said to myself, 'It won't make any money,' so I asked for a fee instead of a percentage. That was the biggest mistake of my career. If I had accepted a percentage of the film, I'd have enough money to make my grandchildren rich. After that, I got offered mountains of scripts in Hollywood, but they were all things Bette Davis didn't want to do 20 years ago! I didn't feel the need to be a Hollywood star. It's all right—the sun is nice and it's nice to have a car sent for you each morning—as long as you don't do crappy pictures and work with crappy directors. I worked with Stanley Kramer on *Ship of Fools* there. He's no Jean-Luc Godard, but he knows it. The truth is, I don't work much because I have a husband and a marriage I have to hold together. We've had stormy periods but we must be doing something right, because we've been together 18 years."

Signoret is 47, the daughter of a Jewish father and a Catholic mother. In 1947, while working as a movie extra in Paris, she married Yves Allegret, a director. Two years later, she met Yves Montand, whom she married in June, 1960, shortly after her divorce from Allegret. The marriage has often been heated enough to make headlines, "but only when we are separated. Don't ask me about Marilyn Monroe. I've had a lifetime of Marilyn Monroe. That happened while we were apart. Now I never take a job during a period when Yves is working. It creates a split. Recently I played Lady Macbeth on the stage in London and I was so miserable being away from him that it was a disaster. The reviews were so horrible I couldn't even read them. We shot *The Sea Gull* in only 27 days, so I wasn't away long. Now Yves will do *On a Clear Day You Can See Forever* in Hollywood with Streisand, and I will stay home and play the actor's wife and enjoy myself. There are people in Paris I wouldn't have a cup of tea with. Hollywood is no different. It just has more idiots that anyplace else, that's all. It's not my place and I don't have to belong. I'm a passenger in transit there. I have no secretary, no maid, no dresser—my only entourage is the bellboys at the Beverly Hills Hotel. In France, my home is a country house in Normandy. Instead of going to Maxim's every night with four mink coats, I have everyone to my home. We show 16-millimeter movies, musicians rehearse there, writers come and write there. Resnais wrote *La Guerre est Finie* there. It's that kind of house. In Paris, I also have an apartment which used to be an old bookstore."

The door opens and in comes a preacher from Dallas who teaches a religious cinema course in a Baptist seminary. Do you love it? He has tried to interview Signoret earlier in the day, but his tape recorder broke. Now he's back. Signoret is bored. "Just say Sidney Lumet has no talent, I hate him, I hate Chekhov, the woman I play is a crook, Vanessa Redgrave is a cute little actress, David Warner is a spoiled brat, the whole thing has been written by a phony baroness, and I did it all for money." She winks and pours another Scotch. The preacher looks as though he has been slapped, but he smiles to let her know he has enjoyed this moment of actressy eccentricity.

The interview continues for half an hour, then Signoret rolls up her sleeves as though she is about to tackle a hard day's wash, and says: "Look. I have no problems with religion. I'm a complete agnostic and I don't believe in God. Life after death is bull and the principle that we should live a certain kind of life in one place because it will prepare us for another life somewhere else is ridiculous! There's no mystery, no heaven, no life hereafter. For others maybe, but not for me."

The preacher from Dallas flees as though he has just

seen the devil himself. Signoret licks her chops, turns on her sinister smile from *Diabolique*, and says, "Now. Where were we?"

Another question is forming when the door opens again, admitting David Warner, who informs Signoret they are all due in an hour at the apartment of Tony Walton, the *Sea Gull* set designer and ex-husband of Julie Andrews. "*Merde! Merde!* Those idiots at Warner Brothers have not sent the car around and I can't get anyone on the telephone." She dials Warner Brothers. "Hello, dear," she says to the operator, "let me speak to the publicity department . . . what do you mean, they're all out? Are they all sick or still out to lunch? This is Miss Signoret . . . S-I-G-N . . . what do you mean, they've all gone home? (Covering the phone.) Do you believe it? Not a soul left in the whole office. Hello . . . yes, I need some money and a limousine and . . . what do you mean, who do I know? They want to know who I know. What should I tell them?"

"Tell them who you know . . ."

"Hello . . . I know Kate Hepburn . . . and the woman who owns the Algonquin Hotel . . . and George Cukor . . . no, no, *merde!* . . . he doesn't work in the legal department . . . he's a *director!*" She slams the receiver down. "Idiots!"

This is followed by a great deal of excitement over sending a telegram to Vanessa Redgrave, whom they plan to join in Hollywood in a few days, and which I have to write, since Signoret insists actors cannot spell. Then she goes into the bathroom and begins to wash her hair. The interview seems hopeless. I pack up my pencils.

"Tell Mr. New York Times to stay as long as he likes," she yells to David Warner from under the soapsuds. "If I didn't like him, I would've thrown him out a long time ago."

I leave where I came in. "Actually," says Warner, tossing his bangs as the door closes, "I never give interviews myself. I made that perfectly clear when I left London. No interviews, I said . . ."

Patricia Neal

Patricia Neal sat on a big yellow blanket in an old chair with the bottom falling out of it and grinned. Watching Patricia Neal grin is like tasting ice cream for the very first time. There is no grin like it anywhere. It starts casually, down deep inside where the clockwork is, winds its way slowly up, catching on around the lips, then pauses, connecting along the way with some part of the brain that thinks sunny thoughts, and finally breaks wide open, letting in the world or the room or wherever she happens to be when she's grinning, and everybody feels at home. In a life full of minus signs, it's been a big plus, that grin.

"Mind you, I wasn't always this happy," she said in her tiny dressing room in the back of an old warehouse on West 26th Street where she was between shots on *The Subject Was Roses*, the first movie she has made since she suffered those three hideous near-fatal strokes three years ago. "When I recovered from nearly dying, I hated life. I couldn't talk, I couldn't move, I hated the nurse, I hated my husband Roald Dahl, who had to do all the housework and take care of all four of the children, I hated God, I lost all contact with religion, I really resented everything and everyone for letting me live to be a vegetable. I hated life for a year and a half, then I started learning how to be a person again and now I've loved life for a year and a half. And I love it a lot."

She waved a goodbye kiss to Pat Hingle, an old friend who had dropped by for lunch served in plastic bags and

paper cups, then sat down again and lit up a menthol cigarette. She was wearing an orange dress and an old brown
sweater thrown over her shoulders and her hair was tied up
in a brown scarf. It was a far cry from the glamorous days
on Hollywood movie sets when she was the hottest thing
since peanut butter, but only one thing seemed important:
Pat Neal was working again. The illness has left her with a
slight limp and when she speaks the words form slowly and
sometimes get twisted around her tongue like bacon around
a fork, a fault she covers up by becoming veddy British
("married" comes out "maddied," etc.). Otherwise, she's the
same staunch, valiant head-held-high lady she always was.
Maybe better. A new strength has crept in where an elegant
Kentucky-born, Tennessee-bred softness used to reign.
"Coming back to New York was my husband's idea. I didn't
choose this film, he did. You know, Frank Gilroy wrote it for
me to play on the stage, but it came at the time when my
little daughter Olivia died and I was too upset to do a play.
But they held out for me when it came time to do the film,
waiting to see if I would be well enough to do it. So Roald
just signed me up without even asking me if I wanted to do
it and now I'm glad he did, because I think it's the best film
I've ever made. I think I like it even better than *Hud* or *Face
in the Crowd*, which are my other two favorites. And I tell
you, being back in New York is the best therapy in the world
for me. I was pretty scared, let me tell you. I didn't know if
I could do it or not. I can't learn lines anymore. They just
go right out of my head. My illness just wiped out my
memory. I didn't even know my husband's name when I
came to, or the names of any of my children. I still can't
remember the names of most of the films I was in or the
names of people I worked with. I remember everything that
ever happened to me in my life, even the things I'd like to
forget, but the part of my brain that was injured is the part
that remembers names. Oh, I remember *The Fountainhead*
and *The Breaking Point*, but not the others. People come up

to me and say, 'I just loved you in *The Hasty Heart*, and I say, 'Let me see now, which one was that?' In *The Subject Was Roses* I have one four-page scene of dialogue where I talk to myself. It was very difficult. Valerie, my companion from Great Missenden, my village in England, came with me. At home Roald had six or eight friends a day dropping in from the village to help me with my lines, and now when I forget, Valerie helps me. She is one of the people who helped me most. She started me playing bridge again and she came with me last year when I made a fourteen-minute speech for brain-injured children at the—oh damn, I can't remember the name of the hotel."

"The Waldorf," said Valerie.

"Oh yes, that big ugly one on Park Avenue. Everyone has helped me. People have been more wonderful to me than I ever dreamed. It sometimes takes a big blow like I got to make people re-evaluate the importance of human beings. On this film alone, I couldn't have made it without everyone's help. I love the actors, I love the producer, Edgar Lansbury, I love the director, Ulu Grosbard, I love my hairdresser, who comes from ten miles away from where I was raised in Tennessee. They've all helped me over the hurdles."

And for Pat Neal, there have been a lot of hurdles. "Listen," she is quick to point out, "my troubles didn't begin with these strokes. So many rotten things have happened to me in my life that sometimes I think I was born under a very nasty star. Nobody else in my family has had the miserable luck I've had, so it's not something that runs in my family. I left home when I was 18, and I haven't lived with my family since, but we are very close. My mother is 68 years old and lives in St. Petersburg, Florida. My sister lives in Atlanta and my younger brother is a teacher in— wait a minute, I'll look up the name of the town in my address book, because I can't remember—Wimberly, Texas. See? I can remember a lot of things. My father died of a heart attack in 1949. I came to New York from Tennessee and met Eugene O'Neill, who didn't use me in the play I auditioned for, but he liked me enough to get me into something else and a lot of people saw me there and I got to understudy in *The Voice of the Turtle* and on closing night I got a telegram to do the Lillian Hellman play, *Another Part of the Forest*. I didn't want to do that play, I wanted to do *John Loves Mary*, which Richard Rodgers was producing. I remember he wouldn't give me the money I wanted and I got so mad I told him Lillian Hellman wanted me for her play and he just told me to go ahead and do it. I love him, but he was the stingiest man I ever met. Anyway, I did the Hellman play and that's what got me to Hollywood, where I bet you can't guess what my first movie was. It was *John Loves Mary* and I was very bad in it. I had been very happy in New York. I lived in an apartment with four friends, then in a fifth-floor walkup with Jean Hagen on Lexington Avenue that didn't even have a kitchen or a john and we used to take baths a block away at a friend's house. The happiest part of my life has always revolved around this town. My troubles began when I went to Hollywood. I started going with Gary Cooper and ended up in analysis. When we broke up, I went to a woman psychiatrist in Philadelphia and nearly had a nervous breakdown. Then I ended up in Atlanta and hid out there for six months in my sister's house and went to a wonderful psychiatrist who saved my sanity and got me in shape to go back to work. I came back to New York and did Lillian Hellman's play— I can't remember the name—"

"It was *The Children's Hour*," said Valerie.

"Oh yes, *The Children's Hour*. That's when I met Roald. You see, this interview is doing me a lot of good. It's making me remember. Let's see. Oh yes, I couldn't wait to get pregnant, but after we were married I couldn't have any children, so I went to a doctor who blew up my tubes—well, my darlin', that's what they *do*, you know—women are so complicated—and then they started coming right and left. Now we're going to stop. No more children. I don't think I could stand the pain of watching misfortunes happen to any more children. First there was Theo, who was hit by a taxi and we didn't think he'd live. The poor little thing lived in a critical condition for two years with a tube in his head to drain the fluid from his brain. He's eight now and he's going to be all right. He has a hole in his arm and bless his heart, he keeps breaking it all the time. But at least he will live. Then there's Ophelia, who is 4, and Tessa, the eldest, who is 11, and the baby, Lucy, who was born two years ago during my strokes. We didn't know if she would live eithcr. My daughter Olivia died of the measles when she was 13 and there was nothing anyone could do. It was one of those terrible fluke accidents. Then my mother-in-law died suddenly. Then I went to California to make a film for John Ford and we had just started shooting when I had the first stroke. I was pregnant with Lucy and if I had not had a husband like Roald I would not be alive today and neither would the baby. He had been discussing Theo's brain injury with this brain surgcon who was my agent's brother-in-law. We had met him at a cocktail party, and I remember thinking, 'I hope he never has to operate on *me!*' When I became paralyzed, Roald recognized the symptoms, picked up the phone and called him, and they rushed me into surgery in Los Angeles. Only quick thinking saved me. They didn't think I'd have any brain left when I got off the operating table.

"At first I simply refused to get out of bed. I hated everyone and wanted to die. They treated me like a child. I was forced to say the alphabet. I had to learn all over again how to spell and how to say dog and cat and hello. I tell you, I was a vegetable, that's the only word for it. But something happens to you, I guess. You just accept what has happened to you and you get stronger and stronger. Everyone was so kind. Mildred Dunnock and Betsy Drake took care of my children before we left California for England. I went to a swimming pool in a military hospital every day to learn how to use my limbs again. People donated their time, and it was all free. I never had to pay for anything but my leg massages and my therapist. And I don't know what I'd do without all the insurance we had through Actors Equity and the Screen Actors Guild. We can't get sick again, any of us. We've used up *all* the insurance. I wore a cast and my legs were held in by big leather braces until recently, but now I'm fine. Working in this movie and being back in New York again, seeing all my old friends, has done more than any braces could do. It has proved to me I can carry a work load again. I don't take any medicine or pills and I even drink better than I used to." A wide grin breaks out like a June morning. "And I *love* cocktails. I love martinis and old-fashioneds, but I love martinis the best. I also smoke too much, but I can't stop. I once had a doctor who couldn't stand cigarettes and he always warned me and lectured me about smoking. He died of lung cancer two years ago and he didn't even smoke. I tried to quit once, for an entire week, and I cried for seven days. The first thing I remember when I woke up from the operations was seeing this blurry figure looking out the window smoking a cigarette. It was Roald. I didn't even know who he was, but I reached my hand out for his cigarette and now he says that was the first sign he had that I would be all right. Now I just try to carry on with my life as normally as possible. I have to dance in the movie and although they wouldn't let me see the rushes, they tell me I was fine. Do you have a light?"

They were calling her for makeup. Melvyn Douglas was arriving at three to say hello. It was a busy afternoon and time to leave. "My darlin', my darlin', listen to me and remember something. All of these rotten things that have happened to me have certainly changed my outlook on life. But I look around me at all the crime and the terrible things people do to each other and it makes me wonder if the world is going straight to hell. If only I could tell people how lucky they are. I've learned to love people and life again and I've learned there is definitely something bigger than all of us up there or out there somewhere that keeps us going. I am not Joan of Arc of 1968 and I sure as hell don't want anyone to think I'm a martyr. I'm opinionated and sassy. They tell me Ronald Reagan may get into the White House. If that happens, I swear I'll give up my citizenship. I hope the last has happened to me for the rest of my life, but my point is I had to have a severe blow to make me learn how to *care* all over again, after I had forgotten how. That's the one thing I got out of all this. I don't think I will ever forget again."

Outside, green buds were poking out on the grimy trees growing out of the dirty cement. Grips and electricians and even the tired studio cop guarding the warehouse entrance chatted gaily. A warm breeze blew the skirts of the girls in their spring dresses. Maybe I'm crazy, but it looked like people were smiling. And why not? Patricia Neal was back. It was a lovely thing to smile about.

Zoe Caldwell

"I don't give a tuppence of crap for being a star," says Zoe Caldwell, who whether she likes it or not, has suddenly become one. Why? Because in spite of her attempts to hide from her own success, she is so remarkable in *The Prime of Miss Jean Brodie* that the public will have it no other way. What's more, she would have been a star a long time ago if she'd only stayed in one place long enough.

Like Porgy, she's been on her way for years. Word would sift down from places like Manitoba about her Mother Courage or Saint Joan. People would bring back paeans of praise for her Ophelia in Minneapolis or her Cleopatra in Canada. Everywhere people would grab their programs, run their fingers along the cast list and remark: "It says her name is Zoe Caldwell, but who *is* she?" Broadway almost found out when she briefly replaced Anne Bancroft as a demented, hunchback nun in *The Devils* in 1965 and later dropped by for a few days in 1966 to pick up a Tony for her waspish Southern society columnist in Tennessee Williams' ill-fated *Slapstick Tragedy*. But then, in typical Caldwell fashion, she went off to Niagara-on-the-Lake and got lost again playing Shaw. That's the way she is. And now that she's back and Broadway's got her (as they used to say in the ads for Clark Gable-Greer Garson movies), people are still wanting to know: Just who *is* Zoe Caldwell?

For clues, examine this. You go to the interview backstage at the Helen Hayes, expecting Miss Brodie—frumpy, middle-aged, with a layer of tub around her middle, held together with a torn corset, hair in a bun, peering down through schoolmarm spectacles and serving delicately sweetened sassafras tea in dainty blue teacups. Instead, you fall into a whirlwind. Here is this sexy—yes, *sexy*—dame (34 years old, and you don't believe it) racing about being photographed by a man with a high-speed camera that sounds like a machine gun going off ("It's like an adventure!" she squeals), with a soft, girlish complexion and what appears to be 8 pounds of red hair, flying every which direction.

Sipping brandy and puffing filter cigarettes, she throws her stockinged legs across the end of a pink and green chaise longue and talks a blue streak. "No, I'm not like Miss Brodie, except for one thing. I've never been married and I'm most certainly in my prime." Friendly freckles sparkle across her countenance and one suspects that, hidden away in the dumpy old-maid schoolteacher clothes she wears as Miss Brodie, there beats in Zoe Caldwell the heart of a swinger. She has had five major love affairs, among them an Australian guitar maker and several leading men in the theatre (In 1961, when she was playing Bianca to Albert Finney's Cassio in *Othello* at Stratford-on-Avon, she was named corespondent in his wife's divorce suit). "Darling, you don't think when I was going to all those places playing all those roles all over the world, I was *alone,* do you?" Right now she is "very much in love, luv" with Robert Whitehead, the producer of *Jean Brodie,* and spends her spare time dashing about with a stray cat named Mop in a yellow jeep with a red canvas top between his New York apartment and his Bucks County farm—"75 acres with a lake and an 18th-century stone farmhouse with lots of fireplaces." Here she glows.

"My life is happier now than ever before, but not necessarily because I'm at last on Broadway. I don't think Broadway was ever a goal. I know I'm an actor—will be one till I go—you know, *die*—and if tomorrow I get a call from Manitoba wanting me to have another go at Mother Courage, I'll go. My next job is always the one I'm offered. The biggest mistake creative artists make is playing it safe. Is this the right play, is this the right part, is this the right place? It's the same in life. Is this the right man for me to love on this particular Sunday? I've never lived my life like that. I want a child—oh please God, let me have a child—and it will be raised with teddy bears and 'Gentle Jesus meek and mild' and all that, but I don't intend to plan out its life. I won't spend my time with mouthwashes and dusting off sofas. I'm a Virgo. Squeaky clean we are.

"I've always taken chances. I began in Australia where there was no theatre. Only two men like the Shuberts who would bring tours over from New York or London. I've been a professional since the age of 9, but by the time I was 18 and ready to go into rep, there was no rep. Then a bloke came out from London and started one and I got to do everything from a tour with Judith Anderson in *Medea* to leads in *Major Barbara* and *Blithe Spirit*. It was good-o, luv. But if I had packed me bags earlier and really *planned* a career, I would never have gotten to play so many roles so young. Then when I went to England, to Stratford-on-Avon, there I was with six years of leads behind me, but all I could get was a contract to do walk-ons. But it never occurred to me to say, 'Hell, I'm only walking on so I'll only make up half me face.' I was an actress and they saw it in my work. Tony Richardson got me all dressed up exotic-like and blew up a big part for me in *Pericles* and in 1959 I went back and played the first fairy in Peter Hall's production of *Midsummer Night's Dream* and worked with Laughton, Ian Holm, Dorothy Tutin."

There was *Othello*, too. Mary Ure was Desdemona and Paul Robeson was Othello—"a marvelous bloke." She leaps to her feet and does an imitation of Robeson trying to do improvisations because "Tony Richardson had just come back from America that year and was mad-keen on the Actors Studio and Robeson just jumped up and down and said, 'Yeah men' and we all thought we were method actors.

"Then Michael Langham rang me up when I was at the Royal Court in London and said a girl at Stratford had become pregnant"—she roars approval at the thought of anyone becoming pregnant at Stratford—"and could I play Rosaline in *Love's Labour's Lost* and I went straight back and worked with Paul Scofield and Kate Reid and then went to Toronto to do a telly with Sean Connery and while I was *there* another bloke rank me up and asked me to come to Manitoba. I didn't even know where the hell Manitoba was, but I went. Most of my career has been just saying yes to blokes on the phone."

When she went home to Australia, she found herself "out of tune with my own country," took off on a vagabond trip up the coast in an old car, ran out of money, got caught in a cyclone, and hocked everything to get to Minneapolis. "I just said, 'Yes, I'll come' on the phone—I'm not very good at signing me name to contracts, but if I say I'll be there, I'll be there. So when I arrived, I discovered Equity didn't want me because I was an alien and for the first six weeks of rehearsals every time there was a union meeting they'd hide me. Even Bob Whitehead's cousin Hume Cronyn voted against me. But they finally let me in and I had a marvelous year playing *Three Sisters* and *The Miser* and then I got that old ding-ding danger signal that things were getting too cozy and I went back to Canada and did a very second-rate tour of little country towns where people buy tickets and never come, you know, like people who pay $20 to the Cancer Fund to rid themselves of guilt. I was miserable."

Back to Minneapolis for starring roles in *The Caucasian Chalk Circle* and *The Way of the World* and Lord knows what else. Then she moved in with the Cronyns in Manhattan and understudied Anne Bancroft as the nun in *The Devils* and one night, when the star wrenched her back, Zoe went on and for the performances that followed audiences went wild. "It was good-o, luv—I'd walk up Fifth Avenue and watch myself in the store windows. One block I'd be me and the next I'd be a hunchback nun trying to have an orgasm"—she walks around the dressing room like a hunchback. Then Alan Schneider offered her *Slapstick Tragedy*. She played the society columnist like a cross between Hermione Gingold and a pelican, won lots of praise, then disappeared again.

"By this time I was already living with Bob Whitehead, so we took off after I did the Shaw festival in Canada and picked up the Arthur Millers and toured the Caribbean for eight months with the Cronyns. It's the first time I ever enjoyed leisure time and just had fun. Once in London, when I was out of work, I got so neurotic I got a job as a mother's help, scrubbing pots and making breakfast. I also got a job in a pickle factory. Acting is what I need to spend my excess energy on, to make me a good member of society. Without it, I'd probably become sort of nympho-maniac or whatever kind of maniac presented itself. I've never been to an analyst. Actors who need psychiatrists are simply not doing enough acting."

Nobody is more surprised about her success as Jean Brodie than Zoe herself. "Actually Bob wasn't keen on me for the part. It was the playwright Jay Allen, whom I'd met through Bob, who convinced him. I was sitting around the kitchen table one night helping them think of the right star and suddenly Jay said, 'I know who could play Brodie,' and we both said, 'Who?' and she said me. I had seen Vanessa Redgrave twice in the role in London—I know her quite well—and it seemed absurd. She's beauti-ful and I've never been pretty. People used to say, 'Give Zoe an ingenue and she'll give her stoop shoulders and glasses every time.'

"But I liked Brodie and that is my only requirement. I like her so much that every night I strip down stark naked and start becoming Brodie from scratch—I pull at my hair here, twist it a bit there, get the feel of her shoes. I couldn't play any part I didn't like. If I had a thing against blondes, I couldn't play a blonde. There are no parts I can't play—Nazis, Lesbians, nuns—I'd like them all. One thing I've never done is play myself. I'd like to play a modern girl now, a part I could create. I'd love to go to Arizona and make a western movie. I don't know how to ride a horse, but I could learn. Oh, the trouble I've had with agents who want me to be a star. I will not appear in the *Players Guide* because they don't know how to label me. Ingenue, leading lady, walk-on—I've done them all. One woman came to interview me. 'What kind of actress are you?' she asked. I thought for a moment. 'Character,' I said, 'I'd have to say a character actress.' 'Does that mean you never get the man?' she said." Zoe grabs my shoe and falls back on her dressing-room chair, convulsed. "Well, I got the man when I played Cleopatra and I was sexy as hell in that, luv."

She is tough on herself: "When critics say I am all technique and no warmth, they are sometimes right. What all those people at the Actors Studio need to do is learn some of my technique and *I* need to go to the Actors Studio. I have a lot of power and a great technical facility. I am never worried that I will lose my strength, but I have to watch my technique or it will push my character off the stage. I did that on opening night. I lost all my saliva and started out on such a high, forced level that I distorted Brodie. When I insult my own taste, it doesn't matter how many people tell me I'm marvelous, I bloody well know I'm not."

But about that success: after all these years, won't a four-figure weekly salary change a girl? "Money! Hah! I have no fur coats, no money in the bank, nothing I can say, 'Look, there's a bit of security.' Look, luv, I used to furnish my whole apartment for 50 bucks at the Salvation

Army. Now I shop at Bloomingdale's. But there's not much difference in the junk you get at the Salvation Army and the junk you get at Bloomingdale's except the junk at Bloomingdale's costs more."

It's time for her to start stripping down to the nude to create Miss Brodie again. "A STAR . . ." she roars, halting me at the door with a voice that is half Jean Brodie, half Thunderhead, Son of Flicka. "I don't think I am a star! But if I ever become one, I think I could cope." She grins so widely that three wrinkles appear in the middle of her pretty nose. "And if I ever had to, I could go back to the Salvation Army next week."

Stars Fell on
Alabama – Again

Selma, Ala.

Saturday night in Selma, when the stink from the paper factory settles over the town like fallout, is usually the loneliest night of the week. Nothing much to do. Some folks go down to the Rotary Club meeting, others wait for the picture show to open at eight o'clock. The teenagers ride up and down Main Street waving to their friends. Moths hang around the street lamps. Folks drink a beer and go to bed early.

But tonight is different. The movie people are in town and there hasn't been this much excitement since the murder of Mrs. Viola Liuzzo put Selma on the map. The movie people are here shooting Carson McCullers' novel *The Heart Is a Lonely Hunter*, and although most people in Selma have never heard of Mrs. McCullers, her novel, or the film's star Alan Arkin, they're out in groups, hanging around street corners, listening to the LSU-Alabama football game on their transistor radios, and waiting for the action to begin.

A few blocks from the now-famous Pettus Bridge, the spot on the Alabama River where the peace march from Selma to Montgomery was halted two years ago by state troopers throwing tear gas, the movie company has set up headquarters for its ten-week stay in an old B. F. Goodrich tire store next to the bus depot. Here Robert Ellis Miller, the director, is finishing his blackberry cobbler. "Frankly, we were worried about coming to Selma," says Miller, picking a blackberry seed from his teeth, "after the unsavory reputation of the past few years. But once he learned this was not a film about racial problems, the mayor said, 'It will give us an opportunity to show the rest of the world we're not a bad town.' We've had no incidents, nothing but cooperation. I think most of the people here are ashamed of what happened. The fire department even sent over a giant new 85-foot-high snorkel crane to shoot over the top of the ferris wheel in the carnival scene. The Coca-Cola people flew down a Sprite poster in their company jet for a scene in an alley. The local people are playing roles in the picture and they are marvelous—the boyfriend of Mick Kelly is a part-time fireman I found at the University of Alabama in Birmingham. He had to do a love scene with a 60-man crew looking on and he *did* it. The biggest surprise is going to be Sondra Locke, the 17-year-old girl who is playing Mick Kelly. This girl is phenomenal. I think she's been in the business 30 years, she knows so much about acting.

"It's the kind of book that needs local color. I read it in college and I always wanted to direct it, but after his success with *Ulysses* Joseph Strick got the job. Then there was an upheaval, which I had nothing to do with, and Strick dropped out of the picture. I had just finished *Sweet November* with Sandy Dennis and was getting ready to rest at the beach when the offer came through. 1 jumped at the chance. If we shot the whole book it would be a 27-hour movie. We're just doing the essence of the book. But problems? We haven't had any. The people of Selma probably realize this film is boosting the local economy by about half a million dollars, but whatever their reasons, they've been lovely. Negroes they've seen. You know what really fascinates them? James Wong Howe, the cameraman. They've never seen a Chinaman before."

Cecily Tyson, a fine Negro actress from New York,

drops by the table. "When I heard they were coming down to Selma I nearly fainted. This is a film that should be made in the South, but why Selma? Also, I had heard about all the horrors the Negro actors in *Hurry Sundown* went through in Louisiana. But the people have bent over backward to be nice. I was in the dime store the other day and this woman introduced me to everybody in the store. One lady said, 'We heard you were afraid to come down here,' and I said, 'Well, lady, wouldn't *you* be?' Then my fiancé Miles Davis came through on his way to do a jazz concert in Spain and the mayor of Selma even had his picture taken shaking Miles' hand. I think the whole mood down here toward Negroes is changing."

The company's main problem has been boredom. Selma has only one night spot with any action and it is owned by one of the acquitted accused murderers of Viola Liuzzo, so the company refuses to go there. Mostly they just sit around in their rooms at the Holiday Inn Motel and watch George Wallace's speeches on TV and cook their food in popcorn poppers. Everyone visiting from New York is instructed to bring CARE packages. Alan Arkin's wife flew down with a Nathan's corned beef, a pastrami, two five-and-a-half-foot kosher salamis, a Reuben's cheese-cake and six dozen bagels, and the whole take was gone in 40 minutes.

But life goes on. The company moves past decaying Negro shacks with holes in the roofs, past Bar-B-Q stands and the Silent Nite Tourist Court For Whites Only, to an old deserted 13-room Southern Gothic white ginger-bread house the color of divinity fudge, which the group rents for $125 a month ("Which," winks a grip, "means if we weren't a film company we'd get it for $75"). Cables line the staircase and stepladders clutter the scuppernong arbor. Alan Arkin, who plays the deaf-mute named Singer, plays cards under a Tiffany lamp in the master bedroom. Sondra Locke, in blue jeans and a denim shirt, leans against a fireplace that looks like it survived the Civil War. She's a cotton-haired, creamy-dreamy moon-pie Southern teenager from Shelbyville, Tennessee, who looks like a young Kim Stanley. Like most Southern kids, she has been playing movie stars all her life. She spends most of her time off-camera reciting to the cast from *All About Eve* and she can practically remember Geraldine Page's entire telephone call to Walter Winchell in *Sweet Bird of Youth.* "I read this ad in the Nashville paper that they were gonna make this movie, so I thought I better go to Birmingham and see if I could get in it. It was 200 miles away from Shelbyville, but I had played Laura in *Glass Menagerie* and Emily in *Our Town,* you know, and my parents knew this was just what I wanted to do, be in a movie, so they didn't stop me. I read with all these other girls for this New York talent scout who discovered the two girls in *The World of Henry Orient* and she asked me come to New York and read again, so they brought me up to New York and put me up at the Y."

"The Y!! Haven't you ever heard of the Plaza Hotel?" I asked, visualizing Warners spending some of those *My Fair Lady* profits at the Y.

"Well, the movie people recommended the Y, I guess 'cause I was unchaperoned. Anyway, I got the part and I still can't believe it. The hardest part is cryin'. You know, I had this scene where my parents told me I had to quit school and I just got so wrapped up in it that I started cryin', but then they stopped the camera and shot it from another angle and I couldn't cry again. I mean some people can just keep cryin', you know? But they had to put somethin' in my eyes. I haven't read the book. I couldn't get through it. But I just love makin' movies. Now I think I'd like to skip college and go out to California because if I wait five years after this movie comes out, people will just say, 'Who are you?!' They forget, you know? But boy, I don't know. Hollywood is a long way from Shelbyville."

Outside in the cold, the crowd stands wrapped in blankets, watching James Wong Howe spray the camellia bushes with sugar and water. "This Southern movie, I see bulleflies," he says, perched on a ladder in a ten-gallon cowboy hat, smoking a cigar and waving a mean-looking bamboo stick. The crew blows smoke into the frosty air in wool coats and mufflers and sips hot chocolate to warm numb lips. So far, nobody has caught pneumonia. "Pneumonia," says Miller to cheer up his freezing actors, "is just a cold handled by MCA."

The scene begins. Alan Arkin, in a light summer suit, walks across the lawn, which has been sprayed green because it's supposed to be summer. The "bulleflies" have discovered Howe's sugar water, and they are swarming in front of his filter lens. Miss Locke, sobbing on the porch, is, in front of the cameras, an actress to the manner born: she has just been slapped by her father. Biff McGuire, the actor who plays her father, has left town on a plane for New York two weeks ago, so she must remember the slap. Arkin pauses on the porch, where Miss Locke screams, "GO AWAY, I HATE YOU!" through a cascade of glycerine teardrops. Howe's camera rises up the side of the house, peers through the organdy curtains as Arkin turns the light out in his rented bedroom. Cut.

"Would you pose for a still, Alan?" Arkin shoots a hard look at the photographer. A red-faced director's assistant rushes over. "Mr. Arkin does not like to pose after he does a shot. If you ask him again, I won't be responsible!" Howe interrupts, poking the photographer with his bamboo stick. "I once asked an actor to pose for a still in the middle of Ventura Boulevard and he told me to go tend my goddam noodles."

Arkin's sensitivity possibly stems from the torturous role he plays. He is the mute around whom the other characters revolve, representing man's inability to communicate. Everyone talks to him, but he talks to nobody in

return, showering his love instead on a mentally retarded
Greek, a part originally planned for nightclub comic Jackie
Vernon, who was fired when Strick walked off the film.
Now the part belongs to 300-pound TV comic Chuck
McCann, who was recommended by Arkin's son Adam.
McCann is so fat that nobody could find a Southern ice-
cream suit big enough to fit him until Miller's wife Pola
hit upon the idea of checking the Warners wardrobe department in Hollywood for Sydney Greenstreet's old costumes. Now moviegoers will see McCann in Greenstreet's
actual mean-man suit from his old Bogart movies.

Arkin himself has studied sign language from an
Alabama man whose parents were both deaf, and now he
knows it so well that he often stops scenes when he mis-
spells a word on his fingers. "It's easier to play a blind
man than a deaf man," he says. "An actor's job is to listen
and I can't listen in this role because I'm not supposed to
hear what anybody is saying. You can close your eyes and
not see, but you can't put contact lenses in your ears. I
visited a deaf-mute school in Montgomery and I learned
they are not freaks. Because his parents were deaf, my
teacher said he used to try to sneak in late at night when
he was a teenager. Every time they'd come in and beat
the hell out of him. Once he broke his foot and couldn't
get out of bed and if he needed something he'd stamp his
other foot on the floor and they'd come running. Most
parents with normal hearing probably wouldn't hear that
vibration. The sign language was the easiest thing to learn.
I got it in a day or two. Now I can talk to mutes who visit
the set. Stereotyped in my mind, they were always people
who were not terribly bright, wildly animated at all times
in trying to express themselves, and undisciplined emotionally. I guess I got that from watching Patty Duke in
The Miracle Worker. Then I met them and found an in-
finite variety in character, personality and intelligence.
Some are very straight-laced, others talk a blue streak. So

there is no one way to play a mute. This character remains a million miles away from me, so I have to look for details in the role to make it real. Like the script said 'He reaches in pocket for loose change.' I didn't feel he would have loose things in his pocket, so we got a little change purse. I carry a watch fob with a gold chain, and a Mark Cross pencil. I planned the way he arranges things meticulously in a little toilet kit in his room. I don't know if audiences will notice these details, but they've made this mute come true for me and sometimes out of my reactions to people there's even humor I hadn't planned onscreen that I never got onstage. Movies have been my first love all my life, I waited for 25 years to do films and I think I'll stick with the medium now. The thought of another year in a play fills me with dread. After three months in a play I start falling to pieces. That's what happened to me in *Luv*. This is the hardest role I've ever played, but as far as playing the mute as a freak, that's out. I've learned that the only difference between them and us is that when they make love they're much quieter about it."

Tom Ryan, the scriptwriter and co-producer, is the man who knows the whole story. For him, the McCullers novel has been the object of six years' hard work. "I closed the book on January 11, 1962, and wrote the movie. In August of 1963, I went to her home in Nyack and read it to her. She loved it. Sidney Lumet was supposed to direct with Monty Clift as Singer. Then we couldn't get any insurance on Monty and it fell through. David Susskind optioned it. Ely Landau optioned it. He wanted Warren Beatty—*can you imagine? Warren Beatty?*—and we could never agree, so he dug in his heels and I dug in mine and we got nowhere. The rights reverted back to me and I was right back where I started. It's got no story. I couldn't interest people by telling them, 'Well, it's about this deaf-mute . . .' Everybody said, 'It's absolutely beautiful and I wouldn't touch it with a barge pole.' Then Alan Arkin got into the act. He had just opened in *Luv* and his agent called and said, 'Alan is the only actor in the world to play Singer.' Three years passed and *Russians Are Coming* was out and he was hot in movies and he walked into this restaurant and said, 'You gotta give me the part now; I've gone to all the trouble of becoming a star just so I could play it.' So I had a star and a script and no money. The only company that liked it enough to back it was Warners-Seven Arts. They said, 'Some pictures you just have to make whether they make money or not!' Then Joe Strick wanted to direct, and we were on. Ben Edwards, the set designer, is a Southerner, so he suggested Selma and when we saw it we agreed. We came to Selma the end of August and shooting was supposed to begin September 19. Then we had an artistic clash about the script. Strick wanted a decidedly homosexual interpretation to the mute's love for the Greek. He saw it very downbeat, depressing. He even wanted the scenes filmed in gray, like the Ascot number in *My Fair Lady.* I had already re-written it 18 times, so I tried to do it his way, but I just didn't believe in it. Strick said, 'We've reached an impasse and I'll make it very easy for you. I'll just quit.' And he did. I never suspected he'd quit. I thought he'd listen to reason. Then Miller, who I remembered from a TV show he directed about a retarded child, took over and now I'm delighted with the way things are working out. Everybody is working for scale except Alan, who is getting half his regular salary. Even James Wong Howe, one of the most expensive cameramen in the world, agreed to cut his price. Fifty years in the business and he wanted to do it because he loves the property. I wrote *Hurry Sundown* and I don't want anything like that to happen to this film. Somebody sent me a theme song with a Tex Ritter-type voice strumming a guitar singing *'The sun is hot, the sky opaque/You feel so hot you think you'll bake/The heart is a lonely hunter, searching for someone to love . . ."* We're not going to have anything monstrous like that. Adolph Green accused me of writing it myself as a joke. I've written the best script I know how to write. It's the first time in my life I've felt that. And it's coming out on the screen the way I saw it in my mind when I wrote it. No writer has any right to expect any more than that. I think—I *hope* —Carson McCullers would be proud."

And so, a few months after her own untimely death at the age of 50, Mrs. McCullers' best novel is coming to the screen. But the problem remains: can they make a commercial Hollywood movie out of a poetic story about a teenage girl so desperate to find her identity that she pulls her baby brother along the streets of a burned-out Southern town in a wagon just to hear the sound of music floating through the windows of other people's houses, a deaf-mute who never speaks, and a mentally retarded Greek whose death results in the mute's own suicide? On paper, it's art. But will they buy it with their popcorn in Cactus Junction? Back at the old house, where they're now shooting the suicide scene, two views. Things are tense. The light goes off in Arkin's room. A gunshot. Miss Locke runs up the stairs and lets loose with a scream so blood-curdling even Bette Davis would approve. Tom Ryan beams under a magnolia tree. "You've either got a great movie or you've got crap. I think we've got a great movie." And out on the street, in the crowd of onlookers, an old codger smoking a corncob pipe turns to his wife and says, "Well, c'mon, Leota, les go home, we done missed half the Dean Martin Show awreddy." Carson McCullers couldn't have written it better herself.

The Golden Globe Awards

February, 1968

NBC's telecast of the Foreign Press Association's 25th annual Golden Globe Awards had to be seen to be disbelieved. This ludicrous event is so suspiciously corrupt even NBC and the Federal Communications Commission have sent lawyers to have it investigated. But award-giving, pointless as it is, is still big business, and it also gives viewers a chance to see their favorite stars make fools of themselves in public, so the Golden Globes were back, minus some of their sponsors, who backed out at the last minute. After a few boring words from the FPA's president Howard Luft (No relation to Sid—this Mr. Luft comes on like a Sid Caesar takeoff on Eric Von Stroheim, interspersed with shots of the stars laughing at him from their tables), emcee Andy Williams summed up what followed: "If you're a winner or a loser, it really doesn't matter too much."

Then Mary Tyler Moore, looking like a buck-toothed Dorothy Lamour, and Peter Lawford, looking like a retarded court jester with his new baby bangs, presented the Best Director award to Mike Nichols, who didn't show up. Nancy Sinatra (No matter how she spends her father's money, she always looks like a pizza waitress) gave the Supporting Actor award to Richard Attenborough, who didn't show up either (tough-broad closeup of Janet Leigh with a cigarette hanging from her lips).

Carol Channing accepting the Supporting Actress award, thanked "Julie Andrews and her wonderful cast," whatever that means (closeup of Julie Andrews, telling somebody a story and not listening). John Wayne staggered onstage to present the Best Actress in a Comedy award to Anne Bancroft, who didn't show up (closeup of Roman Polanski and Sharon Tate, eating). Sally Field, "delicious, delectable, delightful" star of *Flying Nun*, flew in from the top of the ceiling, got tangled up in her wiring, and was left hanging there. Her award went to Best Actor in a Musical or a Comedy, Richard Harris, who didn't show up. "He isn't here," said Faye Dunaway, who didn't win anything. "For once in his life, common sense prevailed."

After some interminable Pagliacci-like suffering from Jerry Lewis, the Best Comedy or Musical Film Award went to *The Graduate* (closeup of Warren Beatty cursing). Then after an insipidly limp medley of song nominees, Andy Williams introduced his wife Claudine, with something hideous in her hair that looked like stringed popcorn. She gave the Best Song of the Year award to a six-year-old song from *Camelot*. Rod Steiger did show up to get his Best Actor in a Dramatic Film Award, although presenter Jim Brown called it "In the Heap of the Night" (closeup of Warren Beatty cursing). Natalie Wood, looking like she had just come from a yoga lesson, gave the Best Dramatic Film of the Year Award to the same film (another closeup of Warren Beatty cursing). Candy Bergen, in a riding habit, looked alternately shocked and amused (as well she should be) when her film *Live for Life* won Best Foreign Film of the Year.

It was the one genuine reaction in an evening of hypocrisy and ho-hum boredom that included a Best Male TV Performer Award, a Best Female Newcomer to the Screen Award, a Best Favorite World Performer Award and, as if determined to prove once and for all what trouble movies are in, there was even something called the "Female World Film Favorite" Award. It went to Julie Andrews, who stopped talking long enough to say a simple "Thank you." The whole blooming agony looked like it would never end.

Just last week *Newsweek* magazine reported denials from the Foreign Press Association that its members give awards to the stars who throw the biggest feeds. "We are not influenced by a glass of champagne," snapped Luft, "Kirk Douglas threw a party last year, and what did he win? Nothing."

This year there was even a special category called the Cecil B. DeMille Humanitarian Award. Who won? You guessed it. Kirk Douglas.

The only award the Golden Globes didn't hand out was an All-Time Worst Evening in the History of Show Business Award. But I guess that wouldn't look nice. You're not supposed to give prizes to yourself.

Oskar Werner

The trattoria shimmered in the Italian sunshine. Just behind Oskar Werner's baby-blond head you could see the ruins where Julius Caesar was assassinated and across the line of tourist buses on the piazza, the stone columns of the Colosseum pierced the sky like fat, timeless darning needles. It was a warm, boozy day in Rome, when most people were asleep: a perfect time to sit under the pine trees and talk to a movie star with the day off. "I'm not vain, I am humble," he said. And yet: he showed up in dark glasses and a khaki safari jacket unbuttoned down to his navel, rearranged everyone under the luncheon umbrella so his was the only face to sip the sun (might as well do the bloody interview and get a sun-tan at the same time) and did five hours on the subject of Oskar Werner, who, if not vain, is at least on close speaking terms with the subject.

He was in Rome to make *The Shoes of the Fisherman*, a super-colossal MGM road-show fantasy about the first Russian Pope. Anthony Quinn plays the Pope; Oskar plays a disillusioned priest who stirs up the Vatican and gets tried for heresy. Oskar himself is a non-practicing Catholic whose own behavior, on and off the set, is so incorrigible his first question, after being introduced to the Jesuit priests in Rome, was "Have you ever slept with a woman?" The script also required him to die of a heart attack during his heresy trial. No dice. "I did that already in *Ship of*

Fools and I never do anything twice, so I made them change it to a brain stroke. I have complete approval of all scripts, so when I arrived in Rome I said, 'This script is terrible. Re-write it or I won't do the film.' They re-wrote it." Such demands have earned him a reputation for being difficult. He admits it. "I am a director and a stage actor first, a movie star second. If a director is nice to me and lets me do a part the way I see it, I give him a whole performance. If not, I only give him half a performance." In Rome, they're calling him the Viennese Orson Welles.

At the age of 45, Werner's talent is so great most directors let him get away with it. *If* they are lucky enough to get him at all. "After *Ship of Fools* I turned down 56 Hollywood projects. I will not make films I wouldn't pay to see myself. Acting is a bit like surgery. You get a part, make a diagnosis, then decide what to do with the corpse. If the body is still warm, I make a transfusion from my own blood to keep the patient alive. Sometimes it still dies." [*Shoes of the Fisherman* has since opened—it didn't survive the operating table.] Werner has very few good things to say about his previous films, either. "In films, we only realize the shadows of our dreams. Thank God the public never knows how bad films are or how many things do not turn out right. If you're lucky, you get 25 percent of the dream. I know exactly what I want when I shave in the mirror in the morning, but when I see my films I'm always unhappy. I tailor my parts. Very few things are ever given to me. After *Ship of Fools*, doctors wrote me letters asking how I studied the heart attack. I didn't. It was only two lines in the script that said 'Fall over from chair and die.' I imagined all the pain, how the throat chokes, how the air stops on its way to the brain." He was silent. Then he lunged forward, knocked the forks and spoons off the table and fell to the cobblestone terrace, giving a perfect imitation of a man having a heart attack. People leaped from their tables in horror. Two waiters came flapping at him like gulls. "You see? I did it myself. Fantasy is my bank account."

He liked his work in *Ship of Fools,* although he admits "others were terrible, so the film was not a success. Signoret and I had the phoniest parts in the world—a dope addict and a doctor with heart disease. We had to create everything ourselves. I told Stanley Kramer I had a bad reputation for being difficult and he said, 'When you get to Hollywood, everyone will tell you I have a bad reputation, too,' so we got along. I changed the role completely. They even had a business suit and tie for me to wear and I refused. I said, 'No Nazi ship's captain would ever wear a suit,' and I ended up wearing an officer's uniform designed for one of the extras."

He considers *Jules and Jim* a moderate success, but the subject of Truffaut sent his fist crashing into the table, upsetting two glasses and creating a dark river of *vino rosso* winding its way along the white tablecloth. "We used to speak, but not any more. During *Jules and Jim* I gave him advice, tried to teach him something, and he listened. Whole scenes, whole pages of dialogue came from me. But when I went to England to make *Fahrenheit 451* he thought he had learned it all. He destroyed that film. It was a 70-millimeter film with an 8-millimeter print. It had nothing left of Ray Bradbury in it. It was ridiculous to cast Julie Christie in two parts. He only did that to save paying an extra salary. Nothing was worked out. The dramatic plot was completely lost. He refused to accept any of my suggestions. I was 15 when Hitler came to power and I *saw* the real book burnings. Truffaut's film was child's play compared to that. Every time I had to register an emotion that was true to my character, Truffaut would cut away with his camera. That's the trouble with these *nouvelle vague* directors. They care nothing about actors. Antonioni is like a man masturbating. He does it all by himself."

For his latest film, *Interlude,* Werner learned to conduct the London Philharmonic and became so adept at it that once, when the camera ran out of film, the orchestra kept following him. "They ruined *Interlude,* too. I did it because music is my greatest love in life and I always wanted to play a conductor. But when I saw it I was furious. They cut most of my conducting and left only the love story. I loathe sex on the screen. There is nothing more tedious in art than to show everything. Sexual intercourse is boring when you have to watch it. Miniskirts are not sexy. It's like watching girls walking in their underwear. I like women in long dresses. The ankles are very erotic. Viennese waltzes are the sexiest dances in the world. Yet films feed on sex. In *Interlude* they wanted me to make love to Barbara Ferris on a tigerskin rug. Naturally I refused."

Naturally. And yet women the world over have made Oskar Werner a new kind of sex symbol onscreen—the great white hope for women over 40. There's not a line in his schoolboy face and sometimes, when he takes off his sunglasses and his baby-blue eyes half close in the Mediterranean sun, he looks like a sleepy wombat. It's a look that could keep him going for years, playing roles that bring out both the carnal and the maternal instincts in female moviegoers. But Oskar Werner is too smart for that. "After *Ship of Fools* the ladies of the press called me the new heart throb, the new matinee idol. I said nonsense, and played a villain in a supporting part in *The Spy Who Came in from the Cold* and they didn't like me in it. So I don't know if I will ever be very big in movies, because I want to play hunchbacks and village idiots. Once I was on a ship and a man asked me what I did and I was so embarrassed to say 'actor' I said I studied. 'What?' he asked. 'Human beings and their destinies,' I said. That was no lie. That's what I do. But I don't want to be typecast in parts. Type parts are for automobile factories."

He was born in Vienna, the only son of a poor insurance clerk. His family knew nothing about the theatre,
but sometimes when he helped his grandmother with the
dishes she would tell him tales of the National Theatre.
One day when he was eight his mother let him cross town
alone to visit his grandparents. He pretended he was blind,
turning his eyes up and feeling his way along the street.
Two people came up and said, "Little boy, where do you
want to go," and he felt so guilty he let them lead him. It
was his first audition and he passed. From that day, his
future was sealed. "I never studied. I loathe acting schools.
You can teach musicians, but actors are their own instru-
ments. Training an actor does great damage. You might
be training a flute to be a violin. I've always said, 'Don't
explain it to me, just show me.' Otherwise, why play Hamlet? Just write an article about it."

When he did his first play he said to himself in the
wings, "Later, when I become famous, people will ask me
what my first line was, so I remembered it." He played a
fireman and his first line was "Where's the fire?" At 18,
he debuted with the Vienna Burgtheatre, Austria's equiva-
lent to England's Old Vic, but in 1941, when he was 19,
he was drafted into Hitler's Wehrmacht. He hated his
uniform, hated himself. Before the war was over, he deserted and hid in terror with his wife and eight-month-old
daughter in the Vienna Woods "without Johann Strauss.
I weighed only 110 pounds, I was secretly married to a
half-Jewish woman and I was only 22 years old. It took
me 22 years before I had the courage to visit a concentration camp. Last year, when I was 44 years old, I took the
train and spent two days in Dachau and it all came back.
People said they didn't know it was happening, but I did.
I watched 70-year-old university professors washing down
sidewalks because they were Jews and after the war, when
the Russians came, I sat in the National Theatre in Vienna
and smelled the dead bodies rotting under the cellar and

we could look out the window and watch the women carried to the hospital on stretchers after being raped by the Russians. They used to rape 20 or 30 women a night."

In 1950, he decided to make "my confession" by doing his first American film, *Decision Before Dawn*. He signed a big contract, but he loved the theatre more, so it wasn't until *Ship of Fools* that he made his second American film. "It was Stanley Kramer, really, who talked me into a film career. He asked me to meet him in Munich, but I still hate Germany so much I asked him to change it to Paris. I feel more comfortable there. We talked five minutes about the film and hours about life, and I said yes. I liked Hollywood, but I've never been back. It was all parties and ye-ye music, and I hate both. If I want to get drunk, I can do it alone. You can't talk to anyone in Hollywood. I don't like films. I only do it for money. I'm married to the theatre, films are only my mistress. Now is the first time the mistress has paid off and she pays very well. Onstage nothing can stop me. You have to fire me to tone me down. I have space. Not in films. I have no control there. I only do them to become famous enough so people will pay to see me onstage. I was invited to bring my Hamlet to America before I was famous and I said I would never bring it in English. If I make a few more films now, I could come to New York and read the telephone book. Now I can have artistic freedom. I will come back and play Hamlet and they will say, 'We saw him in *Ship of Fools*, let's see what he can do.' So I did this film about the Pope and I had the most beautifully paid Roman holiday I ever had in my life. And I made very much money."

He borrowed everyone's cigarettes, rubbed his chest under the safari jacket, tore his napkin into a zillion shreds and threw them on the ground, played with a chain around his neck, and idly forked a rather sickly-looking plate of prosciutto swimming in oil and getting stale in

the hot sun. At several intervals the suggestion was made
by the press agent that it was time to leave. "Stay and
buy me another double benedictine," he said. And so we
stayed, through the afternoon, until the sun came down.
And Oskar Werner kept talking, like a self-appointed
politico doing a marathon filibuster. "I only met Laurence
Olivier for the first time in my life on this film. He has a
very small part, but I asked to give him second billing
and I'd take third. I'm very humble. He gets last billing
now, because that's how film people think. The two biggest dangers are to be vain and ambitious. If there is no
spiritual manifestation in acting, it becomes very close to
prostitution."

He is married to Tyrone Power's daughter now, but
he refuses to discuss her. He pretends not to care about
money, but he lives in Lichtenstein (no taxes there). "I
have a sauna and a pool, but my home is small. I don't
want anyone staying overnight. I'm always working. I
am haunted and hounded by this profession. Last night I
walked until 4 A.M., then I went over to the set to see
Tony Quinn shoot some night scenes and I watched from
the sidelines, playing all the other actors' parts. My motor
is always running. I would never become an actor again.
It is the most primitive profession. You have to depend
on other people. I want to do it alone. I can play Hamlet
alone, because it is practically a monologue, and that is
my greatest role. You can have any Ophelia—a fat Ophelia,
a short Ophelia, an ugly Ophelia. But I turned down Romeo
five times because I could never find the right Juliet. She's
the viola and Romeo's the second fiddle."

He began to conduct an imaginary orchestra playing
Schubert. He hummed. He syncopated. Everyone in the
piazza was looking. "Maybe I will conduct the Vienna
Symphony. Or perhaps I will direct my own films. I will do
a film next about Judas. I can control everything if I direct
it myself. Then I will be so independent I can tell everyone

else, 'Thank you very much, drop dead.' " He drained his eighth double benedictine and the press agent helped him to his feet as he staggered off into the traffic, narrowly escaping a head-on collision with a crazy Italian driver careening through the square behind the wheel of a cabbage truck.

"He'll make it," said the press agent.

And he did, too.

Colleen Dewhurst

It's the day after the not-so-triumphant opening of *More Stately Mansions*, a time when most actresses retire to their sick beds sipping hot tea with lemon with the phone off the hook and the lights turned out. But Colleen Dewhurst is not like most actresses. Most actresses wouldn't have the guts to share a spotlight with Ingrid Bergman (or steal it, according to which reports you believe) on her return to the stage after a 21-year absence, in the first place. And most actresses have not already played Camille, Portia, Cleopatra, Kate, Anne of Aquitaine, Lady Macbeth, Martha in *Who's Afraid of Virginia Woolf*, Miss Amelia in *Ballad of the Sad Café* and Medea before they were 40. Colleen has played them all brilliantly enough to have earned a reputation as one of the best actresses in America. So don't go calling her ordinary. And don't expect, on the afternoon after her new play has been drubbed by the critics, a weepy-eyed actress crying in her beer.

She stands in the middle of the kitchen in her 200-year-old country farmhouse near South Salem hungrily devouring a bacon-cheese-and-egg sandwich and drinking Diet Pepsi from a quart bottle with the three o'clock sun sifting through the dying red maple trees and filtering through the open window into a swirl of rich chestnut hair that looks like it must surely be the decapitated mane of some thoroughbred owned by a queen, and there is no doubt that she will survive. "I tell you, I never read reviews.

G.C. reads them all with glee, but I never do. I don't have to. I can tell if they're bad because the phone doesn't ring. Today I have had what I call a moderately middling phone, so I know they were pretty bad."

Her husband George C. Scott is upstairs asleep and her two sons are piling out of the school bus with leftover bags of trick-or-treat Halloween candy, and the painters and carpenters are moving furniture and running the vacuum cleaner from the mess she made when she left the shower running upstairs and caused the ceiling to fall in, and . . . well, who has time to worry about critics?

"Mommy, did you bring home the good luck things from the opening night?" asks Alexander, age 7.

"No I left them at the theatre."

"How did it go, Mommy?" asks Campbell, age 6.

"*The New York Times* liked Mommy, but not the play," she answers with a wink. "What does that mean?" "Disaster, darlin', that's what it means, *disaster!*" Then she roars her enormous lumberjack roar and everything is right with the world again.

It's that laugh that gets you. It's her most revealing trait, aside from the pants and the baggy sweaters and the strong, covered-wagon face like a heroine from an arty western movie, and the radiant grin that caused one woman in a preview to turn to her friend and exclaim, "My God, she's got a mouthful of teeth!" It's a laugh that starts down deep inside, where it's still a private joke, then roars up through her throat and bursts out like a roomful of daisies, bringing you into the secret and wrapping you up in its warmth.

Yet beneath the glow and the pride and the nice-lady face, one suspects she has lived. From the day she was born in Montreal, the daughter of a hockey and football player, she was her own girl. Rugged, tomboyish, fierce, determined, she wanted to be an aviatrix at five. At Milwaukee Downer College she was so bossy she wrote and directed the school play, and when she got fed up with the girl playing the lead, she kicked her out and played it herself. The dean wrote to her mother, suggesting that life was an endless party to which Colleen had been the only one invited, and begged for her removal from the halls of ivy in her second year. She fled to Gary, Indiana (Why Gary? "I had a friend there") and made $25 a week as an elevator operator, later became a dentist's receptionist and a gym instructor teaching fat old ladies how to shape up. She arrived in New York in 1948, married an actor named Jim Vickery, lived in a $28-a-month hole-in-the-wall in the theatre district, and slowly worked her way into bit parts in summer stock.

In 1957 she got her biggest break playing a promiscuous jailer's daughter in the Circle in the Square production of *Children of Darkness*. One of the actors got sick and a search began for a replacement. Somebody suggested an unknown named George C. Scott, but Colleen wanted a friend of hers to play the role. "Whichever one's home, hire him," said Ted Mann, the producer. Colleen's friend was out, but Scott was home, so he got the job. "It was 'Mr. Scott' and 'Miss Dewhurst' for about four months," she recalls. "He was very distant. He only came in during the third act, but he walked off with the play. I had never seen such talent." Both of them were married to somebody else at the time, so it took them until 1960 before they could marry. Since then, their marriage has not been, to put it mildly, without storm clouds, but they must be doing something right because they've been divorced and remarried three times. The last time was on July 4, 1967.

"Mommy, do you have the paper?" asks Alexander.

"You mean the reviews?"

"No, the sports page in the *Times*."

"No, Mommy isn't buying *The New York Times* this week. She's mad at *The New York Times*."

Alexander settles for a look at the wedding photos, in

which he and his little brother are shown in full Kodak color eating their parents' third wedding cake. "This is our wedding," he says, pointing proudly at the Scotts in their Sunday-go-to-meetin' clothes.

Colleen roars. "I was expecting Alexander during the run of *Caligula* and Campbell came along during *All the Way Home*. I'll never forget *that*. I was supposed to be pregnant in the play, but we had to keep changing the lines from 'You don't show Mary' to 'You show' to finally 'I see you're pregnant, Mary!' I played it until my eighth month. They're not very typical kids, as you can see, but they'll only be actors over my dead body. They came to Bucks County when G.C. and I did *Lion in Winter* there, and later we heard the cook asking them what it was about and they said, 'Well, Daddy is a king and Mommy is a queen and they have two boys and Daddy likes the little boy and Mommy likes the big boy and they fight a lot.' And G.C. said, 'Yep, that's absolutely right, that's what it's all about, all right.' "

She's in the living room now, making great stabs at being a country wife, pouring cream in the tea and chain-smoking Lucky Strikes from a crumpled pack. "The day after an opening I feel like I have a hangover. I want to go into the closet, change my name, and come out again a new person. I get so *involved* in everything and then when the critics don't like it, I die. When *Ballad of the Sad Café* flopped, I went through agony. But this time I'm going to have fun and enjoy myself. I wanted to do this play and I'm not sorry. I love the O'Neill women. They move from the groin rather than the brain. To play O'Neill you have to be big. You can't sit around and play little moments of sadness or sweetness. You cannot phony up O'Neill. And God knows if you fail, you can't lay a quiet bomb up there onstage, you go with a resounding crash. I read it and was appalled at the length—you should have seen it when it ran five *hours*—but I have the utmost

faith in José Quintero and knew he could cut it. He has
survived the most colossal problems in this play—three
actors who want to be evensy-Stevensy, six scripts before
a final one was approved, producers who wanted it to be
a commercial success and still remain reverent to O'Neill,
the problem of bringing down the curtain at 11 because
if you go over you have to pay the stagehands overtime.
Endless problems. But in the beginning I could only see
that role. Then Arthur Hill, who is as bad as I am about
never taking the safety route to a commercial success, called
me and said, 'It's fascinating, Colleen, but scary as hell.'
Then José told me Ingrid would like to do it and I just sat
right here in my living room and stared at him. Then G.C.
said, 'Honey, you know I'm not an O'Neill fan and this
play is a bloody bore, but two or three scenes of O'Neill
are worth all the crap done in the theater every week, so
do it.' Then the first rehearsal came and Ingrid walked in
and I thought, 'My God!' I knew she'd look good but this
was ridiculous. She looks better than I did when I was 30.
You know there are lots of well-preserved ladies in our
theatre, but you get the feeling that if you touched them
they'd shatter into a million pieces. Well, Ingrid is just the
opposite. She's not well-preserved in any unreal sense. She
has her Scotches, she stays up late, she tells jokes, but she
looks glorious. Nothing that she is is the result of any
massage table or any face makeup. Well, she must have
gone into shock when she saw Arthur and me. She had us
running back and forth to the dye shop to look as good as
she did. Even now, after living day and night with her for
three months while the play was trying out in California,
she can walk in after lunch and I just sit there and stare—
'My God, that's Ingrid Bergman!'—and it takes me a few
minutes before I can shake myself and realize it's just
Ingrid. She's that incredible. And *honest!* Whoopsie, is she
honest. Everything you get from her is right in the face,
nothing phony. And thank God, she's tall. When I'm on-

stage with her for once in my life I don't feel like an Amazon charging with my warriors.

"It's been like a strange marriage for the past three months, an incestuous little circle made up of Arthur, Ingrid and me, that audiences can't break into. They tried to build up a feud out in California because of a New York newspaper article saying I was better than she was, or something silly like that. It was like 'Dewhurst is New York's girl, Ingrid is Hollywood's, we give Dewhurst 7 and Ingrid nothing.' I didn't read it, but G.C. told me about it and they tried to keep it from Ingrid. But she reads everything. So I came into the theatre that day scared to death and Ingrid said, 'You know what we should do? We should start a rumor that there's no feud, that we're really having a thing between us. That'll shake 'em up.' That's how close we all were. And that's why I almost hated to see the opening night come, when the public could finally get at us. I can't bear to see little flippy things like bad reviews come in and put us on the line like that after we've worked so hard. What if it is one of O'Neill's inferior plays? The fact that it's O'Neill at all should be reason enough for it to be seen. Isn't that what the theatre is all about? Even today you say, 'Goddammit, next time I'll do *Any Wednesday*,' but it never happens. I've always done plays I believed in and I have no regrets. Money isn't important. I'll do a TV show for thousands just so I can afford to work for Joe Papp in Central Park or do something off-Broadway for $50 a week, and that's my integrity. But I never fool myself. I never say, 'I'll do that trashy TV play and make art out of it.' I just do it for the money. Occasionally something will come along on TV like *The Crucible* and you get both the money *and* something that doesn't stink, and then you're *really* happy. But that doesn't happen often."

It's dark now. Outside, birdcalls in the meadow and leaves brushing the windows. She switches on a reading lamp and the warmth draws out the smell of the fireplace.

Colors lead up dimly: purple, blue and brown, secretly shadowing the great face, half-lit half-obscured. Yes, she could be Cleopatra. Or Lizzie Borden, or any other damn thing you could think of. So why, you ask, has the face been ignored by the movies? She's only done two: an insane creature who tried to murder Audrey Hepburn in *The Nun's Story* and a rather grotesque psychiatrist in *A Fine Madness*. "I'd love to do movies, but quite frankly, nobody's asked me. People are always telling me to go to Europe, I'm another Jeanne Moreau. Hah! And then I get the line, 'You're a real woman!' Sounds great, but then I think, 'In contrast to what?' It'd be nonsense to say I don't want to be recognized in supermarkets. But here I am. I've been here all the time and I'm still not a supermarket star. I don't think they ever knew where to put me. They'll say, 'She's a cross between Ingrid Bergman and Ava Gardner,' but the trouble is, they can't find the pigeonhole. Then they say, 'Your background is mostly classical, isn't it?' and that *really* throws them. Also, I never played roles that would attract a movie mind. I've tried not to fall into a niche, because in America we're so cult-conscious that actors are always expected to be right where they're supposed to be. You either play sex symbols and make good money or you play villains and make good money but you're not supposed to be able to play everything and make good money. The only thing I require in a role is that I like the woman I play. I don't care if she's a Lesbian or a whore or a first-class pig. I have to like her and then know why she went in that direction. I can play all those ladies onstage, but not in the movies. I never saw the two I made because neither of them had anything to do with acting. Also, you're at the mercy of cutters and mechanics in films, but once you're out there onstage it's all yours and a marvelous love-hate struggle begins with the audience. An audience can make you rise to great heights you never knew, the camera can't. So I am content with just being a star in the theatre, and leaving the supermarkets to the other ladies. Then I drive home at night to my Concord grapes and my chickens and my vegetable garden and try to get with it, but I'm not very good at the country life. Every now and then, the kids decide I'm not like the other Moms because I drive them to school in my nightgown with something around my head and come back home and go to bed while the other Moms are making their kids cookies and things. A few weeks ago, when I got back from California, I decided one Sunday to get up early and ship everybody off to Sunday school. It was time to get organized like the other Moms. Well, I left a pair of wet blue jeans on the radiator upstairs and they nearly burned the house down and then I left the shower on and G.C. said, 'Honey I hear a great cracking noise,' and it was the roof caving in under the flood. So I don't pretend to be very good at any of it. When I decided to do this interview it got to be a joke backstage: which Colleen Dewhurst to show? Should we meet in my dressing room to show the dedicated actress or in a bar to show the carefree dame or out on the farm to show the all-American, folksy, genuine wife and mother? Well, it's a good thing you saw me like this, with nothing planned to say and no time to think up anything. I'm not very good at any pose except just being myself. The theatre is the only thing in my life I've ever had any discipline about."

And later, when the kids are fed and tucked in, and G.C. has brought the car out and they're both on their way into the city, he to be dropped off at *The Little Foxes* and she to drive on to *More Stately Mansions,* at about the point where the car angles in under the lights of the George Washington Bridge, she suddenly remembers: "Oh my God! Tonight we get the magazine critics!" A furrowed woodchuck glance into the back seat at the interviewer. "And then I've got next Sunday's *New York Times* to look forward to with Walter Kerr and *you* side by side! Oh Christ!"

"And then," chuckles G.C. maniacally at the wheel,

"you'll read a headline: 'Rather Obscure Actress Kills Self in Remote Westchester Retreat.' "

Then the Dewhurst roar, turning the car, as she does the stage, into instant magic. Half I-don't-care and half Come-up-and-see-me-sometime. And glorious to hear in the hush of the night.

Irene Papas

"One thing I know—
I know nothing . . ."
—SOCRATES, 399 B.C.
—IRENE PAPAS, 1967 A.D.

The soil of Greece is in her eyes. Smoldering with fire and ice, like coals from an ancient volcano, on a tiny Greenwich Village stage no bigger than a discothèque dance floor, they are the eyes of Queen Clytemnestra—tortured and pained with the Greek furies swirling around them in a wind of black crepe—in Euripides' *Iphegenia in Aulis*. But backstage, hiding from the applause of an audience in tears, they are the eyes of a lithe, compact, intense and restless lady named Irene Papas. And here the fire and ice turns to melted snow.

They're trying to get at her, that audience. Sidney Lumet and Peter Shaffer and 20 girls from a Catholic convent are pouring backstage with hands to shake. But the face hides behind a black curtain, the charcoal embers in her eyes turning to frightened ashes. "I didn't know they were coming. Nobody told me. I don't know what to say." Then she grabs a reassuring arm and darts into a taxi for some late supper, seeking answers: "I wasn't very good, was I? Tell me the truth, I can take it."

At Sardi's, the eyes are not appreciated. Lost in the blurry browns and blacks of furs and raincoats, she stands timidly in a corner, thrilled to be in the same room where everybody else is too busy making a fuss over Pearl Bailey to notice a simple Greek lady in a simple black coat. "Did you see Pearl Bailey?" she asks, blushing. "She is very exciting, isn't she?" Pearl Bailey is led to a center table.

Miss Papas is hustled upstairs, where nobody recognizes her except two Greek waiters who treat her as though she were Constantine himself. They bow deeply and bring her a vermouth cassis. Here, in a quiet corner away from the glamour and noise, talking to other Greeks, she is at home. "When I came here last year to do *That Summer—That Fall* on Broadway, there were not so many Greeks here yet. Now they are everywhere—Paris, London, Rome. Like children without a country. And we all stick together. We have to. All we've got is each other. Melina Mercouri . . . Michael Cacoyannis, my director . . . we all know each other. I once played Melina's sister onstage and when I made my first film she gave me a black dressing gown with ostrich feathers. Now we are all in the same tragic boat. I will never go back to Greece as long as the Fascists are in power. They didn't export me—I exported myself! I was supposed to play Jocasta in a film of *Oedipus Rex* in Athens, but I knew if I went something would happen. I knew there would be no elections. I felt it all before it happened. I was in London the day the junta took over. I had gone there to see the producer, to tell him to get me out of this thing. He said, 'Don't be ridiculous!' and what happened? He's the one who ended up locked in the Athens Hilton. Then my film, *For Each His Own,* about the Mafia, was in Cannes, so I went there and spoke. Melina had already spoken out in New York, so I spoke against the junta, too. But I don't know why they have not threatened *my* life as they have hers. I still have my citizenship and my property. Maybe they will kill me on the streets. Maybe they're saving something really *big* for me."

She laughs, but there's no laughter in the sound. "My family still lives there, but I'm over 21, I have to be responsible for myself. I believe in democracy. So I came here. In America, you can be anything, you can even be a Fascist if you like. This seems to be the only free country left. If America goes, there's nothing. In Greece you can no longer play the Greek tragedies. We couldn't do this play there now. In it, we say, 'We are Greeks, we are free!' and the house comes down. But in Greece today the junta doesn't want to hear anything against tyranny or dictatorship, so the great plays like *Antigone* are banned. It will be up to the people now to have a civil war, but they are not rich or self-sufficient. They need the aid of America. If Johnson had stepped in at the beginning, the Greeks would be free today. But today the world obeys and says nothing. That's why I'm in trouble with my life as well as my acting. I don't want to sit quietly by and obey.

"My problem is I'm too obedient. I try to serve the director, make him the hero. That's why I may leave acting. I'm thinking about it. Because I can't stand this dictatorship over me. I think I am too intelligent to be an actress. It's very hard for an intelligent person to act, because you have to be selfish to stand up for what you believe and I'm not selfish. If I had been more selfish in *That Summer—That Fall* perhaps it would have been a different play, but I tried to obey the director when I disagreed with him. I wanted to burst out, to spew out all the tragedy that woman was feeling inside, and go AAAHGGHH! !" She hits the wall with her fist and nearly knocks over a caricature of Noel Coward. "Uta Hagen was like something I never saw in my life in *Virginia Woolf* because she refused to let anyone keep her down. With Cacoyannis I work well—he knows what I have to unleash and he lets me flourish—but not so well with other directors. I think, alas, the only director I will ever accept is me."

As long as she talks about Greece, the eyes glow with some of the grandeur of Clytemnestra. But when the topic turns to Irene Papas, she winces and the eyes become sad, misshapen bullets, avoiding the issue. "Oh, how I hate to be charming for interviews. I never believed publicity had anything to do with acting. I don't believe people want to really know about *me*. Maybe if I liked myself more as a person, I would not mind talking about myself. But I am very vulnerable and open and it's up to you what you do with me. You can hang me in the paper if you want, but I will try to be a good interview for you and tell you what you ask." She stabs a pork chop with a sullen fork and takes a deep breath. "My childhood?" A smile, and the corners of her dark mouth turn into a cave of secrets. "That was a happy time in Greece. I come from a village 100 kilometers from Athens called Chiliomodion." She writes it on the table-cloth in Greek letters for me. "A tiny village, very ugly, but we have a telephone in our house and electricity. My family were teachers. My father is 96 now, on the pension. My mother, who is 66, lives in New York with me. I don't want her to go back now while the junta is there.

"As a child, I was always acting. I made dolls out of sticks and rugs"—she makes a doll out of her knife and fork to show me—"and once a tour came to the village and set up a tent and I saw women tearing their hair in the Greek tragedies and I liked that. After that I would tie black kerchiefs around my head and charge the other children to watch me. When I was 7, we moved to Athens and lived in a marvelous house with a palm tree in the garden. At 12, I went to the drama school and they kicked me out, and said go home and get old and come back. I went back at 15, going to high school in the morning and drama school in the afternoon. In Greece actors are respected, because they have the most education. You can't be a dumb actor there. Then you must get a license or you can't work. It's like becoming a doctor in America. Without a license, the police arrest you. I played Elektra, Mrs. Alving in *Ghosts* and Lady Macbeth, all at the age of 18 and got my license."

She made her stage debut in 1948 in a musical. A *musical*? "Oh yes. I was very funny. I played a high society girl who goes from one cocktail party to the next refusing to speak Greek. Everyone thinks of Melina as a musical and comedy star and of me as a tragic actress, but I'm very good at comedy, and Melina is the best tragic actress Greece has produced. You know what I would like to propose? That we switch roles. Melina playing Clytemnestra and me playing in *Illya Darling*. She would be better than I am and I would be the best Illya you ever saw."

Spyros Skouras brought her to America for the first time in 1954. She did a scene from *The Country Girl* for Elia Kazan, but nobody hired her. In 1955 she came back with a seven-year contract at MGM, where she made only one film, *Tribute to a Bad Man,* which was originally to star Spencer Tracy and the young actor Bob Francis. "We went to Colorado and waited for one month while Mr. Tracy fought with the director. Then he walked out, we went back to Hollywood, and Bob Francis was killed in an airplane crash. Then they had to get a new old man and a new young man. They got James Cagney and a young actor named Don Dubbins. What ever happened to him? I guess he vanished. It's easy to vanish in America. I vanished too."

She came to New York where she was interviewed by Eva Marie Saint's husband for another film, but "he didn't like me either, so I spent the winter going to the Actors Studio. I had some money saved from Greece, but I didn't need much. I don't spend a lot. If I have one pair of shoes, it's enough. I had only one dress when I came here, but I just washed it and put it on again. Who needs a second dress?"

Finally she went back to Greece in despair and toured with the National Popular Theatre for two years in plays like *Inherit the Wind* and *Merchant of Venice* and starred in films like *Zorba the Greek* and *Elektra,* gradually building her protean talents into an international reputation which now requires her to give as much of herself as a 24-hour day will allow. She has no children, although she has been married ("one and a half times," she tosses off, without explaining). Currently she has two unreleased films ("One is a comedy—I don't think they can sell it") and she's making a third during the day in New York. "It's called *The Brotherhood* and it's about the Mafia. I play Kirk Douglas' wife. It's not such a great part, but I need the money. Like most Greeks, I am supporting several people back home."

Has her best work been in movies or onstage? "I haven't done my best work yet" is the simple, direct answer. Then the big black eyes turn moist and she seems on the verge of tears. "Many things I do just for money because I don't know how to make a living any other way. I miss that, not having done something more important with my life. I'm very sad that I may have to spend the rest of my life as an actress. Acting depends on love, and I never know—I'm never certain—if people love me. My sister Elektra is an archaeologist. My other sister, Leda, is a radiotherapist in Athens working on a cure for cancer. Those are wonderful, important jobs. They have done so much more with their lives than I have with mine. If I was in science, making a rocket fly, then nobody could say I didn't do that. But with acting, people are never sure. I feel I am not good enough. I'm always looking into people's eyes to see if they like me. That's my proof of being alive. And that's why actors are so unsteady, so unhappy. It's a profession of doubt. You have no God, no love. Life gives you nothing to hold onto. So every night I feel nervous, nauseated. I'm not a happy person. I'm moody. There is a beautiful word in Greek—*apolotriosis*. It means you are confiscated. You don't belong, but nobody can kill you. That's what I feel every night when I walk onstage. They may hate me and I may fail them, but they can't kill me. I have no ego and no ambition. I'm like a cow you milk milk milk and then it finally gives you a kick. I feel like kicking back, but I never do."

"But now you are more successful than ever—"

"What is success? After *Elektra* won all the international film prizes, I didn't work for two years. After *Zorba* I didn't work for a year and a half. I'm loved and admired, then dismissed with laurels. It's never been an easy life, acting. Blood and sweat, as we say in Greece. I've never made much money. For *Zorba*, my most popular film, I made only $10,000. I am not a star people pay money to see. They take my blood instead and I'm always there to give it. Every time I begin a new project I nearly die. When we started rehearsals for *Iphegenia* Cacoyannis said to me—he knows me so well—'OK, Irene, let's go through that birth-giving again,' and he was right. And even now, when they applaud, I wonder if another actress couldn't do it better. I feel a tremendous responsibility to those young faces in the audience. I wonder every night if I have studied enough history, or read enough books, or lived through enough pain to give them what they deserve. If you are cobbler you know if your shoes are worth the public's dollars, but I live my whole life wondering—am I worth it?"

Gathering up her pride, with no more difficulty than if she were closing a door, she is gone before the answer comes. Home to her 66-year-old mother, waiting in some tiny West Side hotel. And leaving me behind with a lump in my throat, wondering why it is sometimes so hard to say "Yes."

Paul Newman and Joanne Woodward

The hand-painted sign on the sculptured lawn of the sculptured house in Beverly Hills reads: "PLEASE—THEY HAVE MOVED!—THE PIERSONS." Of course, there are no Piersons. The sign is a voodoo gris-gris Paul Newman and Joanne Woodward have put up to discourage the myriads of tourists who drive by with movie-star maps, get out of their Toyota Coronas and trample on the sculptured lawn of the sculptured house, taking snapshots with their Brownie Instamatics. If only they were lucky enough to get inside the house, they'd have a lot more fun.

Standing in the kitchen door at the back of the house is a busy dandelion of a child, a 7-year-old femme fatale named Lissy Newman, who promptly announces: "Mommy's on the telephone. She's always on the telephone. May I have a cigarette? Cigarettes are very bad for you. You shouldn't smoke." Lissy never stops talking and when you meet her parents you know exactly why. Lissy fakes it with an unlit True cigarette as she leads the way through the kitchen, where a chauffeur sits reading the afternoon paper, into the library, where Joanne motions to a sprawling sofa. She is eating chocolate-chip cookies and drinking iced coffee. The female half of the Newman team, she is the star without an image, the girl with many faces, none of which ever get recognized by clerks in dime stores who riot when her husband walks in. She has glorious white skin, twinkling naughty eyes which always clue you in to the fact that encyclopedias are being written behind them, and her hair is long and golden and soaking wet because she has just come from a ballet class she takes with the UCLA football team. (Ballet is Joanne's favorite thing in the world —for Christmas, Paul gave her a complete print of the Nureyev-Fonteyn *Romeo and Juliet* and she will do all the leaps if you will just ask her.)

Lissy is still faking it with the True and explaining in great detail that her sister, a 9-year-old femme fatale named Nell, has taken Baron, the family sparrow hawk, to the bird doctor, when Paul Newman bursts into the room in tennis shorts and a rumpled white T-shirt with a sheaf of papers in his hands and a defeated look on his face. "I'm writing a speech for Eugene McCarthy and it has to be ready in three hours. You don't want to write a speech for me, do you?"

There they are, America's jet-age Doug and Mary, nibbling on cookies in a swank rose-carpeted, paneled library that has nothing to do with the way they live. Jack Armstrong and Scarlett O'Hara in basketball shoes. "Out!" says Scarlett, with a delicate Southern accent that is more pure-bred moonshine and magnolia blossom than hominy grits, to Lissy, who is now standing on her head in the middle of the room. "I have to be interviewed and how can we get anything done if you are talking all the time?" "I won't talk; I'll just stand on my head." "Go help Daddy write his McCarthy speech." Paul scoops up Lissy, still upside down, and carries her out to the pool where her violence won't be so loud, and although by now it is no longer clear what anyone has come to talk *about*, it seems like the interview is on. More or less.

Joanne doesn't really *do* interviews. Even though she's the only member of the Newman family who has won an Oscar, she has always been content to take a back seat to the fame and glamour, preferring to emerge in the roles she plays instead of phony interviews. But like most Southern girls, she's never at a loss for words and in her case the words always sound fascinating. (She has an IQ of 135, higher than 90 percent of the doctors at Bellevue.) And on this summer day, with the California sun licking at the windows like tongues on an Eskimo Pie, she has something worth talking about—a film she's proud of, called *Rachel, Rachel,* in which her performance as a 35-year-old spinster living with her mother above the Japonica Funeral Chapel is so remarkable it could be the beginning of a whole new career. "Paul gets all the wonderful parts, but I always seem to be the after-thought, like the backstop who stands behind the pitcher. You know, even a bad movie takes two or three months out of your life, so I finally decided that if I am going to take that much time out of a life I enjoy, it better be something I bloody well care about. For a script like that, I have to find it myself. Good things are seldom offered to me. When I started, I just wanted to act. That's all I cared about. I did some good things, like *Three Faces of Eve,* but I also did some things I didn't care about. Now the older I get the more I realize that life is like cotton candy. Take one bite and it's gone. Life is too short to worry about the tiny dissatisfactions. They're a pain in the ass. I hate wasting time. Like the tourists driving around on Sunday afternoons looking at movie-star houses. They could get killed tomorrow and what do they have to show for it? They spent their last day on earth looking at Paul Newman's house. I refuse to fiddle away my life in dribs and drabs. One thing I say to the kids—'Tell me anything, get mad, yell at me, but *never* say you're bored.'

"People kept asking 'Whatever happened to Joanne Woodward?' Well, she got bored waiting around. That's why I was attracted to *Rachel, Rachel.* Its theme is that things never stop, tomorrow is another day. I felt very unhappy and discouraged and I felt my career had ended. I'm not a movie star anyway. I've never been the same person twice in movies and Hollywood never really knew what to do with me. So when you're in that boat, you either become an enormously successful established character actress or you do anything you can get. I was determined I'd rather do nothing than just work for the sake of having a job, and I was even more determined I'd never do anything again unless I felt strongly about it. One day John Forman called. He was our agent once and now he, Paul and I have formed a company. We've known him for years. He got me my first job fresh out of Greenville, South Carolina, in an old Robert Montgomery TV show. Anyway, he had read a review of this book called *A Jest of God* by Margaret Laurence, a Canadian writer, and we got the galleys and decided to take an option on it. Paul couldn't believe we had done that. Then when he read the book I don't think he liked it much." Her eyes droop into one of those Poor Pitiful Pearl Doll looks as she imitates Paul: "Not movie material." Then the sun breaks through in her smile and she's as pretty as one of Irwin Shaw's girls in their summer dresses. "Paul had no intention of directing it, but we couldn't get anyone else interested. Stewart Stern, who wrote the screenplay, and I went around offering ourselves to everybody, but I'm afraid offering a package of the script and me was hardly like offering Elizabeth Taylor and Tennessee Williams."

But somehow they did it. They did it because, even when saddled with Hollywood slag far beneath their dignity or ability, the Newmans have always remained individuals, with firm grips on their identities. They both have minds of their own, in a business where actors tend to think collectively. And it would take two nose-thumbing, tasteful, anti-Establishment rebels with strong convictions to make a film like *Rachel, Rachel.* It wasn't easy. Even after Paul put his name in the pot, every major studio in Hollywood turned them down, sniffing with typical chaotic irrationalization, "Newman's a star, it's too big a gamble to let him direct; Woodward's not a financeable name." They both had to commit a chunk of their lives away to

get Warners-Seven Arts to finance their film, but they
have now surprised all the skeptics by delivering their
package for less than $800,000 (a feat unheard of these
days with names like the Newmans involved). And they
have surprised everyone even more by turning out not
just another Hollywood junk collage the big studios grind
out yearly like cheese sandwiches, but a thoughtful, provocative, moving, undeniably *unique* movie. Now the question looming ahead like the Hollywood Freeway—will it
sell?

"I hope it's successful," says Paul, "not because of
any financial reward—hell, both Joanne and I did it for
nothing—but to prove to Hollywood you can make a film
about basic, simple people without sex and violence and
a band of Indians scalping the settlers. I don't know. People get embarrassed by their own involvement. They want
fantasy and they want to keep their cool at the same time.
They can't help but be involved here. But the film represents something we *had* to do and we did it."

"It just kind of happened," says Joanne, watching
Paul slave over his McCarthy speech. "We talked about
it and one day we found ourselves all sitting around in
Palm Springs writing the script. Actually the men did all
the work while in the best tradition of the Southern belle
I sat around and fanned myself and drank lemonade. I'm
not much of a pusher."

She means it. She has always refused to become one
of those sad little dumplings who fall into their swimming
pools and melt there. While other stars are busy hiring
and firing butlers and imported Swedish masseurs, Joanne
dodges the Hollywood scene and spends all of her free
time in her converted barn in Westport, Connecticut, designed by Broadway set designer Ralph Alswang and set
in three acres of apple trees and riverbanks. She hates
Hollywood's superficiality and her frankness on the subject has not always made her popular here. "Listen," she

laughs, scratching her toe, "I've been knocking Hollywood so long it's become a joke out here. I don't like it and that's all there is to it and I don't really know why. Maybe I'm perverse. Life is pleasant, but it's just not me. It will never be home. This house is not me. It's rented out all the time. The kids went to a school that was very proper, all straight A's and Debbie Reynolds was head of the Girl Scouts, you know what I mean? I couldn't wait to get them out of there. I don't like the way Beverly Hills *looks*. I loathe manicured lawns and I *hate* palm trees. We just sold this house and we're moving into a place with a prize-winning cactus and three of the biggest palm trees you ever saw in the yard and I'm having them all cut down and planting magnolia trees and rose bushes. People expect us to have big houses and servants and the whole *schmeer,* but I hate houses with no personality and I feel guilty having servants with nothing to do. I had to let the secretary go because every time I passed the library, she was just sitting there buffing her nails. We have a driver who takes the kids to school, but I have to keep thinking of things for him to do. LISSY!"

Lissy comes in wearing a fresh new pinafore, eating a limb from one of the trees on the sculptured lawn. "Get the driver to take you down to the store and buy some pencils." Lissy leaps at the idea of some action on this otherwise lethargic Beverly Hills afternoon and is gone like a shot. With Paul's three children (Stephanie, Susan and Scott) and Paul and Joanne's three (Nell, Lissy and baby Clea) there are six junior-sized Newmans hanging from the rafters and none of them seems a bit impressed by the fact that they are living with two of the biggest movie stars in the world. "Now that Nell is a movie star herself in *Rachel, Rachel,* Stephanie wants to be one too. She's 13 and just hates it because she's flat-chested. The kids are all marvelous and beautiful and slightly insane —five beautiful blonde ladies and Scott, who is 18 and looks like a French film star. That's what my life is all about. We never read anything that is ever written about either of us in magazines. The only magazine we subscribe to is *Child Life*. We used to take everything, but they kept following us around the world and we had to pay extra postage. I do love the *National Geographic*, though. It was the only magazine as a child that you ever saw people naked in. Paul gets all the fan mail and I read everything that comes to the house. I'm still waiting for the one that begins, 'Gee baby, you were great.' The only fan mail I ever get is from 12-year-old boys. One wrote, 'I love you, I love you, I love you, you're six months older than my mother.' We don't have many kooks hanging around. Occasionally Paul gets the oddballs who want him to take off his sunglasses so they can see his blue eyes, but usually he gets a different breed, which I think is an interesting comment on his dignity as a human being. It must be sad to be an Elizabeth Taylor, who hasn't been to a supermarket for ten years. I couldn't stand that. I remember going to an Actors Studio premiere once for Kazan's film *East of Eden*. Marilyn Monroe was there and it was one of the most horrible sights I ever witnessed— watching her be grabbed at and mauled. That little white face in that sea of hands. We just don't allow that to happen. Oh, there are a couple of things we can't do any more. Paul can't take the kids to Disneyland because he gets mobbed and the kids don't get to see anything. He took them to the World's Fair and had to be slipped into back doors and things and it was no fun. But it's a small price to pay for everything else."

No need to explain the folks-next-door image any more. The room has suddenly turned into a script for "Ethel and Albert." Paul bursts in with a mug of iced lager, beaming like the kid who just won the potato-sack race. "Just got the news! *Rachel* is going to open the San Francisco Film Festival in October!"

"Sit down and eat some celery before you blow your cool," says Joanne, sounding like she was back in the freshman dorm at Louisiana State University. "Paul's trying to stop smoking and he has to eat celery."

Paul is lying on the floor in his tennis shorts, showing me how he keeps his stomach flat after drinking so much beer. We're suddenly both on the floor, raising our legs and pushing our heads through our knees to stretch our stomach muscles while two cats named Snowflake and Black Basil are walking across our chests. "That Black Basil is going to be a great prick when he grows up," says Paul on a deep knee-bend.

"How dare you say that?" gasps Joanne, indignant. "Black Basil has more dignity than any cat I know."

"We have five cats and they're all pricks," says Paul to his kneecaps. "We're the only people I know who carry more dog and cat boxes on planes than luggage."

"We only have four cats now. Cassandra wandered off and we never did find *her*. She was a great striped cat with eight fingers on each toe."

"Eight fingers on each toe," gasps Paul between stomach bends on the floor. "*That* is the most ridiculous thing I ever heard of!"

It is quite obvious by now that the interview is over. The kids are home, flying through the house totally unlike anybody's idea of what Hollywood children were like in the old Margaret O'Brien days, chased by the barkingest, howlingest contingent of neighborhood dogs this side of the Los Angeles City Pound. Two makeup artists from Universal are waiting upstairs to Max Factor Joanne into another of the many faces of Eve for the film she is currently working on, a race-car movie called *Winning* with Paul and Robert Wagner. Dignified? Snobby, now that she is the star of a very important new art-house movie everybody's talking about? "Ha!" cackles Joanne. "We're calling the new movie 'Cool Hand Luke Finds Rachel in the Sack with The Thief!' "

She stands giggling in the kitchen door, with the baby in one arm and two dogs yapping at her bare feet. "I'm the only movie star who still rides the Super Chief. I'm taking the train back to Connecticut next week, then Paul starts a new western in Mexico and I'll come back so he can come home on weekends. If we get rid of him one night, come on over for soul food. Turnip greens, cornbread and sweet potato pie. He *hates* it."

Walking down the driveway into the periwinkle blue California day, I'm suddenly confronted by a carful of tourists reading a guide to movie-star homes, leaning out of a car with Oklahoma license plates. "Who lives there, in that house?" they ask, opening their Brownie cases and staring bewilderingly from their map to the sign on the sculptured lawn.

"Just ordinary people." And behind the door that is being closed by the blonde Scarlett O'Hara nobody recognized, you can still hear the dogs barking as the car pulls away, disappointed.

Joseph Losey

London, 1967.

Notice the eyes. Tired, curved down at the edges, and he rubs them a lot. Joseph Losey's eyes tell the story of a life of hard knocks, a man without a flag and a career applauded everywhere but home, where it matters most.

The name, in Europe, is golden. No Losey film here is just another movie. *King and Country* and *The Servant* both won film festival awards, and *The Damned* won the Trieste science-fiction festival award. For the second time in three years a "Joseph Losey Season" has been held in London for two months this year at the National Film Theatre. The British Film Institute thinks so much of his work that it recently held a special festival just for the showing of his TV commercials. Ironically, he even received the Best Foreign Director award from America's foreign film importers.

Why is it ironic? Because he's not a foreigner at all. He was born in Wisconsin and while he has little taste for America (and no taste at all for most American films) he is still as American as a hamburger. His feelings are understandable. Seldom has there been a case of a native talent treated so badly by the industry that bred him. Educated at Dartmouth and Harvard, he worked as a roving reporter for *Variety*, stage-managed the first Radio City Music Hall show, directed 13 plays on Broadway in the 1930's, and landed an MGM contract in 1938. One of his documentaries won an Oscar nomination, the movie industry began to sit up and take notice, and a series of films resulted which were years before their time. One of these was *The Boy with Green Hair*, which was produced by Adrian Scott, one of the original 19 blacklisted by the film industry during the infamous McCarthy witch-hunts.

The film is now considered a classic (It's still almost impossible to find in America, but the Cinémathèque Française shows it regularly in Paris to standing room only). At the time it was made, however, Scott served a year in jail. Losey was called a Communist and blacklisted too. (Incredible as it may seem, that's the way we used to do things in America, folks.) Losey couldn't get the jobs he deserved, so he directed the late Louis Calhern in *The Wooden Dish* at the Phoenix in New York, and in 1954, he just plain gave up. Gave up trying to sell educated and hard-hitting film suggestions to an ignorant coterie of Hollywood label-fixers who were too frightened to take a chance with a man who had been associated with the word "Commie."

Accident, his 18th film, is now being made the way he makes all of his films in Europe: quietly. A visit to the set in the glimmering green Indian summer of a peaceful Queen Anne farmhouse near London does, in fact, give little indication that a movie is being made at all. Losey likes it that way. The budget is almost invisible. Interiors are being shot at Twickenham, a tiny powder-box studio with three sound stages six miles from London. *Accident* occupies two stages and a murder mystery on a train takes up the third. There is nothing to remind you of Hollywood. No air-conditioned trailers; the stars change in the farmhouse john and the makeup department consists of a wooden table with a hand mirror. Everyone eats on card tables under a cow shed and the film's one luxury (a secretary for Losey) rides a bicycle from the house to wherever her boss is working in the nearby woods.

"We do it the way most of my films are done," says Losey, taking a tea break, "for almost nothing." The actors working that day, Dirk Bogarde and Stanley Baker, sat on the grass with their shirts off, playing with the farmer's kids. "They'll never get rich in my films, but they keep coming back. Dirk has done five, Stanley three. Dirk turned down a Hollywood film worth ten times as much to do this one. He can afford it now. But then there's my continuity girl, who gave up the biggest chance of her career on a picture with a $10-million budget for this. My cutter runs a pub to support his family so he can work with me. I try to surround myself with people who think "we" instead of "they," but I make pictures so selectively that I can't afford to pay them while they hang on waiting. Unusual people with creative ideas get ahead in England. This is where everything's happening in films. People are more informed, more enlightened, freer to do things that say something. Of course that's only half of the film group here. The other half is the same as in America—union men interested only in overtime, and men who want to make a fast buck on a cheap investment."

The sun was hot and the tea with honey heady, so Losey wrapped it up for the day. In the car on the way back to London, more talk about the film and his life in Europe. Unlike the cars owned by most movie directors, it had a straight shift, most of the dashboard had been ripped out and instead of a chauffeur it was driven by a little old man in rolled-up sleeves and denim pants. Losey, worn by the day's shooting, cupped his head in his hands, then massaged his temples. "Working like this over the years, sacrificing the big juicy jobs for the things I believe in, and doing it with no money and little en-couragement—it's been exhausting. This one is turning out well. Harold Pinter did the script, so you know it's extraordinary. I think it's the best thing he's done since *The Servant*. I loathe films with too much dialogue. It's

100 pages long and only about 60 pages of that is talk, so there's room for the visual things."

What's it about? "Well, Dirk and Stanley are two dons at Oxford. They represent people with double lives— academic, dull, defeated, custodians of knowledge who suddenly find themselves in the same impasses as the men in the street. Into the lives of these men, their wives and a young male student comes an Austrian girl who brings out the best and the worst in them all. She is the catalyst, the accident-maker. At one point, they all play the war game, which is the rage on TV here, and it suddenly becomes so real that they attack each other physically. Everyone lusts after the girl. Finally, at one point in the highway driving from Oxford to the farm, everyone's life changes. The boy—Michael York, who just did *Taming of the Shrew* with the Burtons—is killed, the girl simply packs and leaves, and the others are left to face their own guilts. I guess it's really about how civilized and courteous people can often be as vicious underneath as the lower classes. In some way, everyone affects everyone else in life. Sometimes we have the most powerful effect on others when we least suspect. The cast is really first-rate. Jacqueline Sassard, a French actress, plays the girl, Delphine Seyrig is Baker's wife, and Dirk's wife is Vivien Merchant, one of the most brilliant actresses in England. She's really Pinter's wife. Pinter's in it, too. He started out as an actor, you know.

"I hate working in color but you have to now. Without it you get only half as much for the TV sale. I tried it with *Modesty Blaise* and some of the critics said it was the best use of color they'd ever seen, but even after two years of working out the lighting, the rushes were better than any final print I ever saw of it. I've got the same cameraman, so we'll do something low-key—blue-black with splashes of yellow spilling out of a house at night, violent splashes of red blood against sterile white for the accident, lots of mustard and rust at Oxford. Nobody does anything interesting with color these days. I was impressed with *Red Desert's* color, but the film was so pretentious and boring it put me to sleep. I think the best color in ages was in *Muriel*."

The mention of *Modesty Blaise* seemed to set his juices flowing. In England it is considered a masterpiece by some, a mistake by others. In America, some of the hardest-to-please critics think it's one of the year's best. Others think it's hogwash. "It was meant to be the last and final word on the subject of camp, a film to extinguish forever—hopefully—the forces behind the garbage-can syndrome of movies Hollywood is turning out now. The fact that people are taking it seriously and complaining because it doesn't make sense is proof of what I was trying to say. They've been brainwashed by the same kind of movie I'm putting down. As a result, I'm frustrated again. I've had letters from America saying it was degrading for me to have my name on it. Quite the contrary. It was made for a reason. Now the film is being thrown away by idiots who haven't the slightest idea what it is about. Darryl Zanuck loved it, but he allowed his advertising department to destroy it by playing it up as a female James Bond. Sure, the picture has its flaws—I never did get the color I wanted, Monica Vitti had no sense of humor, Terry Stamp hadn't the slightest clue to what I was getting at, and their performances show it. Still, it would've had a chance of finding its audience if it had been sold simply, stylishly, with an op-art design that told nothing about the plot, a teaser with taste—no nudity, no secret-agent stuff. It should have opened in an art house until they knew what they had, then sent out on the circuit. One theatre manager told me, 'The picture's a flop.' 'What do you mean?' I asked, watching the lines outside waiting to get in. 'For every 2,000 admissions, we've had about five complaints,' he said. 'What the hell does that mean?' I asked. 'Normally, we don't get any.' "

Would he ever work in America again? "Only if all the conditions were right. In England, I can make the kind of film I want to make. They may get badly distributed, but they're the ones that interest me. I don't need X millions of dollars and big-name stars, but I must control the advertising and distribution. The film must be mine. When *Eva* was released in New York I didn't even recognize it. Jeanne Moreau and Stanley Baker and I drew up a petition to have our names taken off it. A film must bear the director's stamp, or it's nothing. I'd rather see a bad film with one really distinct style of badness than a film with 50 different kinds of badness.

"Life is OK here. I'm not rolling in money; last week I had to direct a vodka commercial. But I've just taken a house for the rest of my life. I lecture at cinema clubs, do TV panels and film symposiums, and there's a new book coming out on me in France. There's another Losey festival this fall at Eton College in Windsor and a retrospective of my films in Australia. I'm doing a musical on the London stage in January with John Barry music and Sean Kenny sets and a script by another American expatriate, Lucas Heller. I've had lots of wives and although I'm presently married emotionally but not legally I've got a 9-year-old son named Josh and another grown son, Gavrik, who is a production manager for one of the London film studios. Not everybody needs America, you know. Some of us hold our heads up pretty well over here." The car pulled up to an intersection on Brompton Road. Losey waved goodbye. He was off to see the rushes. Alone. (Nobody gets invited to see the rushes on a Losey film.) When the car pulled away, he was still rubbing his eyes.

Omar Sharif

"The new Clark Gable" is what Hollywood calls Egyptian-born Omar Sharif. But once again, Hollywood is wrong. "They are so anxious to make me into a new romantic screen hero like Clark Gable they even sent me to the special showing of *Gone with the Wind* at the Cannes Film Festival this year. But I am like no other man. I am an individual," he says. And to prove it, the first and only actor from the Arabic world who has ever become a star in English-speaking movies has turned out 13 films in which he has never played the same role twice. He was Sheik Ali in *Lawrence of Arabia,* a Mongol warlord in *Genghis Khan,* and Armenian king in *Rise and Fall of the Roman Empire,* a Yugoslav partisan in *The Yellow Rolls Royce,* a Spanish priest in *Behold a Pale Horse,* a Russian poet in *Dr. Zhivago,* a French police inspector in *Night of the Generals,* an Italian prince in *More than a Miracle,* and, most recently, a Mexican heavy in *McKenna's Gold,* Jewish gambler Nicky Arnstein in *Funny Girl,* Austrian crown prince Rudolf in *Mayerling,* a lovelorn lawyer obsessed with Anouk Aimee in *The Appointment,* and—close your eyes—Che Guevara! All adding up, quite naturally, to confusion in the minds of Omar Sharif fans. Who, they ask, is the man born Michel Shalhoub?

To unravel the mystery, some clues. Outside his villa near the Colosseum in Rome, the city is asleep. A cat meows in a nearby garbage can. Stone statues stand motionless in the entrance. At the top of the velvet staircase, "the new Clark Gable" stands in his stocking feet with a Barbra Streisand record in his hands. "I live one day at a time," he says, extending a hand, "I'm a very lazy person." Inside, the Streisand record roars, battling in competition with the television set, which is tuned to the motorcycle races at Monza. Shoes and socks are strewn about the floor. Every table is covered with unfinished jigsaw puzzles. "You like? I had to have this place fumigated when I moved in because it was full of ants. I hate European hotels because they don't let you bring women up to your room. I get very lonely in hotels."

On the outside, he is cool, the master of every situation. He can charm the stockings off even the sternest old-maid librarian. If he doesn't like the direction a conversation is taking, he'll look into your eyes until he hypnotizes you into submission with pupils that bore through you like two pieces of coal. He hulks above his guests with a six-foot frame, and he has skin the color of sable. But something's wrong with the picture. On the inside, he's not so secure. He suffers from a serious ulcer the doctors have been trying to remove surgically for years and he often has to take pain-killers to ease the discomfort. He is restless, often grouchy, and spends all of his spare time playing games and solving puzzles. He takes two pain-killers, washes them down with red wine, and explains why: "I should never have become an actor. My teachers wanted me to specialize in physics. I have a mathematical mind and being a movie star bores me. After I make a few million dollars, I plan to retire and play bridge the rest of my life. I bore easily, so I taught myself to do something between scenes sitting around on movie sets and now I have become an expert on bridge. When I finished *The Appointment*, I toured America with a team of five professional bridge players. We got $110,000 to play in tournaments against other teams. On the set, I have four hands going at the same time and between scenes I play each hand. I am very lonely. I make friends easily, but in this business each time you make a new friend it's time to pack and leave. So I play games. I lock myself in my house until I solve each crossword. In Hollywood, when I was making *Funny Girl,* I spent all my spare time in the studio commissary playing the pinball machines. I even brought a Monopoly set to Rome. Gambling? It's not the same pleasure, because there is no puzzle to solve. But I did work out a mathematical theory to win at blackjack. I went to Las Vegas five weekends in a row, won $10,000 each time, and now I am banned at the casinos."

How he has time for all those rumored love affairs is another mystery. But he admits, "I love sex, wine and food—after a hard day's work, they are my rewards. Some people think my attitude toward women is unethical. But I've had a lot of experience. Women want to be dominated. I like to go with American girls, but they make terrible wives because they are too independent and money-crazy. Then they can walk out and sock the man for half his money. Even in divorce cases, American women get the sympathy of the courts. That makes the man weaker as the wife gets more aggressive."

Omar was separated from his own wife after ten years of marriage, but they are still friends. "I was married at 21 and my wife was a big star in Egyptian movies and since there are only about five stars in all of the Arab world, we both worked on three or four films at a time. It is not easy to keep a marriage together when you are both working in films. The temptations are strong. You are always meeting beautiful and exciting people. Unless you are mature, which we were not, it ceases to be exciting. We both became bored. Then I did *Lawrence of Arabia* and I was gone for a long time and the separation was too much for us. But we are still friends. I built my wife a house in Paris and she lives there with my 11-year-old son Tarek. We have an agreement that if either of us wants to remarry, we can get a divorce. But I have never found a woman to replace her. I know women in every city, but they are always women for temporary periods of time because of the travel. I am a big success now, but I'm having no fun."

For *Lawrence of Arabia,* he spent 14 months in the desert—7 in Jordan, 5 in the south of Spain, 2 in the Sahara living under a tent. For *Dr. Zhivago,* he spent a year in Finland on a frozen lake in 40-below-zero temperatures. He isn't satisfied with any of his films. In *Funny Girl,* he feels he was upstaged by Barbra Streisand. "She's a monster. I had nothing to do but stand around. But she's a fascinating monster. Sometimes I just stood on the sidelines and watched her. I think her biggest problem is that she wants to be a woman and she wants to be beautiful and she is neither." In *McKenna's Gold,* he broke his nose in Kanab, Utah, when his horse bent over to eat some grass. He leaned over to pull up on the reins and the horse raised its head so quickly the great neck tendon slammed him in the face. "So you see, no fun. I have yet to do a really good part in which I can show my talent and be fulfilled. Everyone thought I was going to do it in *Zhivago,* but in 300 days of shooting all I did was react to everyone else. Every day people went to the daily rushes and came out saying, 'Wasn't Rod Steiger marvelous' or 'Wasn't Julie Christie marvelous,' and nobody said a word about me. I was in terrible despair. I was never off the screen, but I never had one good scene. A few more good parts and I'm finished with films. I have made a lot of money, but I'm not financially independent yet. American taxes take it all. I'm too lazy to keep papers so I end up with nothing. When you become a big movie star, you become a corporation, then you get into tax situations, alimony situations. You have to become a fighter. Then you lose your energy for fighting. To maintain your identity you must alternate the terrible spectacular movies for lots of money with the small artistic films for less money. That is why I made *The Appointment* for Sidney Lumet. It is the best part I've ever had in my life and it will kill me if it does not make money. Next, I want to work with Fellini. But I will never make enough money to retire and play bridge if I stop making big, terrible spectacles. And if I make big, terrible spectacles I lose my self-respect. I am now in a real dilemma."

He swallows another pain-killer. And out on the street near the Colosseum, a magazine truck delivers a new batch of Italian magazines blaring the headline: "Omar Sharif —The Screen Hero Who Owns The World!"

Makes you wonder how they get up in the morning.

Miss U.S.A.

Watching the "live from the beautiful Miami oceanfront Miss U.S.A. Beauty Pageant" last Saturday night on CBS, it must have occurred to most sane viewers that somebody was pulling their legs. Of course all beauty pageants are satires on an American dream as archaic as rose-covered cottages and chicken every Sunday. Yet every year the most beautiful (and, one suspects, psycho-sexually disoriented) archetypes of the female species line up on some drafty stage somewhere (usually by an ocean) and exhibit their Clairol hair and their Gardol smiles. They run for Miss Everything.

In an age when the creeps and the freaks seem to be running the show, the old-fashioned American dreams make their claims for survival. And in some bizarre way, remind themselves of their own existence.

The Miss U.S.A. Beauty Pageant was like a cattle auction. The only difference is that the winning cow gets a movie contract. You know what that means. Miss U.S.A. invariably ends up as a topless waitress serving cigars in the background of a Rock Hudson flick. Gives her something to tell her grandchildren. And, in its own way, I suppose it's as valid as telling them, "See this scar under Granny's eye—got that beating up a cop in front of the Columbia chemistry lab."

This year, the pageant looked like a skit from *New Faces*. Sponsored by an underarm deodorant, the 51 contestants were so beautiful they all looked exactly alike. (Beauty queens are like Chinese.) So to make them stand apart, somebody had the bright idea of parading them around a platform in Halloween costumes that looked like they were sewn together at the last minute by each girl's Aunt Tillie.

The idea obviously was to represent some aspect of the contestant's home state. I didn't mind the ones in blue jeans and kilts and monkey fur so much, or the flappers and Scarlett O'Haras, or Miss Washington dressed like an Alpine mountain climber, but things got icky for poor Miss Montana, with pickaxe and miner's helmet. Miss Nevada looked like a cash register. Miss Massachusetts got drowned in an ugly floor-length black Pilgrim gown, Miss District of Columbia wore a miniskirt made out of an American flag (which, even in this madhouse era, must have offended someone other than myself).

Poor, dear Miss Tennessee was pinned into an LP hillbilly record with a big hole through the middle to expose her bust-line, another unfortunate girl came out as a whole life-size Christmas tree with a star on top of her head, and my favorite wore a billboard which looked suspiciously like an "Eat at Joe's" sign. She must have been from Brooklyn. There was not one all-American Negro girl on display, and even Miss Hawaii came from Boston.

After Paul Anka screeched his way through a chorus of "I Wanna Be a Yankee Doodle Girl, Cause 68's a Yankee Doodle Year" about three keys beyond his range or ability, Miss U.S.A.'s answer to Bert Parks came out and introduced himself as Bob Barker. Everyone clapped a lot, like they had actually heard of him or something, then June Lockhart told the girls that "only 15 of you ever get to the swimsuit and formal evening gowns, but each and everyone of you is already a winner."

The Fabulous Fifteen were marched out from their slots in the lineup while the other losers smiled bravely through salty tears. Then Bob Barker asked the Fabulous Fifteen questions. This was the most hilarious part of the show and I doubt if Mel Brooks could have written it better.

Miss Connecticut was interested in astrology, "but I'm not sure it's valid." "I'm a Sagittarius—what about me?" asked Barker. "Frank—giggle giggle—Sinatra's a—giggle giggle—Sagittarius too—giggle giggle." (I saw doom waiting in the wings for Miss Connecticut.)

Miss Alabama, a busty physical type, said she loved diving from high diving boards. "I jes' do some back flops and then some other stuff and you know. You c'n do anythin' with a sweatshirt on." "Why a sweatshirt?" "Cause it keeps ya from stingin' when ya hitcha back." Miss Nevada was a prelaw student dancing in a Las Vegas nightclub. Miss New Mexico sounded like Eve Arden and wanted to be a female James Bond. Finally, Miss Maryland, a dental assistant said, "I love my work except for the ones who bite."

Barker, a real all-around charmer, replied: "Next time I see you you'll be all scarred up." I tell you the show had class.

While they were hustled offstage to get into their swimsuits for the next relay, June Lockhart faced the viewers with the astounding news that: "It's amazing what the girls want to do with their lives. They all want to get married." Then she admitted several want to be movie stars and one might like to try brain surgery. "Their handwriting runs from chicken track to pure undecipherable, and one girl even misspelled the name of her own home town." Dear June. June tells all.

Then they showed topless baby pictures of four girls (What about the other 11? Didn't they have tops?), followed by the "parade of bathing beauties," in which the girls wore identical Catalina swimsuits designed to give them the uniform appearance of underwater concrete statues in an old Esther Williams movie.

Then last year's Miss U.S.A., a has-been already, stepped out to the White X in tears, and when the applause died down, said: "Did you ever see a llama sneeze? I did. I counted the raindrops in Waikiki, slept in a log cabin, climbed the Space Needle, and saw Disneyland. I even met a Green Beret. All I can say is thank you and goodbye."

But it wasn't over yet. We had the annual "super extravaganza number" to get through, with all the girls tap dancing with canes like paraplegics doing an old Virginia Mayo number. In the evening gown competition, there was so much chiffon (Purity of spirit, you know, goes hand in hand with Pepsi) that I almost cheered for one flowered print.

While they broke for a mouthwash commercial, June Lockhart asked the home viewers to get a pencil and jot down their own favorites: "See who's the best judge in your family." In the apartment where I watched the show, there was a mad dash at this point for the hot hors d'oeuvres, while I made a mental note to vote for the girl in the flowered print.

Ten girls were eliminated fast after the tap dancing. (I

lost sight of the girl in the flowered print—dark horses go fast.) The five finalists were Blue Ribbon stock. They had to be brilliant, witty, philosophical, feet-on-the-ground, and gorgeous in 10 seconds, as they stepped into an isolated soundproof booth, like the one Daisy Clover went bananas in, to answer the Big Intellectual Question of the year: "As a spokesman for the Younger Generation, what is the best advice you can give to people your own age?" The dancer from Las Vegas said, "To thine own self be true," and I crossed her off my list. The others looked at Heaven, and thanked their mommies and daddies. Miss Washington, bless her hide, said, "Do your own thing." My vote was in.

After a commercial in which a woman gave beauty advice to all the women in the audience who would never get within 300 miles of Miss U.S.A. or any other pageant by taking a bath in a tub of hot milk and putting cucumber slices on her eyelids, a voice-over talked solemnly about Duty and Honor while the old Miss U.S.A. made her Farewell Walk as an accordion played what sounded like a funeral dirge. Oh, yes. Miss Washington won. I'll be watching for the big cigar scene in the next Rock Hudson flick. Don't forget, I knew her when.

Albert Finney

Smoking cigars in his sock feet and roaming restlessly around in his elegant suite at the Plaza before the opening of *Joe Egg* like an enormously likeable caged bear, Albert Finney looked outwardly disarming. With rumpled clothes, tousled red hair and freckled white skin like crushed cornflakes in a bowl of milk, he was a walking reproduction of an unmade bed. Rather like Tom Jones, in fact—a yoke and an image he has learned to live with. But behind the boyish grin things were obviously going on: thoughts, decisions, self-doubts and a search for identity in the face of wealth and celebrity which had taken him along a road of soft shoulders and detours ahead.

A search which had kept him away from Broadway for four years. "Between *Luther* and *Joe Egg* there just wasn't anything I wanted to do. That's not a cry of desperation. But I have to respond to what I'm doing or I won't do it. And it had to be something more important than just *'Tom Jones* is back.' I think this play *is* it." It's a comedy with music about a man trying to decide whether or not to murder his own child, a kind of spastic vegetable with epileptic fits, to save his marriage. A kind of euthanasia with rhythm, which, even for Finney, is pretty controversial. "It's not a black comedy, though. The spastic child just happens to be this couple's hangup. It could represent other hangups in society. I'm not worried about critics. One can't live his life worrying about *them*. The only critic in London who really panned the play was Harold Hobson and I happen to know he is crippled, so perhaps it was too personal for him. But I think it's healthy to treat a so-called taboo subject openly, honestly, without sentimentality. And here in America there is the whole Lenny Bruce tradition of comedy, so I think the audience can take it."

Finney himself has a 9-year-old son, Simon, by actress Jane Wenham, whom he divorced in 1961. "He's normal, thank God, and I see him often. But when he was born, I felt no relation to him. He didn't need me. To me he was just a little thing who cried too much and needed changing too often. Romantically, I had expected more, but I was uninvolved until the first time he recognized me. Now if a doctor had said to me then, 'I think he may be retarded'—a mongoloid—that's when you say, 'What would I do?' I think I would seriously discuss the possibility of euthanasia, putting it to sleep forever. I wouldn't want my marriage or a relationship to the woman I love to have the extra burden of sustaining a hopeless life dependent on us. And that is what the man I play in *Joe Egg* faces."

The play was an accident. The independent production company which Finney and his partner Michael Medwin formed eight years ago had just produced his new film *Charlie Bubbles* (which Finney also directed) and he was busy editing it when Medwin phoned him about *Joe Egg*, which Medwin had seen in Glasgow. Finney never got to see it, but Kenneth Tynan was also trying to buy it for the National Theatre's repertory, so they acted fast, beat Tynan to the draw, brought it to London, and it was a hit. By the time they were ready to export it to New York, the star of the show, Joe Melia, couldn't leave because his wife was having a baby, so Medwin suggested Finney play the part. "Now I've been trying to convince people a long time that I don't want to do anything but direct movies. So I said, 'I'm retired, I just want to sit in my flat overlooking the river and think about directing my next film.' But I read it again and the part was so good that I said yes. But only for ten weeks. I don't want to get bored." He grinned. "The last time I was here my *Luther* contract was for four calendar months, and it was up on January 23, 1964, a Thursday night. I remember it well. David Merrick had asked me earlier to do an Actors Fund benefit and I said sure, but when the time came for me to leave the show, they told me Merrick had scheduled the benefit for some date in February! I guess he suspected my ego was so big that I'd stay in the play another month just to perform for all my friends on a Sunday night." When did he leave? "January 23, 1964, a Thursday night, right on schedule." He roared. Then: "Maybe you shouldn't mention that story, because if you print it, it will only perpetuate the myth of David Merrick." He roared even louder and his mouth turned into a happy trapezoid.

So we got only 10 weeks of Albert Finney. During which he also unveiled *Charlie Bubbles,* a film about which he was even more concerned than *Joe Egg.* "If people don't like the play, it's no skin off my nose. But *Charlie* is *my* film. If they reject that, they reject my feelings, my attitudes toward life and everything around me. The incidents in it are not autobiographical, but the feelings are." Curious, since it is a film about a man so trapped by success that he is no longer able to feel anything but inertia, while Finney seems to be living life to the hilt. "I wanted to explore a mood and make you feel it moment by moment instead of talking about it or signboarding it. For the last four years I've made a lot of money. But I don't *feel* anything. I want people to question their own lives, find out what their real values are. It started as a 32-page outline by Shelagh Delaney and we worked together night and day. It took a long time to make. Now I wonder if people will be bored. I get bored in Antonioni films, and maybe if I saw *Charlie* made by anybody else, I'd be bored by it, too. But it's like abstract art. You must put faith in your own reactions. I never used to talk about myself. I didn't want people to know about *me*, except through my work. I never did things like the 'Tonight Show' for that reason. But if people go away understanding this film and responding to it, then they'll know a lot more about Albert Finney."

That embraces a lot of things. He can be casual and offhand (When people call him "the new Olivier," he says, "Tyrone Guthrie told me a long time ago, 'Don't try to do it all before you're 35, after all, Verdi didn't write *Falstaff* until he was 75' "), or funny and hip ("I went to see Liza Minnelli at the Empire Room after a night of rehearsal with my makeup still on and she was so great I started crying and then they turned the spotlight on me with the mascara running down my face and I'm sure everybody said, 'Who's this Queenie just come over?' ") But always he's Finney. Albie to his friends. The rough-hewn North Country Lancashire lad whose father, also named Albert Finney, was—and still is—a bookie ("We were always illegal—one week if we had money we'd have a car and chauffeur, the next we'd have to move. No security. Perfect training for an actor's life."), who grew up across the street from a racetrack a few blocks from his friend Shelagh Delaney, flunked out of school, got into the Royal Academy where Tynan called him "a young Spencer Tracy," and ended up a star at 25 in the film *Saturday Night and Sunday Morning*. He was never ordinary. He smoked cigars since he was 15, read Pogo during interviews, carried all his possessions around in one suitcase, changed his address every two weeks, and once onstage told the audience: "Either you shut up and go home or I will." Even when he was getting started and needed money he turned down Peter O'Toole's role in *Lawrence of Arabia* because he "didn't want to become a Hollywood property or spend two years in a bloomin' desert," and went off to Glasgow to play repertory for $42 a week instead.

Four years ago, at the height of his career, he was starring on Broadway to wild acclaim in *Luther* and enjoying unprecedented movie popularity in *Tom Jones*. Then, with multi-million-dollar deals offered daily, he disappeared for one whole year without a word of explanation to anyone. The search again.

"I was told 'Strike now while you're hot or people will forget,' but I just wanted to get away. I figured when I got back I could still work *somewhere*, even if it was a tiny village in the Hebrides. Acting is a life's work, a career is a life of exploration, not just a few hot years. Also, being from North Country stock, I'm very suspicious of success. I had suddenly seen success too quickly and I had a fear of how to handle it. And then there was the question of following up *Tom Jones* and *Luther*—with *what*? What do you do next? So I learned how to do nothing. I traveled to Hong Kong, Fiji, Japan, Bangkok, Mexico, all over the bloody world. It was nice not having to clock in and just wander about. I'm not one of those actors like Dirk Bogarde or Peter Sellers, who must be constantly committed or insecurity sets in. When I'm active I'm so intense I cease to communicate. *I stop reading books!* Too many people were trying to get at me. I became a hot property. You see, this terrible conflict sets in. If you're a celebrity, you limit your opportunity to surprise people with new facets of your ability. Yet on the other hand, you want to be known or you won't get a chance at the great parts. I hated that. And not being a Hollywood star I could chuck it all and leave. You can't do that in America. The cult thing happens quicker here. You've *got* to be successful here or you don't survive. You've got to make a profit or your edges get rubbed off.

"Anyway, what I tried to do was interest myself in the things I wanted to do. I just want to make sure what I do is for myself. Live the life I want to live. I've tried to protect that right and resist the pressure of cashing in." (The closest he's ever come to Hollywood is a day's shooting on Catalina Island and a week in San Francisco last November on a film called *Picasso Summer*, about an architect who wants to meet Picasso. Finney hates any mention of it and says, "It had nothing to do with acting. I just did it to meet Picasso and I never got to meet him. All I do in it is walk around and point to Picasso drawings and go 'Woo, woo' and fight a little cow with Luis Miguel Dominguin.") "I wanted to live out my own neuroses. Well, it didn't work. After five months on my trip, I found myself on an island called Oraietea, an hour and a half by DC-3 jet from Tahiti. I had been there three weeks and all I did was watch the reef all day. If I felt a sudden surge of energy I'd fall into the surf, then climb out and sleep. It was the height of inertia. Then one day I heard a jet and got the same feeling I'd had in New York—I wanted to be on it. I knew I had to start the journey home. However romantic it seemed to be a beach-comber I learned I had to get back to the neurotic society I need in order to function. I didn't find any answers, only more questions. But I came out of it more convinced than ever that I wanted to be my own man."

He returned to England, phoned Laurence Olivier for a job, and landed in the Old Vic, playing repertory again for a fraction of the money he could make in films. Eight months later he made *Two for the Road*. "I had never done a *movie* movie—always it had been for friends in places like Nottingham, and here was this big-budget film all over Paris and the South of France with this big international lady, Audrey Hepburn, and well—it may sound perverse—but I like to come out of different doors."

Which brought up the "unspeakable" subject press agents warn against: Audrey. He didn't flinch. "People are always asking me when am I going to marry her. Well, you tell *me*. The subject and the situation are very tender. Working together was like a well-organized tennis match. I'd throw up a ball and she'd throw up a ball to match. A wonderful experience and a big campy time. But if anything happened to her marriage, I was not responsible. She *was* married to Mel Ferrer at the time, so it became a matter of questionable taste. I've had several affairs and known some marvelous women, but I've never known the need for permanence before. Now I feel I'm changing. It may be something as corny and obvious as loneliness, but I do feel I'm missing something without someone to love. I have a new girl friend—it's *not* Audrey—and maybe she'll come over from London for the opening."

She did. A beautiful actress named Jean Marsh, who calmed him down even after a glamorous first night which he did not enjoy. "I felt almost an immediate resistance from the audience. They weren't prepared for this kind of play. I didn't act well. It didn't work tonight." The old Finney search began all over again as he wandered through the plush Canterbury Pub shaking hands, blushing at compliments, chain-smoking, sweating out the reviews he said he didn't care about. The notices arrived, turning *Joe Egg* into a hit and adding another star to his already overcrowded crown. Then he put on his Argentine gaucho hat, lit another cigar and swept out of the pub in a jazzy long cape on the arm of love—half Aristide Bruant poster, half Bonnie and Clyde. Getting on with the search. And grinning all the way.

Jean Seberg

Baker, Ore.

This summer they'll pour into Paris again, eager tourists and American college boys with slickum on their hair, and the first thing they'll do is head straight for the Rue Scribe, hoping to see Jean Seberg selling the *Herald Tribune* in front of the American Express. But all they'll see is Norwegian beatniks with dirty feet. The real Jean Seberg is alive and well and living with a handful of Chinese poker players, 300 extras, a full-blooded Sioux Indian, a 250-man crew, Alan Jay Lerner, Lee Marvin, Clint Eastwood, a man who bought Laguna Beach for $2.80 and is now being sued for $13 million by the state of California, 250 head of horses from Nevada, 30 water oxen from New England, a bear from Honolulu, an ex-member of the Green Berets, 150 hippies, and the Nitty Gritty Dirt Band. "I'm back," she smiles, "and I don't find America very different. Only decadent. When you start bottling peanut butter and jelly in the same jar, that's decadence."

The golden sunflower girl from Marshalltown, Iowa, who was a star at 18 and an unemployable has-been at 20, is very much back indeed. She's living in the wilderness of Oregon as the star (Winning out over 18,000 girls— how's that for a has-been) of *Paint Your Wagon*, a Technicolor super-extravaganza $14-million musical directed by Joshua Logan. The location is unbelievable. A sleepy little town near the Powder River (population 9,986) was the stagecoach center during the Oregon early Gold Rush. It is surrounded by ghost towns and porcupines and in the morning hours on her way to the helicopter which flies her to work Jean sees real cowboys get thrown out of real saloons for drinking too much beer for breakfast. There are few diversions and no restaurants. "La Grenouille" the actors tell the Teamsters who drive their cars to dinner; then they all meet at the A & W Root Beer Stand. Roughing it is what it's called. But somehow, they survive. Alan Jay Lerner jumps elegantly into a private Lear jet and heads down to Hollywood to score new songs for the film with Andre Previn and confer with Katharine Hepburn on *Coco*. Clint Eastwood rides over the hills on a motorcycle to a ranch where he rises each morning at six to slop the hogs. Joshua Logan takes off his mud boots at night and watches old movies flown in from Los Angeles. And Jean survives because . . . well, because she's Jean Seberg, for whom the experience is just one more sugary question mark in a career full of unpunctuated sentences.

Elegant and golden as a buttery iceberg, she puts on a Ray Charles record and moves into the kitchen of her little rented green clapboard house to bake a pumpkin pie. "I tried to bake one in Paris once, but I couldn't find any pumpkin." She glides through the room like a swan, dressed in pink, munching corn chips, with skin white as winter and blue-gray eyes the color of Park Avenue at dawn. If you expect a jaded *bonne vivante* who leads philosophical discussions in the innovational film philosophies of Jean-Luc Godard, forget it. She gets handwritten letters from André Malraux, wears Yves St. Laurents to eat hamburgers, beats Françoise Sagan at poker and is married to Romain Gary, but the darling of *Breathless* is American as a boysenberry. "I've lived in France for ten years and I still can't write a simple thank-you note in French. Life took me there and I just kind of stayed. But I don't feel French. I still have my passport and I pay American taxes. And I've never really made many lasting friendships there. After *St. Joan* the New Wave boys defended me. They found out I needed money and work. I was their new Jerry Lewis, I suppose. The *cahier* people were kind to me, but I don't know them. Truffaut and I have a bizarre relationship. We write to each other two times a year, but we've never even had a cup of coffee together. Godard is like a Paul Klee painting, always hiding behind those funny dark glasses. They all live very hermetic lives and none of them sees each other socially. I had fun making *Breathless* because Godard would arrive each day with the day's scenes written on little pieces of yellow paper stuffed in his pocket. Belmondo insists he had a mad crush on me, but I was unaware of it at the time. I did another film with him in Marrakesh three years later, playing the same girl I played in *Breathless*. We shot it in three days and he never even cut it. I also did a film with Philippe De Broca and three for Chabrol. They are all very strange little men, but I don't pretend to know them well. I like Paris, but I'm tiring of it now. I feel like an American again for the first time this summer, being here near the farm country. There's a barn outside Baker as beautiful as any cathedral in Europe. It has spires where they store the grain and it changes colors with the sun. I rented a funny little house last winter in Normandy, at Honfleur near Deauville. It had cows and apple trees and farmhouses and it made me homesick for Iowa.

"The most sound advice Otto Preminger ever gave me was to never lose my roots. Josh Logan told me to find someone to model my character in *Paint Your Wagon* after, so I'm using my 80-year-old grandma. She was an orphan who scrubbed farm floors at 13, a Willa Cather character. She still lives in Marshalltown, an incredible lady. I took her to the Sunset Strip to see the hippies and she loved it. This house I'm living in is just like my parents' house in Marshalltown. We have a little piano in this corner at home, and pictures on the walls, and the same kind of upholstered sofa. The Christmas tree always goes *there*. The thing I miss most living in Paris is Christmas. There's never a Christmas I'm not dissolved in tears halfway through Christmas Eve. We always went ice-skating on the Iowa River and had Santa Claus and Rudolf the Red-Nosed Reindeer on the roof, and everyone sang carols and people asked us in for hot chocolate and then we'd end up at midnight church. My four-year-old son Diego loves it. He gets up three times a night and asks if Père Noel is here yet. I never get used to these funny European children who speak three languages. Romain hates Christmas. He's Scrooge. He never gives presents to anybody.

"I go home every chance I get. The people in Marshalltown are very nice, but I'm sure some of them think I'm a lost woman. My family has never changed. My father still makes Seberg's vitamin pills and great bubble bath and hand cream in his drug store. I'll send you some. He still regrets I didn't get a college education. When I did *St. Joan* his only advice was to take my vitamins and be a good girl. One time a story appeared in *Confidential* magazine, some scandal about me, and when the magazines came into the drugstore he burned them all. Then he bought up every copy in town so nobody would read it. I'm sure he never doubted for a minute I was pure as the driven snow, but he didn't want the neighbors to talk. I'm sure I disappointed them when I divorced my first husband, because nobody in our family had ever been divorced. But they have always stayed out of things. My parents sold the house all of us kids grew up in and now going home is not the same. The smells of the rooms and the stairs and the feelings you grew up with for 18 years are just not there any more. It's the most terrible feeling in the world. I took Romain to Iowa and he said the countryside, the blackness of the earth and the cornstalks reminded him of the Ukraine."

Romain Gary was not in Oregon. He was finishing a novel in a new house in Majorca, and already divorce rumors were stronger in the Oregon air than the scent of pine trees. "There is no telephone in the house, so I write him letters in English and we send lots of cables," said Jean, covering up. "Romain sits all day and looks at the ocean. I've never seen a man so tied to the sea. He's going through a terrible human transition now. He's 53 years old, and despite his service to France and his own war record, he feels he was never properly assimilated by the French. He was born in Russia and has always loved America. Then the recent strikes in France made him even more aware of the validity of the questions raised against De Gaulle. He was De Gaulle's private secretary during the war and although he has no loyalty to the Gaullist government he is very loyal to the man, even though when he asked to leave for active duty, De Gaulle said 'OK and I hope you get killed. You won't of course, only the *best* get killed.' Still, De Gaulle has written him a two-page hand-written letter for every book he's ever written. No one is a friend of De Gaulle's, I least of all, but I had tea with him once and he was fun to meet—informed on films, not foreboding, beautiful manners, charming with women. He spends all night watching TV and writes his own protest letters to the networks. He's very vain. Did you know he had a duel once in Poland over a married woman? The Poles still talk about it."

Who would have thought little Jean Seberg would come to this? When Preminger discovered her for *St. Joan*, a role she was too young and inexperienced to play (She had once checked out a Stanislavsky book from the Marshalltown library, only to return it the next day because she couldn't understand it), she was a pretty teenager teaching Sunday school at the Lutheran church and working in her father's drug store so she could read all the movie magazines. Suddenly she was an international celebrity nobody liked. The critics roasted her and the public almost lynched her. If her parents had their way, she would have quietly retired and become a dental technician. Instead, she ran away to Nice, lived on the beach, cried a lot, and married a young French lawyer named François Moreuil. The marriage was a disaster, but it produced two good things: her husband foolishly introduced her to Romain Gary and she became a film idol in Europe. Today she is a mature, scary-bright, firmly footed lady who knows exactly who she is and where it's at. She has made 21 movies —10 in French, one in Italian—and six of them in the past two years. She has studied mime with Marcel Marceau's teacher. She has been a member of the NAACP since she was 14 ("My father thought I was a Communist."). She led the campaign to raise the standards of lower-class Arab workers in France. She has produced two films—one on boxing and one about two Guinean students living in Paris. She's involved in everything. When she returned to America this year, she went to the Watts ghetto and rang doorbells of white liberals asking for aid to establish jobs for Negroes. She went to a huge party in Hollywood to raise money for Resurrection City and alienated everyone by being the only one to ask where the money was going. On the set of *Paint Your Wagon,* she is the Mother Superior of the hippies who live in the nearby woods and make their living as extras in the film. She gives them free baths and bakes cakes for their weddings. She may go to jail before the film is completed, because when she arrived in Hollywood she met an old friend who served time as a conscientious objector in Leavenworth and signed his petition volunteering to go to prison if Dr. Spock was convicted. She was with Bobby Kennedy a week before he was killed "at John Frankenheimer's Malibu beach house—he said he knew he'd lose in Oregon and he didn't think he had a chance at the nomination. He sat on the floor, windburned in Bermuda shorts and a T-shirt, eating lunch with his dog Freckles. It was odd. I was with President Kennedy shortly before his death, too. We had dinner at the White House and he asked Romain a million questions about De Gaulle—he was like

an incredible IBM machine, digesting *everything*. I swiped
a menu and wrote Malraux a long letter about it. A few
days later, Romain was giving a very unpopular anti-Gaullist
speech called 'Love of America' and afterward we walked
along the boardwalk in Nice and saw the news in the
papers."

Jean's own career is jumping. She was just finishing
Pendulum, a social-comment murder mystery with George
Peppard set in Washington, when *Paint Your Wagon* came
along. "It was all an accident, really, but I've had one of
the most peculiar careers anyway, so nothing really sur-
prises me any more. I was getting ready to leave for Paris
when Alan Jay Lerner called me and asked if I could sing.
I bluffed and said yes—I'm quite terrible, really—and I
did a test with Eydie Gorme's voice and now Andre Previn
has written a new song for me and I'm doing my own
singing in the film. It's a wonderful script, quite different
from the play. I play a woman who is deeply and genuinely
in love with two different men. She's sort of a 19th-century
flower child in the middle of the Gold Rush. I really dig
that idea and believe it to be quite possible. Especially with
Lee Marvin and Clint Eastwood, who are totally opposite.
Lee is full of chatter and great tales he tells with his whole
body—when I first met him I thought I was talking to a
Watusi. And Clint is the original quiet man. He stands
back and says nothing, but then he comes out with a statement so intelligent you know he is aware of everything
that is going on. It has completely blown my family summer, but Romain and I agreed I shouldn't turn it down."

Everyone else seems to agree. A few nights later, she
stands, lit by the moon, at a fork in the East Eagle Creek
near 9,000-ft. high Boulder Peak in the Wallowa-Whitman
National Forest, up to her bootstraps in mud. Corn on the
cob by Cartier-Bresson. "I no longer feel the need to prove
anything. I used to take myself so seriously I was almost
catatonic, which showed in my work. Now I just hang

loose and never build up false hopes." The hippies clap their hands and stop playing poker. The Chinese extras stand up to their knees in mud and watch. Alan Jay Lerner smiles. Joshua Logan nods approvingly. Lee Marvin crosses his fingers. And back in Marshalltown, at Mr. Seberg's drug store, business has never been better.

Mart Crowley

The dreamy-eyed author of *The Boys in the Band*
reclines like a lazy salamander in an avocado corduroy
chair, dressed in chocolate brown and sipping a Dr. Pepper.
His eyes, large as cueballs, peer out from tinted aviator
glasses, forming deepening circles in a face that is seldom
exposed to the sun and always poised on the verge of ex-
pectancy. His speech is slow, his voice drips honey, and
his conversation is pickled with pungency. The last person
in the world you'd expect to create the most controversial
(and perhaps the most brilliant) new play in years.

But Mart Crowley is a movie. *The Boys in the Band*
looks like a movie, reads like a movie and plays like a
movie. It has a screamingly funny fairy birthday party, a
"Saturday night douche kit," boys kissing boys onstage,
a 42nd Street hustler dressed like a midnight cowboy, a
hairspray called "Butch Assurance," three flaming queens
dancing the Fire Island Madison, an assortment of selected
homosexual short subjects doing Judy Garland imitations,
Bette Davis imitations, Betty Grable imitations and Gloria
Swanson imitations, and the best bitchy dialogue since
All About Eve. And just to make sure everybody gets the
point that it may someday *be* a movie, *The Boys in the
Band* features a supporting cast—never visible but always
hovering in quasi-madness in the wings—which includes
Barbara Stanwyck, Vera Hruba Ralston, Rosemary DeCamp
and Maria Montez. ("What have you got against Maria,"
lisps one lavender lad, "she was a good woman!")

You might call it a breakthrough. For years, plays about homosexuality have been afraid of their own shadows. From the early Helen Mencken-Basil Rathbone days of *The Captive* (a real shockeroo in the 1920's) through Dorothy Baker's *Trio* (Richard Widmark tried in vain to win the love of a girl involved with a Lesbian and the whole thing got closed down by Fiorello La Guardia) to *Tea and Sympathy* (the "problem" was only a hint and the boy got saved from a fate worse than death by going to bed with an older woman), *The Children's Hour* (the real Lesbian finally confessed in the last scene and shot herself through the head), *The Immoralist* (Louis Jourdan committed suicide after he learned how much more interesting James Dean was than Geraldine Page), *Fortune and Men's Eyes* (bold, but safe, since all the queers were behind bars), *Staircase* and *The Killing of Sister George* (lovable, cartoon cut-out perverts, therefore acceptable as long as nobody had to take them home to *meet* anybody)—and on and on, avoiding the subject and using homosexuality to trigger dramatic situations instead of reflecting real life. Homosexuals have always paid for their sins onstage. *The Boys in the Band* has changed all that. Like Clairol blondes, the "boys" in Mart Crowley's band are having all the fun. They don't kill themselves or want to get married or spend the rest of their lives in solitary confinement masturbating. The only way they "pay" is to know who they are. Then they go to bed with a hangover and start all over again the next day. Like life.

It took a 32-year-old boy from the Mississippi Delta to break the mold, but Mart isn't featuring pulpit preaching this season. "What do I know about social causes? I only wrote it for my own survival and personal fulfillment after years of failure. It's not a confession and it's not auto-biographical, but there's a little of me in all the characters and there's a little of all the people I've known. I never meant it to be a piece of camp, either. Camp is dead. The only camp in it is there because it is indigenous to the characters. The Emory character (who wears Bermuda shorts and eye makeup) is campy because all the Emorys I've known in my life have depended on camp to get them through. I didn't write a satire. Wasn't it George Kaufman who said, 'Satire is what closes on Saturday night'? If you once get over the fact that eight of the characters are overt homosexuals, you know the most sensational thing in it. The thing I always hated about homosexual plays was that the homosexuality was always the big surprise in the third act. Well, life is not like that. Not all faggots bump themselves off at the end of the play."

A year ago, Mart was an unemployed Hollywood script writer at the end of his rope. After four years of analysis, he locked himself in the library of Diana Lynn's house in Beverly Hills and forced himself to write one last effort before the gallows. He turned out *The Boys in the Band* in five weeks. Now the same film companies who wouldn't give him a job are offering him Wall Street to let them do his play as a movie. But Mart has not accepted a penny. "I could take the money, go to the seashore and say, 'Take my play, Hollywood, and do what you've always done— *ruin* it.' Well, over my dead body. I have *had* it with Hollywood. If anybody's gonna screw it up, it's gonna be *me*. One studio offered to let me be a 'consultant to the screenwriter.' I said thank you very much, goodbye. Another Hollywood person said, 'I don't think we should use actors at all, let's just use the people who are in it now.' What does he think *they* are? They told me the same things before we did it onstage—you can't do this play, the stage is not ready for it—I just don't believe it. If this play is made as a movie, it will be made my way, written by me, with me as the producer, and filmed in New York by the best technicians I can find. I'm still improving it. We have a rehearsal tonight. I'm relentless in my involvement, from what's going on the box office to how the posters look in

the lobby. I shopped with the actors to find the clothes
they wear, I bought props with my own money. There was
this wine glass one of the boys drinks from and it had
to be a green Rhine wine glass. They couldn't find one
because they were shopping at Woolworth's. I ended up
spending twenty bucks for the glass at Baccarat. In fact,
the only time we ever fought during rehearsals was over
the light bulbs in the lobby. I am committed up to my neck.
I can't just sell it for a lot of money and play it safe and
go on to something else. I mean, you can't do that with
life, can you? Otherwise, you might as well go back to
Bloomingdale's and sell your ties. This film can be made
for a mere $800,000, no more than the expense budget
on an Otto Preminger movie. If that's asking for the moon,
then I'm asking for the moon. What I want is someone
to give me the money and leave me alone with the artistic
autonomy to do the movie the way I want to do it, or there
will simply never be any movie. And don't give me that
Hollywood stuff about 'You can't make a movie because
you never made a movie before.' Bull. I've been making
movies since I was five years old. I just never had a camera
before."

Meanwhile, a movie of Mart's own life to this point
might do just as well. The first reel begins in Vicksburg,
Mississippi. An only child, his father owned Crowley's
Smokehouse ("which had nothing to do with sausage,
baby")—a pool hall with the motto "Where all good fellows
meet." (He's kept the stationery all these years to prove it.)
He was a sickly child given to asthma attacks ("Haven't
had one since the day I left Vicksburg."), who fished on
Tennessee Williams' famous Moon Lake and drank Grap-
ettes while a Negro man held an umbrella over his head
to keep the hot sun out of his eyes. Like most frail and
sensitive Southern children allergic to heat and growing up
in a cultural eclipse, Mart lived in air-cooled movie houses
from the time he was tall enough to reach the ticket

counter. "The only theatre I was allowed to go to showed Warners and Paramount movies, but the MGM house was a firetrap and my mother wouldn't let me go inside. Every year my father would make us go to the Sugar Bowl game in New Orleans, which I *hated,* so I would sneak off to Loew's and catch up on all the MGM movies." On occasional trips to New Orleans, he'd see Tallulah Bankhead in *Private Lives* or some B-company road tour of *South Pacific,* but movies were his staple diet and he daydreamed of running away on a Greyhound bus to Hollywood and Vine to meet Esther Williams.

At 17, he graduated from high school and under the pretense of visiting a friend's aunt in Glendale, he climbed on a bus for California, found a room in the Hollywood Hills, got a job washing dishes in a cafeteria, and climbed the back wall at Twentieth Century Fox where, for an entire afternoon, he was in hog heaven roaming through the train depot in all the Linda Darnell movies and walking down the Main Street used in *Chicken Every Sunday.* His father wanted him to attend Notre Dame, but Mart wanted to study movies, so being sturdy Catholics, they compromised on Catholic University in Washington, D.C. "I subscribed to *Theatre Arts* and read about Walter and Jean Kerr and all the famous people from there who went on to Broadway and it sounded very glamorous."

It wasn't. The next two years saw a little Southern boy "change from Palm Beach suits to Harris tweeds, going to parties at the Brazilian Embassy and spending the weekends in places like *Larchmont!* One day I woke up and said, 'Just what are you doing here?' " Zap! Back to the California palm trees where he lived over a garage in Westwood, worked on an art degree at UCLA, spent his weekends watching Cecil B. DeMille make *The Ten Commandments* and became friends with the son of Pandro S. Berman. (He was easily impressed.) "I just couldn't believe I was actually the friend of Pandro Berman's son! He was

like a celebrity!" Has he ever seen him since? "No, but I've
seen Pandro." (A roar.) "Anyway, I was still confused.
Suddenly I realized movies were in the West, but all the
people were in the East, and there I was in my Harris
tweeds and everyone else was in *alpaca!*"

Zap! Back to Catholic University, where he wrote a revue sketch with James Rado (now the author of *Hair*), spent
every weekend in New York seeing plays ("I'm practically
a second Collier brother with the stack of Playbills I've
collected"), worked as an apprentice in a Vermont stock
company where Bob Moore was directing, and flunked
Greek three times. One summer when he went to Vicksburg to see his mother, they were shooting *Baby Doll* down
the road, so he followed Elia Kazan into a café called Do's
Eat Place and got him to write a gate pass on a napkin.
After that he hung around the set, asked a million questions
and struck up friendships with people who later got him
jobs in New York.

He moved to the Big City in 1957, lived in a cold-water
railroad flat with lots of roaches and badgered his way into
assistant jobs on *Butterfield 8*, *The Fugitive Kind* and *Splen-
dor in the Grass*, where he became so friendly with Natalie
Wood that she asked him to become her secretary. He
worked for her for two years and her encouragement led
him into a writing career. He went back home to Mississippi and wrote a screenplay for Natalie based on Dorothy
Baker's book *Cassandra at the Wedding*, slipped into a
severe depression, went to live with Robert Wagner in
Rome, illustrated a children's book by Kay Thompson, and
returned to California with French director Serge Bour-
guignon to make *Cassandra*. "Suddenly I was the very hot
young writer about town. Dinner invitations poured in.
Then the movie fell through and I was dropped like a hot
potato. The same thing is happening all over again now,
but I've been around the track enough to know the race
by heart," he says.

Other writing jobs opened up, all ending abortively—
screenplays optioned and dropped, TV pilots that didn't
sell. Then Paramount hired him to write *Fade In,* a film
made in 1967 in Utah. He scouted locations in Moab and
settled down to work with a young director in an office on
the Paramount lot which he calls "The William Holden-
Nancy Olson Memorial Sunset Boulevard Building" and
sweated it out. The front office sent memos that he was
not writing the movie they had in mind, and his director
was fired and replaced by another director who locked himself into another room in the building with *his* writer, the
idea being that the two writers could each write a separate
script and paste the screenplays together. "I ended up getting stoned every day on martinis, sleeping on the couch
in the office and reading *Time* magazine while the director
and *his* writer turned out a completely different script and
nobody ever communicated with anybody else." Mart took
his money and fled suicidally to Acapulco. "Acapulco out
of season when you're unhappy—it didn't work out. I just
switched to tequila and kept reading *Time* magazine while
it rained." He never heard another word from Paramount,
and *Fade In* has never been released.

Finally he pulled himself together long enough to go
back to his analyst, who told him "thinking time is working time," and settled down in Diana Lynn's house to baby-
sit with her children while she was on her yacht in the
Panama Canal. Thinking produced *The Boys in the Band.*
He came to New York last winter with no agent and no
money, just a play about a homosexual birthday party
nobody would touch. Richard Gregson, Natalie Wood's
fiancé, wrote a letter of introduction to an agent who said,
"Maybe in five or ten years, but not now," but showed it to
Richard Barr anyway as a favor. He loved it. Then Mart's
friend Bob Moore (whom he met back at Catholic U.)
wanted to direct it. Things looked good, but they couldn't
get actors to be in it. "They were worried about their images.

That kind of thinking is so Hollywood I can't stand it. You don't have to be gay to play a homosexual any more than you have to be a criminal to play a murderer. Now we have the actors with the guts to do it and they are brilliant and perfect, but it wasn't easy. Cliff Gorman, who plays the effeminate fairy, is happily married. He didn't know how to play it, so he came on at first doing a nightclub act. He was hilarious, but you hated him after five minutes. It was only after a lot of talk and rehearsals that he honed it down to what it is now. These people have lived with this play and they are the people who should do the movie, not stars."

Now everybody wants a piece of the action. Kirk Douglas tried to buy it. Rudolf Nureyev and Margot Fonteyn brought six people one night and couldn't get in, so they sat on each other's laps in one chair to see it. Ray Stark offered Mart a boggling sum to write a film for Barbra Streisand. Even the old *Cassandra* project has been brought out of mothballs and Hollywood wants to film it again, trading on Mart's new status as a writer emeritus. Mart hasn't signed anything. He's concentrating all his energy on the film version of his play. And he has not forgotten the people who stood by him through the trouble spots. People like Natalie Wood, who paid for his analysis once for six months; Dominick Dunne, vice-president of Four-Star TV, who dragged him to dinner parties for free meals and gave him a contract to write the pilot for a TV show for Bette Davis; or Jennifer Jones, who always invited him to her home when he was snubbed by the rest of Hollywood; or Billy Wilder's wife Audrey, who used to give stern advice while she dished up knockwurst and sauerkraut. "These," he says, "are the real friends who are happy for me now. R. J. and Marion [the Robert Wagners] weren't standing in the lobby of the theatre last night crying for nothing. They kept me alive in Rome one winter. Marion used to take me to Gucci and buy me shoes when I was broke. They know how much they've carried me through, how many times I've passed out on their living room floor. My friends are responsible for saving me from death in a hotel room somewhere."

It doesn't seem to bother Mart that the majority of the audience at *The Boys in the Band* looks like it belongs on-stage. "The only thing that worried me was that it wouldn't be funny. The night we opened I got a case of the fears and Bob Moore said, 'Listen, they've been laughing at faggots since Aristophanes. They're not gonna stop now.' Besides, who's gonna be the most interested in a play about homosexuals? *Homosexuals!* Right?"

Right. And even if nobody goes to see *The Boys in the Band* except all the homosexuals in America, Mart Crowley could make enough money to keep himself in Dr. Peppers for the next ten years.

Leslie Caron

Paris, 1967.

It was a bad day for Lili.

Shortly past three in the afternoon the Paramount limousine pulled up to the polished revolving doors of the George V, that gangrenous gilt-edged birthday cake of cupids and cupolas that serves as Paris' finest (and most expensive) hotel. The voice on the little pink-and-cream-colored rococo telephone downstairs announced that Leslie Caron had been detained. Give her five minutes. "I don't understand," said the pretty press agent, "she knew we were expected."

About four minutes later a rather flushed Warren Beatty plunged out of the antique elevators wearing what people in the business have, through experience, come to regard as the Warren Beatty look: high-school basketball player face unshaven, suit rumpled, glasses horn-rimmed, expression enraged. The telephone tinkled bell-like in the cavernous silence of the padded lobby. Leslie Caron was ready now.

The girl-woman who opened the door bore only a slight wispy resemblance to Gigi or Fanny or Gaby or what's-her-name who fell in love with *Daddy Long Legs*. Shoeless, with tired little plum-like bruises under the drooping eyes, long silvered nails picking nervously at the cuticles holding them together, she curled up on a long red velvet sofa in the middle of her vanilla malted milk-colored suite in a

wrinkled mass of champagne ripcord double-breasted
Christian Dior material and looked for all the world like
a tiny piece of icing that had fallen off the top of a rather
overcooked French pastry.

"Take off those glasses, so I can see what you look
like. You Americans—always hiding behind dark glasses,"
she said for starters. "I suppose you have come here to
find out if I am a *new* Leslie Caron. Hell yes, and it's about
time. One can't go on wading in brooks and eating ice
cream cones forever."

New approach. After all the ugly headlines, all the
unfavorable publicity surrounding her divorce from her
second husband, Director Peter Hall, in which Warren
Beatty had been named corespondent, did she think she
had profited by her mistakes? "What mistakes? I might
as well commit suicide if you consider everything a mistake. Living through something dreadful doesn't make it a
mistake. Life is not a production number. Some people,
like myself, take the direct route to what they want. I once
broke a contract with MGM and spent the next eight years
in Europe bearing children. Now I've decided I'm not a
statue. I'm tired of that part of my life and I desire to do
something new. You can call it a mistake, but now I'm
giving my private life what it demands. An actor I worked
with recently came up to me and asked me to go to bed
with him. If I did, he said, it would make him act better
the next day. Well, I only go to bed with people I'm in love
with. I'm not bragging. I haven't the slightest idea what
the public thinks of me and I don't care. People like to get
beaten with whips by girls in leather boots, but they don't
brag about it. What I do with Warren Beatty is nobody's
business. I don't want to talk about it."

What would she like to talk about? The old days at
MGM? "Please! Most miserable period in my life. I hate
musicals. Warren is dying to do a musical, but I'll never
make another. I had toe-shoes on from 8:30 in the morning

until six every night. I was constantly in agony. Ankles big as an elephant's. I was in very bad health, worked under impossibly bad conditions, had to dance on concrete floors and windy sound stages. I had bruises and sprains that couldn't heal. When I walked out of Hollywood, after years of unhappiness, Fred Astaire and Gene Kelly both told me, 'Leslie, you're so smart to quit while you can still walk.' I'm glad those days are gone forever. The only dancers I admire today are belly dancers."

If she hated musicals so, perhaps she was excited about her new status as a dramatic actress. "I thought *The L-Shaped Room* was a pretty good film in spots, but my God, I did it for practically no money at all. Money isn't everything. Financially, I never have to make another film. I have a company, but I don't read the Stock Exchange every morning. I couldn't be more bored about all that. I hate to admit that because then everybody will try to take advantage of me. I'm not an idealist. But I'll never work for nothing again."

What about her latest role in *Is Paris Burning?*—the grief-stricken wife of a Resistance leader who is torn from her arms and slaughtered by the Nazis on a public street? For months, the cinema talk in Paris had centered around nothing else: about how Director René Clément had begrimed areas of the city only recently cleaned up by Minister of Culture André Malraux, about how jack-booted Wehrmacht troops had set off bombs in the Place de la Concorde, thrown hand grenades into the Bois de Boulogne, uprooted the vast *parvis* in front of Notre Dame, even stormed down into the depths of Napoleon's tomb to re-create the last five days of August, 1944. Surely a film costing several million dollars, involving 182 sets and six months' work, in which even Charles de Gaulle will appear as himself, would be worth talking about.

"Leslie was so remarkable, she had everyone on the set and the onlookers in the street in tears," offered the pretty press agent, nervously signaling the star to vitamize the conversation.

"Aaah," groaned the reply. "I said *hell* before I did the scene and giggled right after. Dramatic scenes. I don't enjoy them. Maybe I expect more than I can possibly give, so I become arrogant and contrary. When I see myself on the screen at first I usually catch the flu. When I come out of seeing a premiere of a film of mine I have sore throat, fever, headache and all the symptoms of a very serious illness. I go on with acting simply to prove to myself that I am alive. That's why we all work, isn't it? I refuse to be an image of something I'm not. I'll never forget the day at MGM when they photographed me as a bunny. Yes, a French bunny! The caption was: *Oooh, la la!* and then there was a hoop I was jumping through. Quite funny actually. But when you have to go through it it's simply awful. And so I put my foot down, and said no more bunnies for me. And I was considered very difficult, you know, and very few people liked me. And that to me is the whole of Hollywood, making people be bunnies when they're not."

The telephone rang and the star rubbed her temples nervously, trying to keep her voice down. "I told you, Warren, I'm *busy!* I don't know when. Go out and walk around the block a few times. No. *No!* Later. I mean it." She hung up the receiver and made a face.

"Now I suppose you'll print that I'm having an affair with Warren and we're holed up in the George V doing all sorts of tatty things. Just say we're good friends. No, I have no plans for marriage. It's deeply traumatically disturbing to withstand the kind of scandal the press builds up. I understand the side of the journalists and I understand the public's interest, so I'm not angry or bitter or— you know, it doesn't leave permanent scars on me at all, although I've had to live incognito, James Bond style, at times. But I guess that's the price we have to pay. It's for my children, I mean otherwise what does it matter to me. Do you want to ask me something? *Ask!* I don't know what to say. I'm human and I don't like scandal. Ever since I was sixteen in the ballet—long before Gene Kelly discovered me and signed me for *An American in Paris*—I've been in the press, so I don't know anything else. But you're all a bunch of bastards really, you know. Yes, you are."

Does she like anybody? She thought a moment, scratching at her Sassoon bangs. "Not many. I have few friends. How can I know others well if I don't know myself? When I was doing *Gigi* everybody loved me suddenly because I was Gigi, they *thought!* But I was character acting as far as I'm concerned; I already had one baby and I was already 25. I always wanted to play sophisticated women when I couldn't and I didn't look it, and I didn't have the maturity. So I wasn't really Gigi or Lili or any of those girls. Most of the people I know are not actors. You can't have deep friendships in this business. It's like politics. Also, I don't trust people. For instance, if I'm recognized in the street I am bound to think it's a sex maniac, or somebody—I think why arc they staring at me?"

Mention the war. It's like picking the lock on a cheetah cage. "You Americans. What do you know? You've never been bombed or occupied by an enemy or anything. During the war, I used to make shoes from my great-grandmother's leather gloves. A pair of shoes was something you kept for 10 years. We lived on rations."

"We had rations in America, too," volunteered the press agent.

"Ha! What does that mean? You only got one chocolate bar instead of two? Hunger and unpleasantness and fear from the Nazis because my mother was American and my cousins were in the underground. It's never worn off. I still save Kleenex. When I went to Hollywood for the first time, I was horrified. I had been raised in convents, knew nothing of the world. I had two pairs of panties and every American woman had 18 slips. My greatest luxury now is underwear. It is very hard to feel sorry for you Americans. If you want to, you can always work. I went to Cairo two years ago and it was dreadful. The rich people live in tombs, and they are the lucky ones. But in America you know nothing of this. You've had the best of everything and you know the least of anyone."

Recovering from this attack, there seemed only one thing left to question: the future. "I don't expect anything from that. I think you have to be a moron to be really happy all the time. In order to have great happiness you have to have great pain and great unhappiness—otherwise how would you know when you're happy? Marriage is no solution. I've been married twice. It's just a social habit that we have which makes our children have the name of a gentleman. But I don't think it's a perfect solution for human beings. I think the relationship has more chance to succeed without marriage. It's very difficult to plan a life," she said, ushering us to the door. "Very boring if you do, and more boring if you stick to it. Such questions, such odd ideas you must have of how a movie star lives. Americans. I don't know how to talk to you."

Downstairs, on the curb, Warren Beatty was pacing nervously. "I've never seen her like that before," said the pretty press agent as Beatty bounded past us and leaped toward the elevators.

"Movie stars! Bah!" I mumbled, as the limousine swept us into the sane, welcome reality of the 5:00 traffic jam in the Place de la Concorde.

Burt Bacharach

The room smells like burning toast. It *is* burning. Burt
Bacharach has a cold and he's hungry, but this photographer
is keeping him out of the kitchen by closing in on him with
a camera that looks like a weapon and saying things to
make him smile like "Give me your Michel Legrand smile"
and Burt keeps saying, "When you take *his* picture, are you
going to ask for his Burt Bacharach smile?" Mrs. Bacharach
(better known to cab drivers as "a real tomato" and to autograph hounds as Angie Dickinson) went back to California
after the opening night raves for *Promises, Promises* got
tabulated, leaving Burt to nurse his own cold, get his own
picture taken, burn his own toast, make his own bed and
reject his own Burt Bacharach records on the record player.

The bachelor pad on East 61st Street has a grey December afternoon college weekend frat house look. He lived there
long before he wrote "Alfie" or married a movie star, and
now the rent keeps going up every three years, but he keeps
it anyway. When his wife and two-year-old daughter Lea
are in town, they live in a hotel. But Burt's mother keeps
the refrigerator stocked with lemons and eggs and Pep-
peridge Farm bread and he hides out there when he wants
to get away from the screaming fans and the hit records.
Gold-framed Avedons of Marlene Dietrich signed with
worshipful phrases of adoration line the walls. A baby
Steinway sits in a lonely dining alcove covered with a massive clutter of bills, mail tied together with rubber bands,

and blank score pads for future Burt Bacharach song hits
to be penciled in. "I don't take care of my piano," he says.
"I don't even tune it. I can write songs anywhere. If Angie
is making a picture in Arizona, I can write in the hotel room.
But I can't write anything at the piano. I write everything in
my head and then put it down on paper. Poor piano."

The rest of the apartment is an agreeable explosion
of coffee cups filled with day-old instant Yuban, dirty dishes
in the sink, sleeveless phonograph records scattered like
black vinyl seeds behind the sofa, under tennis racquets,
and across the carpet toward the terrace, which is littered
with last summer's beach towels and old squeezed Bain de
Soleil tubes, and which overlooks the roof of Alexander's.
Everyone hums as the phonograph plays a fresh stack of
Burt Bacharach records. Stan Getz Plays Burt Bacharach.
Cal Tjader Plays Burt Bacharach. Connie Francis Sings
Burt Bacharach. (Badly.) The photographer leaves, still
humming "The Look of Love," and Burt leaps into the
kitchen to make fresh toast. The Colts and Packers are
playing and he'd much rather watch that, but he tries to
keep his mind on the interview. He's the man of the hour
in pop music, but you'd never guess it. For a songwriter, he
neither looks like a John Lennon nor lives like a Cole Porter.
He's rich, but he still drives a 1966 Chevy, prefers quiet
evenings in Mexican restaurants to all the hoopla at The
Factory, and doesn't even know where all of his money is.
"You have to hire people to take care of it and then you
just have to trust them, I guess. I bought a racehorse and a
restaurant on Long Island, but the horse is still in England
and I don't know *how* the restaurant is doing. I guess I
ought to go see if the food's still good."

Except for a few patches of white hair, he looks, at 38,
like Joe College in a Burlington sock ad. Plaid pants, baggy
green crew-neck sweater, white socks, and white U.S. Keds.
Mucking up the joint, throwing raw eggs and coffee ice
cream into a blender, and talking about his new show.

"Somehow I lived through it and I'm still alive. I didn't damage my health too much, although I had pneumonia in Boston and spent a week in a hospital. But this has been the hardest thing I've ever done. The work seemed endless. Since August, my partner Hal David and I have written songs, dropped songs, I've seen my wife six times in four months, I take too many pills, I don't sleep any more, I close my eyes and music goes through my head all night—I'm wiped out by this show, man. Tomorrow we do the cast album and then it's all over and I'll be in Palm Springs by Wednesday. I have no desire to ever do another Broadway musical, no matter how successful *Promises, Promises* is."

He's happy the critics called the show a breakthrough, because "before this show the quality of sound in the theatre was really rotten. I tried to get the right musicians who could play my kind of pop music instead of the usual pit orchestra. I went for younger guys. I put in an electronic booth to control the voices I used with the music. I inserted "Fiberglas" panels to separate the sound from mike to mike and tried to achieve the same conditions you get in a recording session without the isolated sound of music coming through speakers. It's a very complicated electronic system, with echo chambers and equalizers and technical equipment, and David Merrick was great. He spent all the money I asked for."

Although he has been called "too old for the pot generation and too young for jogging," his speech is full of uptights, groovys, and cats words which, like his songs, span several generations. "But I don't like to be called a 'rock' composer. I never wrote a rock 'n' roll song in my life. I didn't try to compose a score just to be commercial. I wrote just the way I always do. I didn't compromise or change gears just because it was Broadway, but I tried to give the audience songs they could remember. I write very simply. If we knocked down a few doors with my rhythms, or the new sound in the show, *great*. Show music has to move on, but I don't mean in the direction of *Hair*. I don't respect the score from *Hair* at all. You get people waving flags all over the place over that show, but it doesn't belong on the same stage with a score like *No Strings*. Same stage? It doesn't even belong on the same record player."

He balances the coffee milkshake and a Dagwood sandwich of burned toast, cheese, chopped liver and butter, and sits under a painting of a woman who looks like Libby Holman. "My mother painted that years ago. She'll be knocked out that somebody noticed it." She gave up art to follow the party circuit with Burt's father, columnist Bert Bacharach, after the family moved to New York from Kansas City. "She doesn't regret it any more than that hokey stuff people ask me about 'Just think—if you had stayed in classical music what you could have composed by now.' I could have gone classical. I studied at Tanglewood and with Darius Milhaud in California, but I started seeing the dedication, the way serious composers had to teach school to live, waiting for grants to be able to eat, the poor money they made. I didn't dig it.

"I got into music in the first place to be popular. I wanted to be like my dad, who was an all-Southern Conference fullback, but I was too short. I ate jars of peanut butter to try and grow taller. I couldn't find one boy shorter than I was, only girls. My folks kept my interest in music going when I hated it. It was very lonely practicing the piano while my friends were out playing touch football and I was inside playing Tchaikovsky's 'None But the Lonely Heart.' Also, I was Jewish and all my friends were Catholics. They always got to do things together, like go to midnight mass, and I couldn't go. Even in a football huddle, they'd say, 'Let's kick hell outta those Jews,' and I'd say, 'Yeah, let's get 'em.' Now I look back and can't understand why it was so important to belong to those guys faking their I.D.'s to get rye and ginger ales at the bowling alley, but *wow*, it was then. So to be the life of the party I played piano in a Friday night dance band and suddenly I was with a real group of musicians, practicing together, meeting people. I used to keep time to the radio with a pair of drumsticks. Music made me belong."

Then came a hitch with Uncle Sam from 1950 to 1952 which has got to be one of the funniest enlistments in Army history. "Somehow they marked my file 'concert pianist' and I ended up playing piano in a tuxedo at the officer's club on Governors Island and gave concerts at Fort Dix. It was the put-on of all time. I had *nothing* to play, man. It was all improvisation. I'd give 'em a medley from *South Pacific* and a little 'Slaughter on Tenth Avenue' and then make up some wild thing off the top of my head and if anyone asked, I'd say 'an unpublished work by Debussy.' " For two years he stayed out of Korea by winging it on unpublished works by Debussy. He lived off the base, drove his own car, and kept all the top-ranking officers happy by playing their favorite tunes. It couldn't last forever ("How many choruses of "Home in Indiana" can you play before somebody gets wise?") so they shipped him to Germany where he wrote arrangements for a German dance band and paid other soldiers to clean his M-1 rifles. "I prayed a lot and it paid off. They never sent me to Korea. If they had, I wouldn't have known how to do a thing."

After the army, he worked as an accompanist for Vic Damone, who fired him, later Polly Bergen, Imogene Coca and the Ames Brothers. Square jobs for a swinger like Burt, but the money was good and he "got to go to Las Vegas twice a year." He also played rehearsal piano for singer Paula Stewart and married her. It lasted three years. While he was playing in Vegas, the record company sharks would fly out to audition songs for the Ames Brothers and Burt would hear them. "I thought they were horrible. Songwriting sounded simple. I knew I could write better than that, so I told myself I should quit, go back to New York, and write a hit. I did and for a solid year I couldn't get arrested. What looks simple and clear and inventive is very misleading. I couldn't get anything published. I was busted. I was working weekends playing for Joel Grey in the Catskills. Three shows a night. I was never home. My marriage was cooked by then. I finally got a song recorded by Patti Page. It was awful. I'd rather forget it." He leaps to the piano, tilts his shaggy head toward imaginary calypso drums, pumps the pedals of the Steinway with his sneakers, and sings. He's right. The song was awful. "Then I met Marlene."

His highly publicized friendship with Dietrich began in 1953 when he was asked to fill in for her regular conductor. "I went around to see her at the Beverly Hills Hotel and I had a cold and she said, 'Iz dot a cold?' in that great voice and then she gave me some vitamins and some medicine and wowed the hell outta me. She now says I started coaching and advising her right then and there, but it's not true. I mean she was a *legend* and you don't walk in and say to a legend, 'Listen, baby, sit back on the second eight bars and take it easy.' I was awe-stricken. She thinks I helped her constructively, but *she* had the vitamin C! I had written a song. She called Sinatra and told him he *had* to record it. Of course he never recorded it, but she said, 'Ah, you will be sorry. He'll be very famous one day and you'll remember I told you so.' It's been like that the whole time I've known her. It's a kind of friendship and love that is very rare and special. Other people get into trouble with her, but I never did. Now I'm too busy to conduct for her much, but she isn't sad or afraid. She just wants everyone to know how happy she is that I turned out to be a success. She bought 35 copies of the reviews and mailed them to people all over the world telling them, 'See I told you so.' "

After Burt's first hit song, "Magic Moments," was recorded by Perry Como in 1958, nothing happened for four years while he preferred to travel with Dietrich. "People warned me that I wouldn't write songs while I was traveling, but I say so what? She taught me a lot about never settling for less. I just watched her—what she went after, what she got. I still conduct for her now when I can. Like going to Warsaw. You land. The snow is blowing, the wind is howling, you've had no sleep because you can't sleep, there's Marlene at the foot of the ladder. Not in the terminal with all the other people, but at the foot of the plane, and in her arms she's got two enormous sweaters because she's afraid you won't be warm enough, and the longest Dior scarf you've ever seen, and a sheepskin jacket and a bottle of Polish vodka which she pours, which you drink, in the snow and wind. Then she takes you to your hotel, only it's not just *any* hotel, it's the hotel where Paderewski stayed and she's gone to all the trouble of getting you *his room!* Then you go to Israel, where no German is spoken or sung ever, and the authorities stop her at the airport and say, 'You won't sing even *one* song in German, will you?' and she says, 'No *eleven!*' and people are hysterical and weeping and it's so emotional you have to do all eleven songs all over again. Traveling with her is not a trip or a job, it's an *invasion!* The time I've spent with her is worth ten hit songs."

The other singer in his life has been Dionne Warwick, for whom many of his hits are specially written. He met her six years ago when she showed up for a record date to sing background music for a vocal group called The Drifters. "She had pigtails and sneakers and great cheek-bones and said, 'Who we singin' for on this record?' and I said, 'The Drifters,' and she said, 'Oops, I don't wanna blow my cool!' We've been friends ever since." When she made her debut in Paris, Burt wrote to Dietrich and asked her to look in on the shy young Negro gospel-turned-pop singer. Dietrich not only looked in on her, she took her to Balmain, bought her a gown, took over her opening, introduced her to European society, and—*voilà!*—another star is born, touched by the Bacharach magic. "I'm very proud of Dionne and the kind of lady she's become," he says. "Our careers kind of rose together."

In 1962, he decided to leave Dietrich and "take on the total responsibility for a career." Result: three Oscar nominations, millions of record sales, movie scores, an upcoming TV special. None of which seems to have gone to his head. "I turned down 25 movies while I worked on *Promises, Promises.* Then after all the illness and all the work, I sat down on one of the swivel chairs on the set after the opening and felt like crying. I didn't know if I had it or not any more and I didn't even care. Now I'm going home to California to rest. I'll be scoring the Jack Lemmon film *The April Fools,* but I wish I didn't even have to do that. Angie will be making a film, so we can get up together at 5 A.M., I can get to know my baby again, we can have a home life. The baby was born three months premature and weighed only a pound and ten ounces. They gave her a half of one percent chance to live through the first night. Angie was a very sick girl, with an infection through her whole body. I almost lost them both, but they made it, and now that gratefulness, that vivid remembrance, not impaired by the passing of time, is so strong that I will never take what I've got for granted. I'm very sentimental about my family. Looking at them I see things that are much more important than writing hit songs.

"I'm not worried about being in today and out tomorrow. The groovy thing about pop music is it's wide open. Anything can happen. Eric Burden and The Animals were red-hot, now they're ice-cold. The Yardbirds? Out of it. They come and go. It's this year's arranger, this year's record producer, this year's singer. Who knows? A year from now Frankie Laine could come back with a hit record. I don't worry about running out of gas. I gave up classical music to write songs, then I stopped counting the hits five years ago. Now I just got an invitation from Leopold Stokowski, who wants to commission me to write an original work for the American Symphony Orchestra. My mother burst into tears when I told her. I'm really knocked out by the idea.

But I've gotta get off by myself. Broadway made me a sick man and I need time to reflect." He blows his nose on a piece of blue Kleenex, swallows a vitamin pill, and sighs a deep, hoarse sigh. "There's just so much you can do in life. I used to not know the meaning of the word 'No.' But I'm learning to say it now."

George Sanders

It started, the way almost everything else starts these days, with a phone call. "George Sanders is in town!" said the press agent excitedly.

So?

"So he has vertigo, and he's convinced he's going to die soon, and he just played a homosexual-transvestite cocktail-pianist spy in John Huston's *The Kremlin Letter* and he's only in town two days before he retires from the movies forever!" He sounded persuasive. After all, George Sanders is the closest thing we have left to the bitchy memory of Clifton Webb and Monty Woolley. So, figuring it might be fun to ask the cantankerous *distingué* how it felt, after winning an Oscar for tongue-lashing Margo Channing in *All About Eve,* to finally *play* Margo Channing, I showed up at the Drake at 10 A.M. Breakfast was promised.

There is no way to prepare anyone for George Sanders, but in the elevator, the press agent bravely gave it the old college try. "You may find him difficult, child-like . . . no memory . . . he remembers absolutely nothing about his movies . . . he's very short-tempered . . . he's 63 years old and this is his 40th year in films . . . he's played more than 80 roles, almost always cads . . . he was married to Zsa Zsa Gabor and Ronald Colman's widow Benita Hume, who died of cancer in 1967 . . . he says the only thing he remembers about Zsa Zsa is that he could never talk to her because she was always under the hair dryer. . . ."

The room was gray. Gray light from a gray Manhattan sky shattered the windowpane in gray, blinding splinters. The rug was gray, the lamp was gray. George Sanders, the only spot of elegance in the room, reclined on rumpled gray sheets in an impeccably tailored gray suit, his pearl gray eyes staring at the ceiling in an expression which could only be described as gray. "No coffee, no breakfast, none of that nonsense!" he growled at the press agent, who interrupted his call to room service as though he had just touched an electric fence. "Let's get this thing over. I'm a sick man and I'm on my way to a hospital in Boston. I'm taking a plane as soon as you finish. Do you want to ask me anything, or did you just come here to order coffee?"

Pow! I lit into the questions. *First, let's talk about* The Kremlin Letter. *Did you enjoy making it?* "No."

But the part of a transvestite was certainly a departure from your usual character. How did you go about it? "I'm a spy and I play cocktail piano in a San Francisco night club which was actually located in Rome, that's all. I did it in drag, how do you think I did it? You play a man in drag, you have to be in drag. What a silly question."

The press agent laughed uneasily. "Actually, the club was called The Kinky and after Mr. Sanders showed up in basic black with a choker and a dress slit from ankle to thigh, it became the most popular club in Rome."

Sanders raised himself in bed with the aid of a cane. "John Huston had a different idea, but I've got good legs, so I asked them to slit the skirt in order to show them off. It will be amusing, but I really don't understand the film. It's too modern for me. I just do what I'm told." He lay back down. "I didn't read the book. I started, but couldn't finish it. The part wasn't written for a transvestite originally, but I ended up with a blonde tumbling-down wig and modified sausage curls, sitting at the piano because of my magnificent baritone voice."

"Just like Dagmar," said the press agent.

Sanders let out a great sigh of agony. "They finally used a woman's voice instead of mine. I don't want to talk about that. Don't ask me anything else about *The Kremlin Letter*."

You've made some very impressive films—Dorian Gray, Uncle Harry, Hangover Square, Samson and Delilah, Rebecca, *etc., etc.*—*do you have fond memories of the pictures you've made?* "No."

Not even All About Eve? "No. Why should I?"

Well, it's the only film you ever won an Academy Award for, and it certainly holds fond memories for most moviegoers. "Well, *you* may have fond memories of it, but it was just another picture to me."

Did you enjoy working with Bette Davis? "No. She was all right."

Which of your leading ladies did you most enjoy? He grimaced and slashed the air with his evil-looking rococo cane. "Oh, all right—Lucille Ball! Lucille Ball was my favorite."

What film was that? "I don't remember the name of it."

The press agent leaned forward with a slight trace of panic in his voice. "It was *Lured,* Mr. Sanders—the movie was called *Lured!*"

I understand you were a great friend of Tyrone Power. . . . "Who told you that? He died on the set of *Solomon and Sheba* but he was just someone I knew. One knew lots of people. Every film is like an ocean voyage, a transatlantic crossing. You swear you will meet each other again, but you never do. I have no friends, no relations, no family. Everyone is dead. Now *I* am going to die too."

He looked like the picture of health to me—pink rosy cheeks, ruthless twinkle in the eyes—so I asked him what was wrong. "Maybe it's pernicious anemia. The doctors will have to tell me what it is."

How has it affected you? "I CAN'T WALK! That's how it's affected me!" He leaped out of bed and stalked from one side of the room to the other, leaning on his cane. "See? I can't move without a stick! This cane belonged to my wife. Now it's my turn. But anyway, that's none of your business."

I changed the subject. *There was great excitement at one point about your coming to Broadway in* Sherry, *the musical version of* The Man Who Came to Dinner. *What happened?* "Oh my God, do we have to go into that rotten fish? There must be a boring psychopathological explanation somewhere. I have a wonderful voice. People kept grabbing me and saying 'You must do a musical.' They told me if I was ever going to do one I'd be perfect in the Monty Woolley role. Of course it wasn't perfect and I never should have gone *near* it, but I did. Then my wife became ill and I left the show before it ever got to New York. She died a year later. It was a horrid show and a horrid experience."

Does the theatre interest you now? "No, not at all. Not in the least. I was also announced for *South Pacific* but I refused to do it. I have this wonderful voice, see . . ."

Do you sing around the house to keep your wonderful voice in shape? "No! I'm dying now, so I never sing around the house or anywhere else. I have no intention of becoming an octogenarian baritone."

Do you remember your first film? "Yes, I was the wicked husband of Madeleine Carroll in *Lloyds of London* and I've played nothing but wicked bastards ever since." (Actually, his first film was *Strange Cargo* in 1929. He doesn't remember it.)

Didn't you even like That Kind of Woman, *the Sidney Lumet film in which you actually played a sympathetic character who gave Sophia Loren her freedom to run away with Tab Hunter?* "No. The only thing I remember is how hot it was. We filmed it in 100-degree temperatures here in New York in a horrid little studio with no ventilation, and on a stage which was not air-conditioned, and they had to keep my head wrapped in ice packs. Absolute agony, and all because the woman Sidney Lumet was married to refused to go to California, or something like that, so we had to sweat it out here."

What was your last film before The Kremlin Letter? "I don't remember. All I know is there were some planes going over, some parachutes fell out of the planes and there was a big mystery of some sort because there were no bodies attached. I was playing a general or something, because I remember looking through binoculars and saying 'Good God!' and a lot of rubbish like that. Before that, it was a film in Mexico City. Phone up and find out if you care. I don't know what it was. I never see any of my films."

Do you think a lot of the fun has gone out of film-making today in comparison to the old days? "I think all the fun has gone out of *everything,* but I'm not qualified to comment on films because I never see them. I *loathe* the theater and I *loathe* movies. I will never make another one."

What will you do then? What would you like to do with the rest of your life? "Nothing. I would say I'd like to do nothing. The only reason I ever acted was because some agent would ring up and say 'There's this picture, and I think I can sell you into it.' I will never miss it, or feel out of it. I feel out of it when I'm *in* it and can't wait until the whole damned thing is over."

But while hating it, you also made quite a bit of money at it . . . "I don't want to talk about money. Money or ex-wives."

Are you still friendly with Zsa Zsa? "Not very."

I read once that she considered you the best of all of her husbands. "I was."

You now live in seclusion in Majorca. Why did you choose Majorca? He yawns. "Must I have a reason? All right. Because it has a nice climate and a nice airport. Also, nobody speaks to me there. They leave me alone. I never

see anyone. I don't want to be uncomfortable. I'll do anything to avoid discomfort. I have an English butler and
his wife who look after me and a native boy who helps out.
The people there are not like stupid Americans, always
rushing about like *fans*, asking for autographs." He smashes
his cane into a copy of *Time* magazine with Temple Field-
ing on the cover. "*He* lives in Majorca, too, but nobody
ever pays any attention to him there. You have to come
to America to find out what your neighbors are doing. He
writes guide books. I know that from reading *Time*. But
nobody knows *what* he does *there*."

"Mr. Sanders has a wonderful solution for the war in
Viet Nam," volunteered the press agent enthusiastically.

Sanders' eyes brightened to a saucy shellac: "Send
over from here some long-range planes, drop a few can-
isters of nerve gas on the whole country, and kill everyone
in it, including half a million American troops, and that
would eliminate any problem of whether to lose face by
bringing them all back home or not. Furthermore, they'll
all be killed anyway. Even if they tried to get away now,
they'd be machine-gunned on the beaches as they tried to
get into the transports. This way it would be noiseless,
odorless, and tasteless. You just wake up in Heaven."

With that, I began to gather up my pencils, but he
seemed excited for the first time. He was pacing the room,
pointing his stick threateningly. "I'm a cynic. Our values
are all false and life is simply a matter of pretense. Take
the subject of these young people burning down the colleges.
I don't know what their problem is, or what they want, or
who isn't giving it to them, but I understand them. They
say 'Tell it like it is' and they look through their parents'
keyhole and watch them doing everything, then the parents
pretend such things don't exist and refuse to let their
children see it in the movies. I was in *Forever Amber* when
they got so upset because Linda Darnell showed cleavage."
His eyes rolled back and he sent a sigh of ecstasy toward

the ceiling. "Ah, cleavage! Now they do everything in movies but they are rotten to the core because they still wear jock straps. The whole world wears a jock strap. It's either so dark you can't see, or you see their naked backsides. The whole world is a sham. It's not erotic, it's just boring! I don't want to see a pornographic film unless it shows *everything!* I don't know where society is going and I don't care, I'm just happy I won't be around to see it."

He sat back on the bed, spent, like a gruff child who has been lashing out at everyone because he stubbed his toe—sad, passionless, exasperating, but strangely touching. As I left, I wished him luck. "Don't bother, I shan't need it. I have no friends, I have no interests, I have no plans, I already wrote my life story called *Memoirs of a Professional Cad* so I have nothing left to say. I won't be bored, because I'm bored already. I just want to be left alone."

Which, surrounded by gray, is exactly the way I left him.

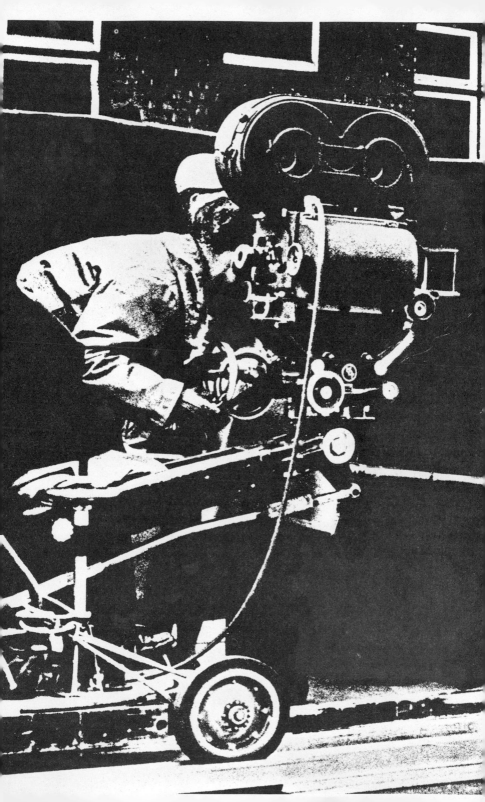

Paint Your Wagon

As soon as we climbed out of the helicopter, we heard the music. "Hand me down that can of beans . . ." roared the goldminers. "Make them sound like the Red Army Chorus," said Alan Jay Lerner. And up on the hill 250 extras jumped and leaped and fell in a ton of mud.

At a fork in the East Eagle Creek, near 9,000-foot Boulder Peak in the Wallowa-Whitman National Forest, Hollywood has come to make a $14 million super-extravaganza movie musical of *Paint Your Wagon*. The setting is one of the greatest natural fir and pine forests in America, yet the trees on the set are from Hollywood, the horses are brought in from a place in Nevada that teaches horses to act, the water oxen are from New England, the bear who plays a role in the wrestling scene is from Honolulu, the cows are from Texas, and the set designer is from Australia. The first things you see when you climb out of the mini-chopper are the towns. Two Gold Rush mining camps have been built by one of the biggest construction companies in the world at a cost of $2.5 million. One is called Tent City, complete with gold mines. The other is No Name City, which is Tent City seven months later (after the intermission)—a total town built on wires and pulleys, like an Erector set. The saloons, the churches, the whorehouses, everything does tricks. The roofs fly off, the ceilings cave in, and everything blows up and sinks into the river in a big climactic scene like Sodom and Gomorrah. In case they miss the shots (God forbid!) the buildings all snap back into place for a retake.

The entire location has to be seen to be believed, and it was all designed by John Truscott, who won some Oscars for *Camelot*. Not bad for a 30-year-old Australian, but what does he know about the California Gold Rush? "We had gold in Australia, too," he grins, knee-deep in mud. Sen. Wayne Morse thinks the whole thing is so impressive he's legislating to preserve the location for an Oregon tourist attraction after the movie people leave.

Not everyone is delirious, however. Nearly 600 people are here, living 47 miles from the set in a remote country ranch community called Baker (Pop. 9,986). It used to be a stage coach center during the Gold Rush. Now it is surrounded by ghost towns and porcupines, which keep giving all the Teamster's Union drivers flat tires on the dirt roads leading into the mountain trails. Baker has no recommendable restaurants and the actors always climb into their cars after washing off the mud and cow dung at the end of a hard day's shooting and meet at the A&W Root Beer Stand for taco burgers.

The best food in town is at Josh and Netta Logan's house. (The Logans were smart enough to bring along all their servants.) Or at Jean Seberg's, where her Spanish maid from Majorca, makes great gazpacho. Clint Eastwood rides a motor cycle and lives on a ranch, where he rises at dawn to slop his own hogs. Lee Marvin simply opens another can of beer.

Jean Seberg had dust poisoning when she arrived, but now she's falling into the country routine like Linus with a new blanket. "The first week I would have packed my suitcases if anyone had invited me to a cookout," she says cheerfully. "Now I'm going to a barbecue my neighbor, Mrs. Johnson, is giving next week. I'm part of the local scene."

In the film she breastfeeds a baby on screen, rides horses, and sings a new song written for her by Alan Jay Lerner and André Previn. She wears Ungaros to the grocery store and the locals park in the driveway of her rented green house to see who comes and goes.

"I called my folks and invited them to come and fish and I told my mother she wouldn't even have to get used to the place. It's just like Marshalltown."

Most of the extras love the location because they don't have to shave. Dirt and long hair and no deodorant are the order of the day. Shortly after the company arrived, 150 hippies showed up in the nearby woods passing out goldenrod and living on berries. Logan has hired most of them for the movie and Jean has become their Mother Superior. Next week two hippies will be married under a waterfall and Jean, Lee Marvin and Clint Eastwood will all be in the ceremony while the wedding march is played by the Nitty Gritty Dirt Band. Along with some of the other crew members, the Nitty Grittys have moved out to the woods near the set in a trailer. They eat in the commissary, set up like picnic tables, and fish, ride horses, and swim in the icy streams of melted snow. "It's a long way from the Sunset Strip," says the Number One Nitty Gritty, "but they pay us the same money for a room in town and we've seen enough of that town to last the rest of our lives."

The temperature is 35 degrees tonight. Josh Logan stalks through the slime in baggy blue jeans, cowboy boots, a polo coat and a New York hat. "I don't know what the hell I'm doing here," he said, "all these extras, all these unions to contend with. You're afraid to give anybody an extra line to say or the budget goes up $10,000. You have to organize all these horses, all these cows, all these people, get the shot during Magic Hour, while the sky is light enough to silhouette the nature you've come to photograph. I'm living each day to the next. I can't wait to get back to civilization."

Ten men haul in more mud and throw it all over the extras. Netta Logan turns to Alan Jay Lerner: "Why, Oh why couldn't we have gone to Arrowhead? Or even Lake Tahoe?"

"It's got to be difficult," quips Lerner, clutching the finished scrip for Coco on his way to a private Lear jet which will fly him back to Los Angeles for conferences with Katharine Hepburn. "If it's not difficult it's not worth doing."

And you think musicals are easy to make. Spiders crawl across the ground. Jean Seberg sits near an oil lamp, playing poker with a full-blood Sioux Indian named Eddie Little Sky, a former member of the Green Berets, and a hunchback Chinese named Peanuts. Karen Lerner announces she's just driven over a pine stump and knocked a hole in the oil pan of a new Continental. Word arrives that one of the helicopters has gone down in the mountains and the crew had to walk to a farmhouse to phone for a mechanic. "Never a dull moment," says Jean Seberg, who is a long way from her fashionable house in the Rue du Bac in Paris, and even farther away from Truffaut and Godard.

On the way down the gorge, a porcupine galumphs across our path in the road like a lopsided old man. "Hand me down that can of beans . . ." roars the Red Army chorus through the virgin wilderness, and the mikes bounce the music up to the snow-capped peaks above the pines. And up on the rise, for the 45th take, like witches in the moonlight, they're still jumping in the mud.

James Earl Jones

"Are you the black hope?"
"I'm black and I'm hopin' . . ."
—from *The Great White Hope*

As a boy picking cotton in Tate County, Mississippi, he had two choices. He could tear off through life down a Jimmy Baldwin trail of fire-next-time, knocking white heads together and spouting a lot of militant racist mumbo-jumbo. Or he could try to win them over with intelligence and kindness so that by the time he had polished up his extraordinary talent to a point where he was ready to tell the world who he was, the world would be there listening. James Earl Jones chose the latter, and that is why, at a preview a few nights before the opening of *The Great White Hope,* they were all crowding into his dressing room backstage at the Alvin, waiting for The Man, ready to say thank you.

There they were: NYU students; Bill Cosby, chewing on his cigar like a gang czar; beautiful actress Ellen Holly, calling his performance "legendary"; white girls nervous about whatever it was they might say; Negro girls eyeing the white girls suspiciously, not worried about what *they* would say, but about the man they would say it *to.* All of them worshiping at the shrine of that new 20th-century hero, the black man who is "making it."

The dressing room was hot. There were flowers dying in the cigar smoke, knee pads, barbells, boxing gloves big enough for the Jolly Green Giant to wear, and oxygen tank for instant energy revival, and bloody towels on a make-shift clothesline. The only differences from being backstage at Madison Square Garden were the books by Gertrude Stein and Sigmund Freud and the fact that when you got close enough you could see the blood was only red enamel spray paint.

The fans and the students and the actors paid their compliments in quiet, hushed tones, with all the respect and dignity of an elegant funeral, and after they filed out, he put on his engineer's cap, stuffed a book into his Alitalia bag and we grabbed a cab at the corner. How did he feel? Humble? Smug? Satisfied? Like winning a medal in school? He laughed. "Well, none of those things, really. I often come home depressed because I know the audience stood and cheered but I want to be sure they do it for the right reasons. I want it to be for the play and for the company, not me. As for me, I rehearsed for six weeks in Washington, then played it seven weeks at the Arena Stage, and I'm only now beginning to see with a third eye where I belong. But I'm not there yet. I probably never will be. If you ever think you've achieved perfection, it's the end of the road. There is no star in this company. I'm not a star and I don't want to be one. There are 65 stars in this play. That's the old guard Broadway that talks about stars. The old guard is on its way out. This is a renegade group and by throwing all the old concepts out, I think we're gonna kick Broadway on its ass. Broadway seldom attracts everybody in one audience. Where are the black people? They don't go to the theatre because there is nothing for them to identify with, man. A great number of black people would like to see a play about a white racist Southern family, but nobody has written one. Broadway is accused of aiming at the whites. The Negro Ensemble group downtown is accused of aiming at the blacks. I want to be associated with something that can talk to *both* audiences so they can each share in a common emotional experience together, and *The Great White Hope* is bringing them *all* in and they're *all* involved. I'm proud to be lending my energies to something both races can identify with, and *that's* what I want them to applaud."

We arrived at 30th Street and tipped the driver, who looked us over quizzically and drove off in a roar of gasoline. He lives in a rundown neighborhood which he apologizes for quickly and unnecessarily. "I don't care how much money I make, I can't see spending it all on rent." A drunken Negro woman reels out of the house next door and nearly knocks over a garbage can. "The neighborhood is full of whores. The only thing I worry about is Julienne coming home alone at night. It could be dangerous. She doesn't exactly look like one of the local hookers."

She certainly doesn't. Julienne Marie came downstairs and let us in with one of those radiant ingenue smiles she's been lighting up comedies and Richard Rodgers musicals with for years and we made our way up the stairs into a charming $125-a-month apartment as warm and inviting as a country house. It was already Julienne's place before she fell in love with Jimmy onstage playing Desdemona to his Othello and married him last year in Washington. It has a lemon-yellow fireplace, cornflower-blue walls and antique farmhouse chairs and now this is where the off-stage Jimmy Jones breaks down the adulation and goes back to real life. The walls are full of books ("I was never interested in sports, I always read books and poetry; I seldom read them all the way through, but I haunt the indexes—I'm a nibbler—I just love to have them around.") and the talk is diffuse, ranging in one night from the urban school crisis to psychiatry (Julienne went to a black shrink before she married Jimmy, but he has never needed one) to "The Problem," which, although unnecessary, usually becomes the thorn in the side of all Negro interviews. "I always feel like white reporters talk to Negro actors to solicit black information. Then they go and print that every Negro actor is having a feud with Sidney Poitier. Well, don't print that about me. Sidney came backstage and said, 'You've accomplished what no other actor I know could do.' Then Bobby Hooks, who is a completely different kind of cat, said, 'Hey man, cool it!' and I knew what he meant, you know? Tonight Bill Cosby, a third member of the Black Rat Pack, came."

"Oh, what did Bill say?" asked Julienne, pouring coffee.

"He said he was sitting there and people started getting up at the end and shouting bravo and he said, 'Hey, sit down! Just sit down!' Maybe that doesn't sound like a compliment, but I understood what he meant. We're all club members, all black actors, and we should all get on board, you know what I mean? What I said in the cab about Broadway. It can work both ways. You can learn from the old guard too. Last Sunday there was a big picture of me in the *Times* with my hands up holding a champagne bottle right next to a big picture of Marlene Dietrich with *her* hands up and our bellies were touching, and I looked like Hello Dolly, and I liked it. I really dug it. There was no scene like that in the play, but now there is. I hold up the champagne bottle now and the audience loves it. What I mean is, you can always learn something. You can't go through life closed off from people and ideas or even prejudices. You have to learn to make them work for you. Godfrey Cambridge was a cab driver and once he got so mad he ripped the door off a cab. Then he used it in a comedy act and it made him successful. When people used to call me a nigger it ruined my whole year. That's stupid. You're only as big as what makes you mad. Being called a nigger? That's nothing, man. After Dick Gregory used it for a book title, it's not even such a terrible word to *say* anymore. Nigger. *Nigger!* Think of how scary it can sound. I could use it another way and terrify people if I wanted to. NIGGUH! Not sissy nigger, but NIGGUH!" The eyes rolled back and the whites of his eyes stared out like thumb tacks, the powerful arms crossed across the massive legs like a Buddha god, the black lips rolled out like a black assassin in a Bagdad sultan's torture chamber, and the spittle flew across the room as all 200 pounds and six-feet-plus of James Earl Jones screamed out the word "NIGGUH!" and frightened the two white onlookers into silent submission followed by nervous laughter. "See what I mean?"

He went off to take a shower, analyzing from the bathroom why people like him. "I have the advantage of playing a character in this play who is an American folk hero like Johnny Appleseed or Joe Louis or John F. Kennedy. The first Negro champ. They made him, then they destroyed him. America is afraid of the unusual and Jack Johnson asserted himself and his fame as an individual and people couldn't adjust to a Negro who didn't fit into their image. You can say times have changed. Jack was a big success, he had a white girl, and the world beat him down. I'm successful, I have a white wife, and they accept me. But I don't know if things have changed that much. Sure, they liked Floyd Patterson and Joe Louis, but they were great *white* hopes, not black hopes. They conformed. The public hates Muhammed Ali's guts because he doesn't conform. They like me because my social mask is a gentleman. I don't like to offend people. But I don't blame Cassius for being himself. Here I am married to Julienne, but I don't know if we should even take an auto ride together through my home state of Mississippi."

"I'm not going, darling."

"Well, let's consider it. Let's see if people *have* changed. Let's not assume anything—"

"I've already considered it. I'm not going."

Would he protect her? "Ha," she giggles, "that's a laugh. When we got married, we never discussed race as a social issue. The subject never came up. But he did tell me once 'If you are ever with me and someone insults you, *run!* I'll catch up with you in the next block.' That's the kind of husband I've got."

"I figure I can clean up two guys," says Jimmy, coming out of the shower drinking a quart of grapefruit juice in a white T-shirt with great bear-like feet sticking out of white chinos. "But my philosophy is provoke but never flaunt. Never back a guy against a wall. I hate fighting. I believe wars should be fought by men over 50. We should send the old and the feeble-minded to Vietnam and wire them with electrical devices to make them respond to enemy advance, then wire their trigger fingers to fire on response. People will hate me for saying that, but I feel it's a worse alternative to send young men with future potential and destroy them so they are of no use to anyone."

Although he has a build that would delight a fight manager, he wouldn't even go to a gym to train for his role as a boxer. "Fighters have the wildest egos in the world and you can't learn anything from them. My understudy is a former professional heavyweight and a sparring partner for Floyd Patterson and Cassius Clay and he taught me everything. I even shaved my head to look more ferocious and somebody said, 'You look like a newborn baby.' It blew the whole thing. I guess I don't look too mean, do I?"

Not really. But that doesn't mean he's a softie. A hard childhood taught him a sense of justice, but also a kind of gentle toughness. It's how he survived. "It was a feudal isolated farm system in Mississippi. We never saw white people until the day we took the cotton into town. We had to tow a certain line. The white kids were *never* punished if they lost a wheel on their wagon, but *we* were. I remember catfishing, floods, eating persimmons and hickory nuts and grasshopper legs and if you dug down under the ground past the worms, the dirt was very clean and we'd eat that too."

His father was a prizefighter who went North to seek work, so when he was six he was adopted by his mother's parents and moved to a farm in Michigan. "It was a common thing in black families and I didn't mind being adopted. My grandparents were black people who had a hard job to do nobody else could do and I took care of the livestock and learned masonry as a trade. To them, the theatre was something irresponsible. I got into it because I stuttered so badly I couldn't communicate, so they were glad when I got interested in speech and forensics. Hard work was all they knew. I read Jules Verne and once drew up some blueprints for a subterranean machine and my grandfather burned them. To him, I was a Galileo who had to be stopped. It was a great place for the mind to start cooking and until you found something to stimulate you out of it, it wasn't really a bad life."

But he knew there was more to life than that. He worshiped his Dad, who represented to a small boy on a farm the black man who got out. Once he was thumbing through an old *Look* magazine in high school and came across his picture in the cast of *Strange Fruit*. He had become Robert Earl Jones, Broadway actor, and it made him a big celebrity in school. "I remember once when I won a public-speaking contest *and* a scholarship to college on the same day, the little agricultural school I went to gave me the money to call my father. They dropped me off at a drug store and it took me an hour to get up the courage to phone him." He studied pre-med on a University of Michigan scholarship but failed ("I loved the idea of being a saviour, but I didn't care about the names of all those bones") and switched to drama. He graduated in 1953, narrowly escaped being sent to Korea, spent two years in the army instructing mountain climbing in a ranger station in Colorado, and when he came out worked as a carpenter in a stock company on the shores of Lake Michigan. Whether he realized it or not, he was already following in his father's footsteps. It beat milking cows.

He made a beeline for New York, moved in with

his Dad, who had him reading Iago to his Othello before you could say Paul Robeson, and picked up the father-son relationship that had never existed back home. He studied for two years at the American Theatre Wing, auditioned for seven years straight for the Actors Studio but never got in. "Rip Torn and Geraldine Page kept saying 'We gotta get some black folks in here,' but all they took were Diana Sands and Sidney Poitier." He took every off-Broadway job he could find and he's never been out of work since. "I respect people who hustle for a livelihood, but I don't believe in integrated casting unless the parts can be played psychologically *and* physically by Negroes. Otherwise, it's unemployment, not art. The day will come when black actors will enter the psyche of white characters and vice versa and we'll play the hell out of it until your hair stands on end. But you can't integrate a Tennessee Williams play by having a black Blanche and a white Stella. That's not the way to do it. To play Hal as a black man in *Picnic* the play would cave in. I'd like to play it in workshops, but I don't want to sell it as a definitive statement of me as an actor. My father and I played in *Of Mice and Men*. I was Lenny. He's a character in any country, any color, he goes beyond a social theme. Integrated casting is fine as long as it doesn't distort the scope of the play. I thought Diana Sands probably knew more about the psyche of a French peasant girl in *St. Joan* than any white actress, and it worked. It was good for the audience because it allowed their imaginations to stretch. The psyche is more important than the image projected. Integrated casting is fine as long as it doesn't distort the scope of the play, but I'm not out to prove anything and I don't want to be used to further causes because I'm black."

It was 5 A.M. when we moved into the kitchen where Julienne served scrambled eggs and whiskey sours. "I don't want to be condescended to because I'm a black success," he said. "People assume they can use you to sell something." He fingered two telegrams. One was from Tony Bennett, inviting him to a nightclub opening. "That's all right, because we know Tony and he sent it to the theatre because he didn't know how to reach us anywhere else. He didn't do it because I'm a sudden success he'd like to have at his ringside. But this other one makes me furious." It was from the Citizen's Committee for Hubert Humphrey. "They make it sound like if I don't use my influence to get black votes, Wallace will get in. Well I'm not so sure that's such a bad idea for this country at this time. I don't know. But I don't want to be used. I don't want to let suspicions rule my life. I played Macbeth in the ghettos, and the kids threw Coke bottles and paper clips at me, then came backstage and said, 'Hello, Mr. Star,' and tried to shake hands with single-edged razor blades in their palms. But if I had let those suspicions rule me, I couldn't have performed.

"Even if this play is a success, I won't let it change me. I'll have to fight temptations to make big money and fight a lot of people to retain my freedom, but I intend to go right back off-Broadway. I don't get along with the smooth goodness of Broadway and Hollywood. I'm happiest in shoe-string budgets in off-Broadway basements. I've been in positions before where I could have been an overnight success. But people never see me in one role in terms of another one. I didn't look the same in *Othello,* and with a beard I could look like a completely different man if I played Malcolm X. I've never been hounded by mash letters or autograph hunters. Most of the people who come back-stage are usually students who want to give me information or trade an experience. I think people also are perhaps a bit afraid of me physically and unsure of where I stand politically. I am an unknown and I enjoy that. I don't want Broadway and success to change anything. And I try to be that way in my private life. My Negro-ness does not rule my life. If you are happy, people more readily accept you as who you are. If you are hostile and show fear, they want to find out why. I rarely notice hostile glances, do you, Julienne?"

"I have recently."

"Everyone has prejudices if you scratch deep enough, but who wants to scratch that deep? I don't ask that much of people except that they be themselves."

"It's because you're a Capricorn," said Julienne, yawning in the pink glow of dawn through the kitchen window.

"You're hard to believe, you're so good," I said.

"Then don't believe me. Be suspicious. But it's my way of keeping peace with myself. I don't claim any altruistic labels. My reasons are purely selfish. But I passed the point a long time ago when I would cry when somebody called me a nigger. It's what's ahead that counts."

A few nights later, *The Great White Hope* opened. One minute he was a great big sweaty bald-headed Sambo, howling, raging, sobbing. The next minute he was a dandy, all gold teeth and double-breasted suits and carnation boutonnieres, high-kicking like a Cotton Club Stepin' Fetchit. He was king of the world, and you could hear the bravos all the way over to Eighth Avenue. When the cheers died down, everybody gathered downstairs in the lounge. There were beautiful black women. Beautiful white women. And a beehive of forgotten husbands and boy friends of both races, sipping hot Scotch and waters in plastic cups while the beautiful women waited and swooned over the man who didn't want to be a star.

His Dad smiled shyly in a corner. "I'm very proud—he's—well—yes, *proud.*"

"He's the end," said a slinky redhead in a $35 copy of a last year's Pucci.

"Goodbye Sidney Poitier," said a man with a Nazi cross, who looked like a Black Muslim.

Julienne looked bright as a Jell-o salad in a silver and lavender chiffon sari she made on her own sewing machine.

"I've seen it 12 times and I've never seen it like tonight. Jimmy went up like a rocket and stayed up there all night. People cried and the critics stayed through the applause and everything. They didn't even run up the aisles to get out."

"I got news," said a matronly blonde, flapping through the crowd, "my maid is watching TV and Channel 5 said it was 'a play all America should see.'"

"What about the rest of the world?" sneered the Black Muslim.

Applause. And in the middle of the noise, there he was, in a black suit, black turtleneck sweater and a grin as wide as a watermelon slice. He tried to say a few words, but you couldn't hear him. It was clear from the grin "The Problem" was not on his mind. In fact, no problems were. Then they swept him away in a tide of adoration and all you could see was his bald head shining. Black as a panther in the jungle night. Still too good to believe. "Be suspicious," he had warned. But nobody was listening.

China Machado

China Machado!

The name sounds like an endearment drawled mysteriously through a vapor of pomegranate incense in an old Veronica Lake Orient Express spy movie. Yet the girl who fits it has probably never even heard of Veronica Lake. Too busy for trivia. One of the busiest career girls, in fact, in the fashion world. Busy, interesting, powerful, and revolutionary. As one of the senior editors of *Harper's Bazaar*, her influence over what every woman wears is inestimable. Haute couture designers woo her. Models seek her advice (She's the only ex-model fashion editor in the business and to them she represents "making it"). Photographers send her expensive gifts (They'll do anything to get into the pages of *Harper's Bazaar*). She swears she never reads *Women's Wear Daily*, yet her close friends on the *Bazaar* staff insist she wasn't at all unhappy when its pages recently called her "the Buddha high priestess of Seventh Avenue." China Machado is a name that is at once feared and revered. "We have to cater to her," says one top designer, "because whether we like it or not, she's God in this business. If she likes your work, she can make you a star. If she doesn't, one word from her memo pad can kill you in the magazines." And this from one of the top editors of *Vogue*: "China is an absolute goddess. She's the epitome of what I tell my editors they should look like, act like and be like. Of course, you won't print my name, will you? *Vogue* would kill me for deifying the competition."

The girl-woman they're all talking about doesn't look like a demagogue at all. That is, if you're lucky enough to get close enough for a good look. In a business where being seen in Adolfo harem pants or photographed leaving El Morocco in a Jean Barthé hat and Yves St. Laurent see-through lace pajamas is what the business is all about, China embroiders her net of mystery like an elusive butterfly. It is next to impossible to schedule an interview. "You have to see me in action," she says. And she's right. But one week she's lunching at the White House, the next week she's off to some island hideaway off the coast of Mazatlán. A Friday afternoon coffee date is canceled by a harassed secretary: "China's in Mexico City photographing the Olympics." A Wednesday morning sketch appointment is off because "Darling, I have to catch the Emeric Partos fun-fur show at Bergdorf's. They're doing something absolutely *wild* in beige broadtail mink walking suits."

So come along and catch her quick, before the Friday morning caterpillar turns back into a weekend butterfly. If it reads like a movie about the fashion industry, just remember it also plays like one. The fashion industry and all the glamour you see between the glossy covers of *Harper's Bazaar* is a movie more bizarre than anything MGM ever turned out. And China is the star.

• • •

SCENE ONE: China's office at *Harper's Bazaar*. A map of Vietnam covers the door. The room is small and dirty, something you'd never expect a fashion magazine office to be. It overlooks Madison Avenue, with one soot-covered silent air-conditioner braced in the window. Other editors have lacquered their offices with decorator colors—lavenders and lemons, creamy beiges and delicious pinks—like the fruit-flavored lipsticks gleaming from the pages of slick magazines. China's office is drab. No time for such nonsense. Boxes of accessories—bracelets, earrings, gloves —sit idly on the windowsill. Walls of photographs beam down in black-and-white coldness—layouts for future issues, men in motorcycle glasses, etc. China bombs in, looking like a glamorous cobra, eyes narrowed and slanted like slivers of almonds, arms lithe and flying, sipping Chock Full O'Nuts coffee in a paper cup, wearing a brown turtleneck sweater, a plaid mini-skirt and a man's wrist watch with a black leather band. "I go through stages of dressing," she explains. "I feel like sweaters this week, so I'll probably wear nothing else. We're beginning a new issue this morning, so you can see everything for the first time right along with us."

In comes Hiro, the Japanese fashion photographer who is one of the centrifugal forces behind those revolutionary fashion pages you see in *Bazaar*. Hiro is small and round-faced, with a slash of straight raven-black hair jetting across alert and inquisitive eyes that peer out from a pair of enormous black horn-rimmed glasses. China works with all the top fashion photographers, but it is clear almost instantly that Hiro is her favorite. In comes a teenage model in a Luba mini-raincoat. Hiro isn't too happy about it. "I want white. I see white." In comes a girl who looks like a concentration camp survivor ("Models are getting skinnier every year," sighs China) in a white silk John Moore evening gown. "May I see the side?" instructs Hiro. "Now the profile? The back? It has a long draped back. Is Lawrence of Arabia coming back this year? Every year we get either Lawrence of Arabia or Dr. Zhivago." Gwen Randolph, *Bazaar's* fashion director, says "Russia's always good."

China hands Hiro some photographs of models who will be considered for the layout. "I know this one, she's a young Jean Shrimpton type." "She'll do. I don't know this other one," says Hiro, flipping through the photos and résumés of hopeful models. "I have three girls in mind I want to use. Book them on Wednesday and the rest of the week will be tentative."

By now several of China's associate editors are standing in the room, sizing up the clothes on the showroom models. "Where's our leader?" asks one, referring to Nancy White, *Bazaar's* editor-in-chief. "Our leader is shopping," says China. There are eight major editors in charge of such departments as accessories, shoes, beauty, etc. China is the senior fashion editor, in charge of haute couture and millinery. This means she must select the fashions shown in the pages of *Bazaar*, choose and book the models and photographers, arrange shootings, and dress the pages. The other editors work around her, decorating her fashions with the right jewelry, shoes, handbags, etc. China must also play den mother to photographers like Hiro, who often have their own creative ideas. "They want me to go underwater," he pouts. "I won't go underwater."

In comes another girl in a lemon-yellow John Moore with a hood and cape. "You have nothing graphic this month," announces Hiro. Three women fly at the model trying to make her look more graphic, while China answers some of the phone messages stacked on her desk. "I need angles, flaps, sides, backs," says Hiro. "I knew I should've done this in Paris." "When you take a crew to Paris," says China, "you have to do it like reportage. Here, we can have some choice." Then she turns to me: "You see, the problem is we work so far ahead of schedule the designers can't keep up with us. Now we're photographing for spring and most of them have just finished summer and winter collections. Donald Brooks is in Hollywood, Bill Blass has only two people working in his showroom, Geoffrey Beene is out of town. They're on holiday and we're ready to work. Sometimes we have to make up the designs and invent the clothes ourselves. Then we ask the designers to make them up. I know them all well, so they don't mind." "Also," adds

Hiro, "*they* get the credit. They *all* want to be in *Bazaar*."

In comes a model in a navy blue and white two-piece Dior. "This is chic, what someone might buy," says China, touching the tip of her pretty nose with a crisp yellow pencil. "We've got to stop using just crazy clothes. We also have one other possibility—a Rudi Gernreich." "Probably with four bosoms, two in front, two in back," groans Hiro. China laughs. "I'll think about that one and tell you later." In comes a girl in a Mylar plastic evening dress that looks like a banana split that just exploded. Hiro: "That looks like seaweed." China: "There are two more things coming —a Dior on its way over with feathers and a culotte suit by Simonelli." China phones Geoffrey Beene long distance in a moment of desperation. "OK, Geoffrey, have a nice weekend—you're too harassed now—I'll talk to you on Monday."

China is frantic with no clothes Hiro wants to photograph. "We've got to think of a way to make this issue more interesting without being too crazy. Maybe we could use muslin hats or clocks on the legs. Rudi Gernreich and Oscar de la Renta are both designing special clothes for us, so maybe they'll come up with something!" "How do you feel about that first raincoat, Hiro?" asks the sportswear editor. "NO!" "No!" repeats China, "then *that's* out." It becomes increasingly more apparent by the minute that the photographer influence exerts an enormous pressure over the magazine. China's success is partly due to her dedication to the whims of the men who illustrate her pages. She knows them all and, unlike most fashion editors who were never models themselves, she knows what they can do for clothes, how they can make them zip right off the page in a good layout. "It's a great experience to work with a great photographer. He inspires me to be more creative, and teaches how to look at a dress in a completely different way."

She also knows when to keep them in line. "I want

evening dresses because they blend in better with my photographic concept," says Hiro. "Mrs. White doesn't want
evening clothes this month. They won't buy evening dresses
in April," says China flatly. Out comes a Simonelli culotte
suit in boat-deck blue. Hiro: "I can't have any fun with
that!" China: "Fun!! We're not here to have fun!" The
other editors circle the suit. "I hate those buckles. They're
tacky." "Those shoes will have to go, even if they are
Gucci." "We could re-do the belt and give her some snake
gloves. Snake is in again." "Maybe some shoulder pads,
so she looks like a parachute." Hiro: "I'd like to make them
all look like Indians with papooses on their backs. I saw
a girl walking in Central Park yesterday with a red mini-
skirt and a baby on her back and it looked great!"

Hiro explains his concept for the spring issue. "It will
be a computerized photographic essay showing the point
of view of a fashion design from three different sides, all
done by remote control radio. I want faces in back of the
head for a three-dimensional effect." China pulls her hair.
"Do you hear right? Did I hear what he's saying? How can
I get a face in back of a girl's head?" "We could use masks,"
says the accessories editor. "I am a creative man," yells
Hiro. "I refuse to photograph Sears, Roebuck catalogue
pictures! Everything is geared toward business here!" "It's
not that," soothes China, "we have to do things that will
sell." Hiro leaps from his chair in a burst of inspiration.
"I see nuns! Wrap all of the girls' heads in gauze and put
motorcycle goggles on them . . ."

• • •

SCENE TWO: Monday. China relaxes over lunch. She
has just returned from a five-mile hike through the wholesale showrooms on Seventh Avenue, a futile search for
fashions which has turned up nothing interesting. "I've
covered all the design houses and nobody has anything

new to show me. We'll just have to jazz up the clothes we have and make them look more interesting with accessories. Our budget is nil. Hiro and I traveled all over the world once with five people on a budget of $2,000. Sharing a bath, staying in horrible hotels. You can't imagine what we go through. *Bazaar* knows that I always tell the truth about everything, so you can print anything I tell you. I will be absolutely honest. Every girl who comes out of college wants a job with a fashion magazine, but it is not a glamorous, exciting business all the time. I love it, or I wouldn't be here, but it is also very hard work. Salaries are starvation wages. You start out at about $60 or $70 a week as a secretary or an assistant of some kind. The most you ever work up to is an average salary of $120 a week at the top. I don't know a single fashion editor who lives on her salary alone. Most of them have rich families and they already dress well because they can afford it, or they have husbands and don't need to work. Also, it is not a good job for romance. I would say that 75 percent of the fashion designers are homosexual, and although all of the *Bazaar* photographers are heterosexual, most of them are already married. But fashion work also has its advantages. It is a very feminine job, which can make you really feel like a woman. It's like playing paper dolls, where you dress your doll, comb her hair and make her look beautiful all the time. You get all your clothes wholesale, you get to travel everywhere and meet everyone. So a fashion job does have its advantages too. But it is not a job to get rich quick in."

The more you're around China the more you're convinced she's the right girl for the job. She has beauty, wit, charm, intelligence, a super figure that never counts calories, and the stamina of 20 farmhands. She has traveled to Brazil, Africa, India, Spain and Europe with 27 pieces of luggage, two models and a photographer on a bread-and-water budget. She lived for a week in Russia on caviar and goat's milk. She was the last person to ever photograph the women's quarters in the Sultan's palace in Zanzibar, a week before the revolution. To photograph an emerald necklace once, she bribed the bellboys of a hotel in South America to catch lizards, then placed them on silver paper around the necklace inside a shoe box. It became one of *Bazaar's* most talked-about pages. She's tuned in to everything. Separated from French actor-photographer Martin La Salle, she has two daughters—Blanche, 8, and Manuela, 5. She attends off-Broadway plays like *The Beard,* hangs out in Salvation and the Electric Circus, avoids expensive restaurants and fashionable watering holes, and usually ends up grabbing a steak at Casey's in Greenwich Village or eating Chinese food at Pearl's on West 48th Street. She owns a $200 jukebox that plays her own favorite top 40 hits, and lives like a Eurasian princess in an elegant, high-ceilinged, 11-room *palatia* in a 58-year-old building on Central Park West. Obviously she doesn't live this well, with a car and two maids and a luxury apartment and a country home on Long Island, on her salary alone. As one of the most sought-after fashion experts in America, China has been able to triple her income with outside fashion consultant jobs in television. She changed the whole look of TV commercials by organizing the famous Bell Telephone spot in which all the pages of *Harper's Bazaar* came to life, filmed by the same photographers who had shot the still pages. Instead of scolding her for making money on the side, *Bazaar* was so thrilled it has now made China head of its new film division, which will utilize her services and advice in movies, still photography, ads and commercials. Through determination and hard work, she has made fashion pay off. "I wasn't one of those rich girls out of college with family connections," she says. "I started out as a workhorse and I had to think of a way to make it pay off."

China was born in Shanghai; her mother was Siamese and her father was a Portuguese diplomat who also dabbled

in the import-export business. As a child, she lived in
Argentina and Lima, Peru. Already she was on her way
to becoming a jet-set *bonne vivante.* When she was 17, she
went to Paris to study art, instead ended up singing in a
nightclub and acting in B movies. The directoress of
Balenciaga met her at a cocktail party and saw modeling
possibilities in her unusual non-Caucasian beauty. For two
years she was Givenchy's top model in Europe. Then, in
1958, she came to America for the first time. She arrived
at 8 A.M. By 11, she was in the office of Diana Vreeland,
who was then the fashion director of *Harper's Bazaar.* Mrs.
Vreeland had been on the scene for 27 years, but she had
never seen anything like China Machado. By sunset, she
had introduced her to Richard Avedon, who made her a
super-star. China became the highest paid model in the
world. Avedon called her a "Barbarian Beauty" and photographed her on blocks of ice and snow in a frozen lake in
Canada in snow leopard, Mongolian lamb and white fur
Eskimo parkas. The photos became so famous they are now
in photography collections. When Diana Vreeland went to
Vogue in 1962, China became the first model to ever join
the editorial staff of *Bazaar.* She's been there ever since.

"I was making $30,000 a year as a model," she says,
"but a model's life is a short one. Most of them are good only
for about three years, then they quit and get married. They
used to have a career span until they were in their thirties,
but times have changed. Now the photographers devour
models until magazines are sick and tired of them. They
discover a new face and do 20 pages of the same girl. Then
new styles in faces come in and their careers are finished.
We're taking them at 15 now, and making them look 25.
Jane Hitchcock is the big new look right now. She's only
15. They make $60 an hour up to as much as $120 for
certain products like cosmetics, then they save their money
if they are smart and retire. When I was the highest paid
model in Europe, I made a lot of money and life cost me

very little, so I saved it. There were no taxes, no agencies, no unions. Now it is very expensive to be a model."

Since China has come to *Bazaar*, the magazine has been visually overhauled. She was the first editor to photograph models of other countries. She speaks seven languages, so she could interpret for working models everywhere from Spain to Brazil. She is the first editor to ever photograph a Negro. She discovered Donyale Luna, who is now a Hollywood personality. "When she walked into my office three years ago, she was a skinny pickaninny who couldn't even make up her own eyes. I took her to Richard Avedon and we combed her hair for months before we could do anything with it. But she had a certain bizarre look that was perfect. Now she has been to Paris and she doesn't even speak English any more, even though she is from Detroit. *Incredible* girl!"

• • •

SCENE THREE: The following Wednesday. A creaky freight elevator carries me up to the fourth floor of a dirty old warehouse at 110 East 58th Street. Then I walk up another flight of stairs and I'm in Hiro's studio. Dave Brubeck music is piped through the walls. Several models with their hair in curlers are reading paperbacks while they buff their nails. Hiro is lining up his three cameras at once, to show what a dress will look like from the front, back and profile at the same given moment in time. China sits at a tiny wooden desk. For a high priestess of fashion, her own outspoken attitudes toward the subject are considerably controversial, often showing up in the pages of *Bazaar*. She opened the door for miniskirts, vinyl, plastic and high boots, and her famous "prediction issue," with a girl on the cover in a Pucci space helmet copied from a Braniff uniform, was so popular it sold out across the world in three days. "Malraux wrote for a copy, the heads of

Paris Match wrote for copies, you couldn't find one. It was called outrageous, but if you don't exaggerate things in photographs they don't come across. What I've tried to do is bring every kind of woman into her own fashion scene. I've tried to teach women that fashion is a feeling, it does not make a woman fashionable to own a Paris original. Paris died three years ago anyway. Now the American designers have come into their own. I see wealthy women look like *schmucks* in a $1,000 dress and others look great in a $120 dress. The individual look is in. You can wear crazy things only if you have a marvelous body and a strong look. If not, you can't carry it. It depends on how amusing you are. If you have no personality, you can fake it with fake hair and thousands of rings. I want women to have a freer attitude toward everything and I try to reflect that in *Bazaar*. Four years ago, the models all wore these pointed things under their bras. Now they won't even wear bras. Girdle manufacturers are almost going out of business. We started the trend toward health in fashion. Now even the older women are on diets, taking yoga classes, going to gyms. Before, you could only buy dietetic foods if you were sick with diabetes. Now you can buy everything at the A & P. I've tried to wake women up to the joy of the body. I have so much nervous energy I have no weight problem. I eat like a horse. I used to take liver injections, I was so thin. My one *de luxe* in life is breakfast in bed.

"I'm always late for everything and doing a thousand things at once and I don't have time to fool around with myself. I have couturier originals, because many of the European designers do special things for me for nothing. I can't afford to buy them, but when I was a model I never charged some of them, I always asked to be paid in clothes, so now they give me things to hang around in. But I'm just as happy in bell-bottom bluejeans. I only wear black, white, wine, brown and purple, then I color my outfit with a necklace or a scarf by Bill Blass or Cardin. I don't let

fashion rule my life. I always tell the magazine to expect
me when they see me and after five o'clock I tell everyone
to forget about me until the next day. I never see a single
fashion person out of my office and after work I don't really
give a damn what I have on my back."

Her favorite designers in Europe are Ungaro and St.
Laurent in Paris, Valentino and Federico Forquet and Pucci
and Simonetta and Capucci in Rome. "But my greatest
peeve in fashion is American unions. They have made it
impossible for the great designers like Bill Blass and Oscar
de la Renta and Pauline Trigere to produce inexpensive
fashions. Bill Blass employs people who are on such high
scales in their sewing unions that he has to charge $150 for
a dress when Stanley Mort of "Mr. Mort" can put out the
same dress for $20 and charge $39 for it because his union
scales are not so high and he can turn out large quantities
of the same design. The unions are ruining everything."

A Donald Brooks original arrives, made overnight from
one of China's own sketches—white crepe hostess pajamas
with red and black sections sewn into the legs. Hiro sits
on the floor cutting black and white paper dolls out of large
pieces of cardboard while the lights are being set up for
the shooting. China orders lunch and devours hot chicken
soup, roast beef, Russian dressing and tomato on a hard
buttered roll. "I feel sorry for the models who sit around
all day waiting to be photographed. You have endless fitting
sessions all day for showroom modeling, but for photography we don't have fittings. In most of the fashion
photos you see in magazines, everything is pinned up with
straight pins and safety pins. The worst part of modeling
is the unbelievable contortionist positions you are placed
in. I used to get cramps in my body and couldn't move
because it would spoil the photograph."

By 4 P.M. Hiro is ready. He has built a cocoon for
the girls to stand in, constructed from four rolls of white
no-seam paper which line the ceiling and floor. Three
cameras are placed at a triangle inside the cocoon. Hiro

squats on the floor, near a switch control, peering through tiny squares in the paper. When he presses a button, all three cameras flash together, as a beautiful model inside the cocoon runs, leaps, and dances barefoot in midair in white crepe Donald Brooks pajamas. "I told you if we can't find the right clothes, we design them ourselves," reminds China, pointing to the pajamas she sketched herself the night before. She smokes filter-tip cigarettes and drinks cold coffee. Hair flying. No makeup. "You have to have patience for this job," she yawns.

A nearby table bulges with plastic op-art jewelry—dominoes, clock watches, sundial bracelets, big glass square rings. China selects a bracelet made of white plastic with ball bearings rolling around inside a glass clock. "It looks like a barometer," I remark. "You see," says China, putting it on her arm so the dial points toward the ceiling, "if we show this, people will call it 'far-out.' Of course it's far-out. But look what a work of art it is. Graphic fashion. We're out to startle people, have fun. Who is going to show it if we don't? *Seventeen?* Of course not. We have to be the magazine to do it. For each sitting, I tell the accessories editor what I want—black and white, color, etc. Then she brings things in she wants me to see and we keep them in the wardrobe room. During a fashion sitting, everything is typed up for credit for the advertisers. After the final photo, the editors check all accessories and list them in the magazine. One sitting may be repeated many times until all the earrings and gloves are perfect."

Another model comes out in a belted yellow silk dress by John Moore. After three pairs of shoes, China decides on strap pumps. Hiro shouts instructions while the girl leaps. Her earrings keep falling off. Hiro: "China, we need something *wild!* What does Gernreich have new? If only we had a topless!" China: "A *topless!* That's old-fashioned." Hiro: "Well, even something transparent." China: "We've got Rudi's new pajamas coming tomorrow, but Nancy White doesn't want them because they don't go with the other fashions." Hiro: "But it's the photography I'm worried about—the *photography!* I don't care about the clothes!"

The first girl returns in a white cape culotte suit by Modelia with an enormous Mr. John hat. Hiro shoots like crazy. It all has to be reshot because China doesn't like the shoes. She crawls under a makeup table on her hands and knees, searching in the half-light through a suitcase full of shoes. Once a girl is in front of the camera, China's job is usually over. The photographer's ego takes over. Those distorted views you see of models looking like rubber gazelles are usually the photographer's idea, not the fashion editor's. "You have to use photographers you trust," says China, "or they'll ruin your pages."

Both models stand back to back now in white Garbo cloches and capes. Hiro shouts as he flashes his camera: "Pia, you hold Biddy's left hand with your right hand." They get tangled up like they are going to fly out the window. "No, no, that doesn't work—you look like two Lesbians. Bend your arm down—down more—don't smile —too long—you're grinning like an idiot—you're supposed to look sophisticated—move your legs. . . ."

It's after dark as I wave goodbye to China, her hair flapping about her head in the soft rain, on her way uptown to meet some writer and painter chums for dinner at Elaine's up on Second Avenue. "I hate posh places. I never see fashion people socially and I haven't been to El Morocco in three years. We'll finish this up in a few days and then I'm off to Capri, Japan, Hong Kong, Nepal, Africa and Europe for a month's vacation." She waves for a taxi and heads uptown. And on the way home, I'm thinking about fashion: "Let's see . . . maybe for fall raincoats, they could use the Berlin Wall as a backdrop, with Russian guards aiming machine guns at the new Balenciagas . . ." And remembering Hiro's last words: "Don't forget, fashion is a feeling. Next time I'm going to shoot all the girls in tattoos."

Tennessee Williams Took His Name Off It

January, 1966

SCENE: Seven A.M. in the heart of the old French Quarter, where a film crew is setting up cameras for *This Property Is Condemned*. Black marsh rain beats down on store windows. Along the street, signs advertise Dr. Pepper at a nickel a bottle, gasoline at 12 cents a gallon, eggs at 10 cents a dozen, and the main feature on the marquee at the Delta Brilliant Theater is *One-Way Passage* starring William Powell and Kay Francis. The crew has worked hard to achieve the ambience of the depressed Thirties.

Suddenly white klieg lights cut through the rain and fog. Someone yells "action" and Hollywood golden girl Natalie Wood darts from a stone courtyard, looking like a rich man's Dixie Dugan, with 1930 ankle strap pumps, low-cut blouse, straight black skirt, mesh stockings and a beaded bag. As she hurries along, 300,000 gallons of water are sprayed on her head from a hose on the back of a moving truck. When she reaches the corner, five assistants rush to cover her with a yellow bathrobe. Onlookers cheer from under their umbrellas.

Sipping a hot buttered rum, Miss Wood dries her hair and collapses in the portable dressing room in her trailer. "Great way to grow old, shlepping around in the rain at 7 o'clock in the morning. I'll bet the local yokels think we're nuts. As if the rain's not bad enough, James Wong Howe, who's photographing this clambake, has to pour more water on me. He says real rain doesn't photograph unless it's back-lit with Hollywood lights or painted silver. My co-star, Robert Redford, is in bed with fever, the director is coming down with pneumonia. I ask you, is this a helluva way to make a living?"

Two weeks of New Orleans rain was the least of the 77-man company's problems. Back at the studio, six people had already written and rewritten the script, about a girl named Alva Starr who grows up in a world of daydreams and gauze butterflies in a dull little Mississippi railroad town during the Depression. Then Tennessee Williams, whose original one-act play provided the source for the two-and-one-half-hour film, took one look at the completed script and refused to allow his name to be connected with the picture, either on or off the screen.

In Bay St. Louis, Mississippi, where the cast spent five weeks shooting scenes in Alva's boarding house, a petition was filed by a local newspaper publisher to deny the company access to the public roads, and the local mayor used his influence (unsuccessfully) to try to drive the group out of town. In New Orleans for background scenes in which Alva runs away from home and falls into a life of prostitution, the company had another misadventure. One local citizen pushed a cameraman off the sidewalk in front of her French Quarter apartment, shouting, "I'm clean living and I'll have no part of a dirty Tennessee Williams movie around my property."

Plagued by endless miseries which would be thorns in the sturdiest of sides, 33-year-old director Sidney Pollack was taking it like a man. Sitting half-hidden behind the sanctuary of a banana tree, he looked very much like a young Arthur Miller—eager smile, set jaw, black horn-rimmed glasses, Ivy-League corduroy trench coat. "When I was a director on 'Ben Casey,' we never had problems like these. But I still prefer working on location. My only previous film, *The Slender Thread*, was shot in Seattle and my trademark in future films will always be locations. It's costly because you work slower. On a sound stage you can get five takes in ten minutes, but here you're lucky to get five in an hour. But this New Orleans, this crazy broken-down city— you could never duplicate it in Hollywood. Everywhere you look you see history." He pointed up, above the street, to the side of a sagging old building which, untouched by any movie crew, still read: "Uneeda—National Biscuit Co.—5¢ a package."

"Look at that sign, it's pop art!"

Across the street, an animal trainer turned loose a carton of pigeons for the next scene. They hobbled along sadly, wings clipped, pecking at grain mixed with tranquilizers. "Poor little dopes. But we can't let them fly up in Natalie's face and ruin the scene," said snow-haired James Wong Howe, who, according to the crew, had threatened to walk off the picture twice since the company had arrived in New Orleans.

"He's a testy little bastard," said Pollack, "but he knows his business. He's one of the world's greatest cameramen, a member of the old school, used to calling the shots himself. We've had a few blowups. I'm very progressive. To him I'm a 'hipster,' and it's hard for him to take orders. But I think he's pleased with the results. The main problem is making the story more contemporary than its Thirties setting. It could've been just another out-of-style *Summer and Smoke*. I'm not sure I can get away with it, but I'm changing styles in the middle of the film. The New Orleans scenes are done with a liquid dreamlike flow because they show Natalie's downfall. I've cut out all the soap opera Camille stuff, where she dies of a lung disease, and jazzed up some of the shots. The end, for instance, just kills me— it was shot on the railroad tracks from a hand car with a helicopter which takes off from the hand car and photographs the whole town and countryside. Then there's a five-page dialogue scene between Natalie and Redford that will be shot in six different locations without stopping the dialogue, right through eye-level sunsets in Pirate's Alley and light filtering through magnolia trees. Pretty Truffaut-ish, but that's the miracle of film. Everything comes out different."

Inside her trailer, Natalie Wood got the word that it was raining too hard to shoot any more that day. "Come on up to the hotel with the gang," she said, "where things make sense." Later, around dusk, she sat on the floor of her suite at the top of the Royal Orleans Hotel, dressed in a leopard-skin nightgown, her all-American face scrubbed and shin-ing, heartily attacking an order of eggs Benedict on the coffee table. Surrounding her was her entourage: Mart Crowley, an ex-secretary (male) who was passing through town from Jackson, Mississippi; photographer William Claxton, who occasionally takes a picture Natalie will eventually have to approve before it can be published; a male hairdresser named B. J., who works on all of her films; and a maid named Blanche who, Natalie claims, "has worked for them all, even Jean Harlow."

Somebody phoned from Hollywood to read the reviews of her last picture, *Inside Daisy Clover*. She squealed with glee, repeating portions of the conversation to the gang in a Shirley Temple voice. "Best film ever made about Holly-wood — oooo — instant identification — ooo — grabs them where they live, eh?" The entourage danced around singing "Curtain up, light the lights, we got nothin' to hit but the heights . . ."

"Actresses!" Miss Wood grumbled, flopping on the floor again. "We work our tails off and the best scenes get cut and we're the last ones to know. That's why I never go to the daily rushes any more. I can't tell what's good and what isn't. They pay me a lotta money, I go everywhere for loca-tion shooting, but it doesn't have any relation to anything. You can't get thrown by the glamour part. I went on my first location when I was 6 years old, with Orson Welles in *Tomorrow Is Forever*. I was in New York, and I remember I fell madly in love with Louie, the headwaiter at the Carlton. I was in the Macy's Thanksgiving Day parade, and I had chicken salad for breakfast, lunch and dinner. It's been like that ever since. This is the hardest role I've ever done —it's probably the closest I'll ever get to playing Blanche DuBois, so I'd better make the most of it.

"Alva is a great character, always ordering Sazerac cocktails and longing for the excitement of the big city. She wants out of her small town with a capital O, and she'll do anything to get away. There's plenty of room at the bottom if she stays. My own life hasn't been so different. There was plenty of room at the bottom if I'd kept making those Tab Hunter movies. I had to fight for everything. I was once on suspension for 18 months, but at the end of it I did *West Side Story*, so it was worth it. You get tough in this business, until you get big enough to hire people to get tough for you. Then you can sit back and be a lady."

Outside, it was still raining. Up above the city, Natalie Wood, super-star, had just received a bottle of Dom Perignon champagne from her producer, Ray Stark, in New York. The note read: "Dear Natalie: As long as it's pouring so hard, pour a little of this." She tossed the note aside and ordered a bottle of aspirin from room service.

The others had left for a night on the town. "Movie stars, ha! There was a period in Mississippi where all the emotional scenes were building up in one week and I kept thinking, I'm a grownup lady, what am I crying all day for? Down here they give me a chauffeur and a limousine and a gorgeous hotel suite with three bedrooms, a den, living room and kitchen. Maybe Natalie Wood the star is worth it, but I can't believe Nat the girl is. What does it mean? If I go to restaurants, my food gets cold while I sign autographs. If I go antique shopping on Royal Street, a crowd gathers. On the other hand, I've got a healthy bank account, a couple of oil wells, a professional reputation—you give up one thing to get another. I guess from here you've got nowhere to go but down."

She took her Juicy Fruit gum out of her mouth, replaced it with a thermometer, poured a glass of Dom Perignon, looked down at the birthday cake colors of the French Quarter and, like most super-stars, wondered what the night would bring.

Oliver Reed

Can a werewolf make good? Oliver Reed, who looks like a cross between a Sunset Strip hippie and a medieval minotaur, is one who did. Five years ago he was nobody, just out of the British Army, playing a rather Freudian wolf man with a cold nose in a low-budget horror film called *Curse of the Werewolf*. Sure, he was the nephew of British film director Sir Carol Reed, but Sir Carol's last film had been *The Agony and the Ecstasy* and he was having troubles of his own. No time for family pull. So Oliver took the wolf-man job. It was the first time England had seen a method werewolf scratch and howl and paw the ground (and the necks of young ladies) with enough passion to make the Old Vic jealous. And, by Jove, he was sexy, too.

Well, the excitement he stirred up sent his stock soaring so high that the roles he turns down alone could now keep half the film actors in England in fish and chips and a good cuppa for the rest of their natural lives. He is now starring in *Oliver!*, Columbia's technicolor movie version of the stage musical, which is already such a lavish project for England's usually modest cinema sound stages that local film-watchers are calling it "Great Expectations with tap dancing." He is the hip-hep comet to watch with the action set in London (and catching up fast in America) because of two other films, *The Girl Getters* and *The Jokers*, and has three more in the releasing stage—*The Trap*, in which he plays a hairy brute of a fur trapper in the

241

Canadian wilds who is tamed by a mute (Rita Tushing-
ham); *I'll Never Forget What's His Name,* with Orson
Welles, about a man with a wife and three mistresses who
returns through boredom to his former life on a small
literary magazine only to discover the people there were
phony too; and *The Shuttered Room* with Carol Lynley,
which he says is "so bloody awful I didn't even see it myself." Soon he'll play William the Conqueror in a European
spectacular, and he has three films committed to Paramount and eight others to Universal. Impressive. And all
because people forgot werewolves could be groovy.

"It was the cold nose," he says. "When I sniffed, the
birds fainted." Then, seriously, "Everyone told me not to
do horror films. But I wanted to act. I remember standing
on a table blowing bubble gum as a child and everyone
applauded. I liked that. My granny was an opera singer,
my grandfather an actor and my uncle was Sir Carol, so
it was like an involuntary muscular action, like going to
the bathroom. But I had the army ahead. The British army.
What a joke. I had a lot of tight-fisted ideas about military
society, so they sent me to a psychiatrist. I was a featureless soldier in a featureless army. Then when I came out
I went to my uncle and he said to go into repertory if I
wanted to be an actor. It was good advice, because I ignored
it completely. I don't give a damn for the theatre, films is
where it's at. I took my photos around and got a bit in
Dr. Jekyll and Mr. Hyde and played in a lot of the Hammer
films—wicked earls, pirates, swashbucklers in Sherwood
Forest. Then I tested for the wolf. They knew I looked the
part already, so I got it and learned a lot. We had strict
discipline, strict budgets, and turned out those horrors in
six weeks. Used the same sets for each one—just painted
the rooms a different color, nailed a new border on and—
presto!—a new movie."

We were talking on the *Oliver* set out at Shepperton,
where Broadway choreographer Onna White was twirling

350 extras through a massive labyrinth of Victorian London streets, Hollywood conductor Johnny Green was leading a symphony orchestra through a sweep of brassy marches and Oliver's uncle, Sir Carol, was directing three chimney sweeps to sit in a tub of water with their pants on fire. "I see my father's mannerisms in him," said Oliver. "I come on the set, we have a chat—'Hello, how are you?'—then *boom*. I blow." Then he zipped through the cobblestone streets in his lemon-yellow Jaguar, crushing cabbage leaves and horse dung beneath his wheels, passing 1840 snuff shops and pubs filled with extras in stovepipe hats, and angled in under the wash of Dickens' London hanging raggedly on the washlines near the studio commissary, where he slid into a booth next to James Coburn and James Fox and ordered a tomato salad.

"It's you Americans who did it. Nobody in America remembers a werewolf, but I did *The Girl Getters* and *The Jokers* for a young director, Michael Winner, and got discovered there. Then I had a bad fight in a bar, got my face cut up and didn't work for eleven months. I was picked on by this drunk who was trying to impress his girl because he recognized the werewolf of London. Now I just buy them a drink if they tease me. It's easier. Anyway, it's the recognition in America that counts. I've done a third film for Winner and now people are beginning to wonder about our relationship. But I've got 15 scripts on my desk and I'm making more money for *Oliver!* than I've ever made in my life. I could never go back to making horror films now. I don't like starving. That period was filled with wet stockings hanging over strings to dry and living on tomato catsup poured over spaghetti and saying 'Darling' and 'Sweetie pie' to people I hated in bad Italian restaurants just to get a job. When I met my wife she was engaged and I was so poor I tried to get her to sell her ring.

"I'm getting good roles too. People want something new. That old mystique of movie stars in silk-lined caravans is over. Hollywood is full of dog-food commercials now. Filming is an international word. Thank God for it, it's giving the O'Tooles and Finneys and Richard Harrises a chance. Hollywood's last stand was the musical. Now they're bringing Johnny Green over here from MGM and spending eight million on *Oliver!* because we've got the talent. The old marquee names are getting old and I'm getting *my* chance, Charlie. We need American money and they need our talent. Like a wedding. But I'd rather marry a rich girl than a poor one, wouldn't you? I'm being drawn to America now~because my expenses are getting bigger. I have an accountant, a personal secretary, a gardener, a handyman, and a maid, because movie stars' wives don't scrub floors. When you make it you come home and they say, 'All right, Big Daddy, where's the money you promised when you got famous?' You spend every penny and end up famous and broke. This country takes everything in taxes. Then everyone wonders where have all our British actors gone? They've gone to Hollywood. We're all being driven out of the country.

"I haven't lived long enough with this much money to know who I am yet. I don't know if it's big cars or gambling or fast women I want, so I try them all. People ask if I'm a hippie. I don't know. But I hate clothes. I sort of live out of old film wardrobes they give me after each film. I'm no dandy. I own a lot of boots, but only one pair of shoes at a time till they wear out because you have to go to the cobbler and look for your ticket and I always lose mine and end up in a bloody row and get thrown out. I don't like swinging London. I went to the Ad Lib once and it was all actors in tweed hats and corduroy pants who dribbled all over my wife's hand and I thought, 'Christ, is this a mirror? Am I like that?' Actors are bores. I can only take them in twos and threes—no, three is too many— because then they start telling you about all the parts they turn down. I'd rather go to Wales and talk to the miners than to the Mirabelle or someplace 'in' and posh because there's no bull there. When I was in Montreal making *The Trap* I went to San Francisco and lived three weeks in Haight-Ashbury with the flower people before the American press found out about them and the phonies moved in. They were gentle people. No racial tension. If this is the effect of LSD, then swing, babe, do you dig? It produces gentleness, whereas alcohol produces violence. The bars in America are like puke houses, with everyone ordering side-cars and screwdrivers and all that crap. That's why Americans flip over our pubs. Pubs were my acting school. I got all my characterizations that way. You walk into a pub at 5:30 and a man in a bowler hat with a briefcase and creased trousers will go through every stage of mankind before he finishes his bitter.

"Actors used to have to go to the Royal Academy and have a very prissy background. Then war came and everyone was employed as full-time murderers and the Noel Cowards with their chiseled noses and lavender water and Brylcreem hair were out, because the newsreel cameras were shooting men crawling out of trenches. Then after the war everyone sighed relief and escaped for ten years into a world of crinoline and scarlet pimpernels and remakes of old Hollywood three-musketeer movies. Then the children of the men at war took over and the Tony Richardsons were in in British films. Now after the kitchen sinks and the contraceptives and the rooms at the top crying out for recognition, we need another escape, so it's spies. You just saw one at the next table. James Coburn. Faces like his and mine are in. I've got a face like a dust bin, but through the help of the hippies people are learning that if you kick a dust bin over and rhododendrons fall out, it's glorious. Dust bins *can* make love. It's more real to today's kids to love a pop singer with acne, long hair and a guitar by throwing jelly beans at him because he's more real and personal than a Rock Hudson movie idol. It used to be more respectable and secure to have short hair and a business suit, but now men know it's not necessary. Those men were not gentle. And women react to gentleness. So my kind of face has a bigger future than ever, do you dig?"

He walked out into the rain, his beard gleaming and his long hair bouncing in the breeze. The weather and the kids and the musical numbers were back in full force on the streets of *Oliver!* He scratched himself and grinned. "I think I'll give it all up when I'm 40 for a long think." Then he went back to work. It beats digging peat in Ireland.

Mickey Mouse's Birthday Party

Mickey Mouse was 40 years old this week and the Walt Disney fantasy hour on NBC gave him a party. It wasn't a very good party, because like almost everything else the folks at Disney do, Mickey's party turned into a bloated billboard to advertise other Disney products. But it was not a party without its high spots. During the celebration, there were 1925 film clips of Walt Disney drawing roomfuls of scampering little mice, one of whom would eventually become the Star Rodent of the World. Disney himself posthumously added comment behind the original organ music that accompanied Mickey's debut in *Plane Crazy*. There were scenes from Mickey's first synchronized sound cartoon, *Steamboat Willie*, in 1928, shots of Mickey being adored by Will Rogers, Shirley Temple, Laurel and Hardy and the Barrymores, and fond memories of his first Oscar in 1932, when he was only four years old.

Success and new clothes changed him over the years. He developed expressions. His voice changed from a beep to a chatter. He received more fan mail and sent more autographed photos than any other star in Hollywood. During the early Thirties he turned out a new movie every two weeks. His books were read by kids in 20 languages. He practically revolutionized the wristwatch industry. He even played talent scout, discovering Pluto, Donald Duck and Goofy. (It is interesting to note that of his three discoveries, only Donald Duck is still popular, because his perpetual frustration, anger and violence are very "in" today—in Berlin, Donald Duck Film Festivals have them lined up for blocks on the Kurfurstendam.) He was also very educational for children. If it had not been for Mickey, many kids would never have been exposed to classical music. There were shots of him conducting the William Tell Overture, and one lengthy film clip from *Fantasia* in which he performed to "The Sorcerer's Apprentice" (one of Mickey's greatest roles, someone reminded me). Kids often found him too subtle, but grown-ups loved his unique comedy. The saddest thing of all was his demise in the Fifties when cartoon characters suddenly became real, identifiable paste-pot creatures who got involved in situations. Mickey Mouse never had a personality.

I would much rather have seen an absorbing documentary on how the entire Disney empire was saved from bankruptcy during the depression by a single mouse, topped off by a better character analysis of the decline and fall of an American hero (which Mickey certainly has come to be considered). But instead the whole thing degenerated into a bowl of mush, as most Disney shows do, with several disorganized events occurring simultaneously. The now-grown Mouseketeers from the old Mickey Mouse Club showed up, and what some of them have turned into over the years I'd rather not mention. Then it all turned into a circus of advertising gimmicks for Disney World in Florida. Disney coloring books, Disney toys, Gulf station Disney magazine giveaways free with a fill-up of gas, and more Disney products and forthcoming Disney movies than the brain can remember.

Mickey Mouse should have celebrated his 40th birthday with a roar. Thanks to the greediness of commercial television advertising, he couldn't get a squeek in edgewise.

Jon Voight

The midnight cowboys squint in the afternoon light.
Neon pierces the sky on the Accutron sign as a gang of
toughs shove an old lady against the plate-glass window
of a pornographic bookstore which announces "Paperback
Special Today—*Dyke Farm!*" "Shocking! Lustful! Unusu-
ally Excellent!—Variety" blasts a movie marquee as the
smell of sour custard and cheap perfume and onions fried
in stale grease permeates the air. This is The Street—
peeling and rotting in the harsh glare of daylight. The
same 42nd Street that wore out the taps on Ruby Keeler's
shoes has a different face now, its energy re-channeled
from tango to torment.

Faster than a bullet, the image is punctured. Standing
in the film of nausea settling over Times Square, Jon
Voight looks as distinctly out of place as if the white knight
in the Ajax commercials had suddenly stepped out of the
tube and found himself in a tenement living room in Harlem. His blond hair and pink fingernails are so clean they
sparkle in the sun. His pants are pressed, the navy-blue
knit turtle-neck sweater he wears under his corduroy blazer
makes a distinctive decorator contrast to eyes clear and
blue as periwinkles, and his teeth are straight and white
as sugar cubes. People stare suspiciously at the invasion
of all this sanity and good cheer, because in the teeming
violence of The Street he looks like the captain of an
Olympic swimming team who has just stepped off the
wrong bus.

This may be the last time Jon Voight ever walks The Street without being mobbed. After *Midnight Cowboy,* he'll be like Paul Newman—a movie star for whom anonymity is only a nostalgic memory. From now on, they'll stare—but for completely different reasons. In the movie, he plays an orphaned Texas hick named Joe Buck who, among other things, gets gang-raped on the hood of a car by a bunch of toughs, comes home from the Army to find himself alone in the world, heads for New York to be wined and dined by beautiful women because somebody told him he was "one helluva stud," and ends up on The Street, cheated and kicked around by the coldness of New York until he builds a wall around himself and his only friend, a deformed, crippled, diseased wino named Ratso, played by Dustin Hoffman. It's a tough movie—grim and hard to take, and the worst indictment against the city of New York ever captured on film—but Voight plays a male hustler with such heart-piercing naïveté and humorous tenderness that it is not possible to dislike him for a single moment. It's the kind of role that makes super-stars out of nobodys.

He walks, happy about the few last days of his terminating anonymity. "Look at these people. Do you believe this?" he asks. His blue eyes swallow everything, like a child at a birthday party. "John Schlesinger brought us down here to shoot *Midnight Cowboy* and I came several times on my own, dressed in my cowboy stud clothes. I learned a lot about this place. Men would come up to me and try to pick me up and I would keep them talking for a long time before they would get the message and go away. You wouldn't believe some of the stories I heard. It's like a real community unto itself, you know? Crowds would gather around us when we were shooting, like a family neighborhood, and we'd film them doing their things. I really felt good about some of the things we learned here."

He stops in front of a blood bank where the 42nd Street flotsam sells its blood for enough money to exist for another few days of clockless eternity. "One night we shot a scene where I sell blood. In the movie, they show somebody else's arm with a needle in it, but it shows me going inside. This woman started coming down the street right toward the camera. She was overly made-up and singing and dancing—a bizarre creature you could only find in a place like this. She had really freaked out. All the things than can happen to you in New York had hit her very bad and she had left the scene goodbye. When the crowd saw her, they started laughing. But it's like they laughed *with* her, not *at* her. And when she saw the camera, she just stopped singing and said 'Nope!' and walked away like a completely different person. Even in her madness she had dignity. I was really proud of her. She was goddam right not to let us photograph her. None of these people should have been used unless they wanted to be used. It felt undignified somehow to exploit them. They all stick together here. The hostility we encountered from these people was directed at the cameras and actors, not at each other. *We* were the phony world. We were spoiling their street, invading their privacy.

"The thing I learned rubbing elbows with these people is compassion. The person Dusty plays in the movie is ugly. You see people like him every day and you don't need a translation. You look at them and see them for what they are. But if you were taught to look at them a bit differently maybe you could learn to understand why they became that way. Then when we understand what happens to people maybe we could rid ourselves of the callousness that seems to be everywhere. I'm no psychologist, but I feel if we could break down some of our prejudices we'd learn we're not too different inside from these people on 42nd Street. We all hurt in the same places."

A matronly woman eyes Jon curiously, walks quickly

ahead of him, then turns around and stops him. Will she
scream rape? Will she beat him about the face and eyes?
No. She's just a moviegoer who saw his picture in the
ads. Jon grins sheepishly. Then the woman does ten minutes on how she's writing this doctor's thesis on "Victorian
Literary Responses to Renaissance Art." She moves on.
It's something he's got to get used to but isn't yet. He's
still worrying about it when he accidentally trips over a
drunk moaning in a garbage-strewn doorway. He doesn't
run, repulsed. He kneels down and screws the top back
on the bum's wine bottle. "You OK, buddy?" The bum
groans and rolls back his eyeballs. Red mucous runs down
his cheeks, making a river in the dirt. Jon moves on,
obviously touched. It's a quality he has which saves *Midnight Cowboy* from being the most depressing movie ever
made, and now it seems obvious—the quality does not
stem from a screenplay based on James Leo Herlihy's
novel, but from the pure deep-down apple pie niceness of
Jon Voight. "A few years ago, when I was in a revue
called *O, Oysters* in the Village, I got to know some of
these bums. They used to hang around on the Bowery
and take care of each other like a gypsy band. There's an
unwritten law in the Bowery—every bum has a buddy
and they split everything 50–50. It's very beautiful. Like
the relationship between Dusty and me in the movie. It's
really a love affair, although it never becomes sexual. But
it's still love. Loneliness can drive people to feel a lot of
things. Everyone wants to be Mr. Terrific and I'm no exception, but there will be people who don't like me because
of this character. I can't worry about them. I want people
to go away from it realizing that people like these have
a kind of stature, you know? I don't want people to merely
be glad they are better off. I want them to have compassion for the ones who aren't."

Jon Voight has always been lucky. He has never been
a midnight cowboy. He's never even been a 12:00 noon

cowboy. He was born in Yonkers 30 years ago and his father, who is the golf pro at Westchester's Sunningdale Golf Club, started him off as a caddy, hoping he'd follow in the old footsteps. "For a while I played in the low 70's, but I was a rebel. Then I played an 80-year-old man in a school play and acting was all I wanted to do after that. Then my family wanted me to be a lawyer—anything as long as I had some kind of status. But I came to New York in 1960, after I graduated from Catholic University, and studied with Sandy Meisner and, although they disapproved, they put up with my first sophomoric on-my-own arrogance. I guess they realized I would never be a lawyer, so they adjusted. People always do. They have to. But I never had to be a bartender or wash dishes to pay for acting classes. I always knew I could get money from home if I needed it. I always had security. And I worked in projects I was interested in. I was lucky. I never had to do a TV series or anything like that."

Like Dustin Hoffman, he was no overnight sensation. He's done a lot of things nobody remembers. Like singing "Sixteen Going on Seventeen" to Lauri Peters in *The Sound of Music* for six months on Broadway. "My instincts were good but my singing was lousy," he grins. He married the girl. It lasted five years. Roles followed in the off-Broadway revival of *View from the Bridge* and with Irene Papas in Frank Gilroy's ill-fated *That Summer–That Fall.* He has two other unreleased movies, a low-budget job called *Out of It,* and Mike Nichols' *Catch-22,* in which he plays a young Nazi type. All of it leaves him confused, intense, critical, too intelligent to hitch his wagon to any particular star. Even *Catch-22* fails to set him on fire, although everything about it impresses him except his own contribution to it. "I was down in Mexico with all those guys sitting around all day with nothing to do, and I felt intimidated. All that cleverness and wit. It rained a lot and Mike Nichols and Dick Benjamin and Buck Henry and Art Garfunkel and Martin Balsam would sit around all day and tell jokes and I couldn't think of anything to say. I don't have that much to do in it. It's Mike's picture and I only have a small part of the puzzle. So I'd just listen and finally it got to the point where everyone was talking about each other because there was nothing else to do. The night Orson Welles arrived I remember they all wondered what it would be like if he sat up talking all night and somebody said about five in the morning, he'd probably say, 'And then I was four . . . ' "

But *Catch-22* is a long way off. Right now, he's got *Midnight Cowboy* to think about and the kind of stardom Dustin Hoffman had handed to him in *The Graduate* staring him in the face. "My friends tell me I'm avoiding stardom, that I'm self-destructive," he says, staring at a pair of lace panties in a window with the derrière missing. "They say I don't give in to vanity enough, or enjoy compliments. That's true, I guess. I'm neurotic about all that. I distrust it. I want to avoid childish game-playing and make all my statements through my work. Dick Benjamin has been able to do that, and Dusty. I really like Dusty. I was around watching it happen to him, all the fans pulling his clothes and all. He has really developed a wonderful way of coping with stardom. Of course, he goes to a psychiatrist at least five days a week."

Somebody grabs him around the waist suddenly and lifts his six-foot-plus frame off the sidewalk. It's Raymond St. Jacques, on a day off from shooting *Cotton Comes to Harlem*. "Hey, baby, I hear you're too much in *Midnight Cowboy!*"

Jon blushes and changes the subject. The old put-down again. "He taught me fencing at the San Diego Shakespeare Festival one year."

"You were a great Ariel," says St. Jacques.

"That shows what a crummy actor I must've been," says Jon, as St. Jacques vanishes in the crowd. "I played

Romeo that year too, but he doesn't even remember. It was nice of him to come up to me, though, don't you think? When you make it, people's attitudes change. His didn't. He seemed genuinely glad to see me, don't you think? Maybe I won't create much excitement with this movie after all. That would be a blessing. Then I could go on with my life the way it has been and never give anybody a chance to get an overblown opinion of me."

He's still putting himself down as he wolfs down two hot dogs at Nathan's. Two mippy-dippys at a nearby table get so zonked out over his movie-star looks they spill mustard all over their vinyl raincoats. He tries to ignore them. "My looks inhibit me. I can't play real people. I'd like to play a Greek or a Jew but I'll never be able to do much with age or ethnic characters. I hate type-casting. Rosencrantz and Guildenstern should be played by Simon and Garfunkel, like Borscht-circuit comics. I think everybody should play everything, but it doesn't work that way. I wanted to play the Al Pacino role in *Does the Tiger Wear a Necktie?* They want people today who look like Dusty. I want to be a character actor. I will *never* let them turn me into a Tab Hunter and I will never go to Hollywood unless they offer me the right properties. I want to go back to class. I may direct a rock musical version of *The Tempest* with wild lighting and a new kind of theatre both constructed by Jerry Brandt, who built the Electric Circus. After *Midnight Cowboy* I felt drained. I didn't know if I ever wanted to work again. I had so many doubts about everything I did. I felt I made a lot of mistakes. I still feel that way. I know there are so many things I have still got to learn."

Night is falling and out on The Street the creep show is in full swing. Jon Voight wanders past the windows where the "Last Four Days Before Close-Out" signs have sucked in the tourists for the past five years, watching what his movie is all about in action. Past the 15-cent pina colada stands and the 25-cent all-girl nudie peep shows. From nowhere, a butcher steps into the crowd from a doorway, fresh blood running down his white apron. The Street fills with hawkers and drunks and pimps and prostitutes and girls with wild, vacant panics in their eyes and needle bruises on their arms, all looking like vampires in search of a transfusion. It's as though the doors of Charenton are suddenly flung wide open and all the inmates are running free.

"See that drag queen?" says Jon, pointing to something in purple stretch pants with an orange wig and a face full of acne scars. "You wonder what a person like that does at night, what he picks up on a street like this, where he goes. But there's something to be said for being ready to admit to anything being possible. If you cared enough to stop him and really talk to him, I'll bet you could learn to understand him. That's what *Midnight Cowboy* is about. I wanted to try not to intellectualize the study of loneliness and insecurity, because it wasn't that personal a thing for me. In a way, I feel I have no right to be in the picture at all. I don't know anything about homosexuality or transferring the feelings I've had for girls in certain sexual situations to what I might feel for a boy. I think it's a love story, but I'm not enough of a psychologist to explain how I felt about it. It's not whether I *am* that person or not that matters; it's whether I have the compassion for that kind of person or not. I don't want to say to an audience who doesn't know anything about hustlers 'I'm right and you're wrong.' I just want to say 'Let's share something.' "

He heads for a taxi, which will take him uptown to the garden apartment he shares with Jennifer Salt, the actress who plays Crazy Annie, his old girl friend back in Texas, in *Midnight Cowboy*. He turns and takes one last look at The Street. Three imitation midnight cowboys with their flies unzipped dance by, running pocket combs through the streaks in their hair. Jon Voight, who has just played either one or all of them in a role which may make him a celebrity for life, does not laugh. "I have this apartment, you know? It's nice and clean. Very comfortable. I'm very aware of how comfortable it is. But then I think of all these people who don't live that way, and I know having a nice apartment or being a great success has nothing to do with me as a person. These people have their own kind of dignity." He closes the taxi door. "Dignity has nothing to do with where you live." Soon the midnight cowboys are just dots in the rear-view mirror.

Offering the Moon to a Guy in Jeans

On a recent muggy, breezeless morning, a bearded 27-year-old Italian boy from Great Neck named Francis Coppola ambled into a crummy warehouse on West 26th Street, wearing sandals and a red T-shirt with the word "Underplay" across the front. He looked like an organ grinder. Or a hot-dog vendor. But never the sort of fellow Seven Arts would entrust with a $1.5-million wide screen, Technicolor movie called *You're a Big Boy Now!*

Still, there he was, the Orson Welles of the hand-held camera, making like a director, smiling through his furry foliage: "I can't get used to coming to work every day and watching all these people making more money than my father made in his lifetime and they're all waiting for me to tell them what to do."

They were, too. Geraldine Page sat on an apple crate reading Edgar Allan Poe. Julie Harris tiptoed about looking young enough to play Frankie Addams again tomorrow, ready to go into a scene in which she has her arm broken by a demented rooster. Elizabeth Hartman, as a sadistic discothèque dancer whose prize possession is the wooden leg of an albino hypnotherapist who raped her in her youth, sat in a corner chuckling fiendishly. A rehearsal began: "Am I embarrassed to be here?" asked Tony Bill, who is discovered by the camera in a Chinese bathrobe in Miss Hartman's Greenwich Village apartment.

"No, enjoy it," said Coppola.

Peter Kastner, the young Canadian actor whose only previous film exposure was in *Nobody Waved Goodbye,* swallowed a hunk of hot pastrami. "I don't have to kiss anybody today, do I?"

They were joined by a floppy sheepdog with a Beatle hairdo. "Sit, Emily! *Sit!*" cried Peter. Emily plunged into the wall. "If you hit an E-flat, she sits."

"Maybe it'd look better if your hair was wet—like you were taking a shower when Peter comes in," said Coppola to Tony Bill.

"Then I could have my hair wet, too," giggled Miss Hartman.

"Yeah," said Coppola, his eyes lighting up with visions of directorial sugar plums. "Then everyone would think you were taking a shower together!"

Slowly, the scene began to take shape. Kastner fell down a flight of stairs carrying roller skates, tennis shoes, two suitcases, a typewriter, a briefcase and an abstract painting. "Come, dog!" he instructed Emily, who was all over the set, licking everyone. "Gee, Francis, that sounds funny. How would Audie Murphy say it?"

The rehearsal stopped dead while everybody sat around gloomily, trying to think how Audie Murphy would say it. It looked, to an outsider, like group therapy. But then nothing about *You're a Big Boy Now!* has ever been conventional.

According to Coppola, the whole thing started a year ago in Paris, where he was helping Gore Vidal write the screenplay for *Is Paris Burning?* He had already attended UCLA, won the Samuel Goldwyn award for screenwriting, and nurtured a love for movies since he was old enough to toddle to the box office. His grandfather came to America as Caruso's pianist and his mother had acted in Vittorio De Sica films in Rome. "As a child," she says, "Francis would hold out his little hands like he was lining up a shot every time I came into the room."

Armed with a lot of technical knowledge but no experience, Coppola set out to make a low-budget nudie film called *Dementia*. "It was filmed in a motel room and when I finished shooting at the end of the day, I would sleep there because I was so poor." The film played 42nd Street, but nobody noticed. So he turned to writing full-time, and sold some high-priced film scripts like *This Property Is Condemned* and *Reflections in a Golden Eye*. Then, while in Paris, he completed the script of *You're a Big Boy Now!* at night while working on *Is Paris Burning?* during the day. "I wanted to film it in Europe, but Seven Arts wasn't interested in a $20,000 movie shot there in black and white with a hand-held camera and unknown actors, so they made me come home."

Back in New York, the moguls decided to take a chance on Coppola's offbeat script with a beginning budget of $250,000. As one press agent observed: "You should have seen it. Typical conference-table session, with all these stuffy executives sitting around offering the moon to this funny-looking guy with a beard in blue jeans."

Without the moon, Coppola might have ended up another faceless member of the popflick set, the ones who still think *Hallelujah the Hills* is really a movie. Breaking away from accepted slickness with their shaky tape recorders, blurred sound, sloppy editing, and boring repetition. But Coppola gobbled up the moon like Popeye's spinach. Without introduction, he called up Geraldine Page and Rip Torn and Michael Dunn and Julie Harris, talked them into accepting small roles, and suddenly the budget was up to a million and a half. Never hesitant to rush in foolishly where most show business angels had feared to tread, Coppola talked Mayor Lindsay into expediting license and permit procedures and cut through miles of red tape. He got the N.Y. Public Library (bong!) to open its stacks for Peter Kastner to roller skate through, persuaded May's 14th Street store to let him shoot a chase scene through its midday rush hour with cameras hidden in paper bags and delivery carts, even managed the coup of the year by arranging for the Accutron signs over Times Square to interrupt their news headlines and flash the name "Barbara Darling" through the air for a night shot.

On the first day of rehearsal, he presented the cast with not one but two scripts—the first for actual shooting and a second with extra dialogue which he produced on-stage like a play, taped on a video recorder with a zoom lens, took home to a dark room and studied. "It taught me a lot—how to make shortcuts, how to turn fat characters into thin ones, how to shoot three and four scenes at a time, how to handle the actors. That's why writers often make bad directors—they have to film it the way they saw it on paper. Not me. I have no ego. Back at UCLA, while the others were always sitting around talking about Eisenstein, I was stealing the keys to the cutting room."

Outrageous? David Benedictus, the young British novelist on whose book the film is based, says "I never thought it would get off the ground. I'm so shocked I'm hysterical. It wasn't a very good novel. The ending was very downbeat and the tone was black comedy. Now instead of being scarred for life by this sadistic Barbara Darling, the young hero will get a nice girl in the end. Still, I think there have been fewer concessions to public taste than in most American films. Francis is wild. He used to call me up in London from Hollywood in the middle of the night and say, 'We've been offered Warren Beatty and Natalie Wood and an $8-million budget, but I knew you wouldn't be interested, so I turned it down.' I'd groan and turn over and go back to sleep. I never believed it would see the light of day, but with Francis anything is possible. He is so determined you'd be afraid to say no to him."

Geraldine Page, who says she did the film because she believed in the script, is the most amused. "I get scripts daily, but this one made me laugh. Really *laugh!*

I had never met this young man. But I trusted him implicitly. I play a woman named Marjorie Chanticleer who is so monstrous she sends her son a lock of her hair every day so that by the end of the film her wigs get shorter and shorter. Once he directed me in a moving car. He would lie on the floor and begin the scene by clapping his hands, as I drove through the traffic. Of course I'm the worst driver in New York. But it honestly worked. The boy is marvelous, really *marvelous!*"

Elizabeth Hartman, who normally plays mousey, vanilla pudding types—as in *A Patch of Blue* and *The Group*—is the most shocked. "This perfect stranger called me up and said he wanted me for this sadistic *sexy* woman who destroys men with one glance. I nearly cried. I said, 'Have you ever *seen* me? Do you know what I look like?' Everybody else sees me as either pregnant or blind. I was so overcome by the part during rehearsals that all I knew how to do with it was go around for three weeks playing it like Lady Macbeth."

Peter Kastner, who looks like a rather startled wombat, is the most exhausted. In the film he gets choked by a tie-eating movieola machine, runs up a down escalator backward, chases kites in Central Park, gets attacked by a rooster and knocked down by a hideaway bed, falls into the sailboat pond in Central Park, gets chased on roller skates by the cops down Fifth Avenue through the 28th Precinct Police Athletic League band playing "Bewitched, Bothered and Bewildered." "I run about 40 miles in this picture. To keep in shape, Francis makes me run for an hour every morning at seven through Riverside Park. I think when it's over I'll check into a hospital for a while and get some sleep."

At the center of it all is the refreshing young Coppola, who is still so new at the job of being a director that he hasn't yet learned to tell diplomatic lies. "I can make $100,000 a year as a scriptwriter," he said. "If the movie's a bomb, it won't destroy my reputation as a director because I don't have any. There won't be the old story of the studio taking the print and botching it up, because nobody's going to know where it is but me. If it's lousy, I'll burn it. What can they do, sue me? I've got no money. My idea of making a movie is you take four guys and you go out and grab a movie. But there's so much money involved around here that I go around all day depressed. There might be five ways of knocking a chair over, but when you got people like Page and Harris waiting for you, you got no time to experiment. I forget things like yelling 'cut' at the end of scenes. This whole thing is over my head. Everyone wants every shot to be perfect. Every time I turn my head the actors are putting on more makeup. Well, maybe some scenes are not supposed to be perfect. With all these big stars and all these producers with dollar signs in their eyes, I don't know what I'm doing any more."

He scratched his armpit, pressed his fingers to his temples, then relaxed in the glow of a klieg-light smile.

"Yes I do. I'm turning out the most expensive underground movie ever made."

Carol White

Carol White was tired. She had a terrible cold, tears ran from her alpine-green eyes every time she sneezed, and she'd had a rough day. The people at the Johnny Carson Show had shut her in a smoky room for half an hour and told her she could be on their sacred cameras if she'd go home and think up five cockney jokes and learn five cockney songs, then canceled her appearance in favor of New Orleans District Attorney Jim Garrison ("Who's he?" she asked wearily). Even the press agent had doubts, something press agents are not paid to have. "If only she were not so shy, if only she were a bit more Auntie Mame, she'd be easier to sell."

But Carol White was a brave soldier. She came to town to plug *Poor Cow* with her husband and two children, and people liked her anyway. She stood in the receiving line at Le Pavillon and shook hands with people she would never see again. She raced in and out of limousines every ten minutes, tried to be entertaining talking to Virginia Graham and "two women whose names I can't remember" on "Girl Talk," smiled wanly when the reporters asked her how it felt to be the new Julie Christie, and even saw her name on a movie marquee on Broadway from a taxi-cab window.

"I'd much rather be in bed with a good book," she sighed in her suite at the Sherry-Netherland. The nanny was chasing her sons—Sean and Stephen—around the

room in pajamas and commando helmets bought at F.A.O.
Schwartz by their father, Michael King, a singer with the
British pop group, the King Brothers. "Michael has seen
more of New York than I have. He's been to the zoo."

She sipped soda water. She pulled off her vinyl boots
from Countdown and rubbed her sore feet. She grinned
a lot and blushed a bright stop-light red. "I don't know
what people expect me to be like. They all want me to be
a sex symbol. I've always been shy and terrified of everybody. If all of this crumbled tomorrow, I'd just go home
to my kids."

"It used to be really awful," added Michael, taking
off his dark boutique glasses and tugging itchily at his
turtle-neck sweater. "Always she's had a terrible inferiority
complex about acting, her looks, her cockney accent,
everything. A year ago you would have met a different
person. She never opened her mouth. It was becoming a
neurosis for her, her shyness. She was driving me crazy!"

Poor Cow helped. "The director, Ken Loach, had
worked with me before, so I trusted him," says Carol.
"Everyone thinks I was discovered by Joe Janni, who discovered Julie Christie in *Darling*, but Ken is really the one.
He made the film in a semi-documentary style with a very
loose screenplay and absolutely no camera directions. We
just talked out each scene before we shot it, then we improvised. It was a family affair. Nell Dunn, who wrote both
the novel and screenplay, was an old friend, I had once
had a romance with Terence Stamp—I've know him
since I was 16—and the little boy who played my child
at the age of one and a half was really my nephew Simon.
Simon hated Terry and every time Terry had to come near
us, Simon would cry. Remember the scene at the waterfall?
We had to add music to cover up Simon's crying. Then
when the child grew to the age of three, we used my
own son, Stevie."

"Did Stevie like being an actor?" I asked.

"I don't know. Ask him."

"Huh?" said Stevie, age 3.

"The man wants to know if you liked being an actor."

"Huh?"

"I never act," volunteered Sean, age 4. They were both sent packing.

"The movie is a true story," said Carol. "Nell Dunn wrote it about a real girl she met in the slums. Gosh, I hope her husband in prison hasn't seen it, because she'll really get it. I guess he has, though. Do they show movies in prisons? We wanted to show what can happen to a girl in the slums. These people really exist. They don't ask for much in life, but their own lack of knowledge about life and their own ignorance about how to get a job and get out of their environment does them in. Even if you're pretty, your accent loses you the job, and you fall back on the easy way out—stealing or nude modeling or hitting the streets. I could've ended up like that. I was born in a terrible slum and went to an ordinary council school which has since been torn down. But I was lucky. My father was a fairly successful scrap metal merchant who sent me to a stage school when I was 11. The school had an agency that sent me out on acting jobs and the first week I was there I got a job in a children's circus film that paid for all my school fees. I stayed until I was 16, then got a big break in a Peter Sellers film called *Never Let Go*. I made 20 pounds a week (under $60) and I thought I was rich. But I always lived at home. I still go home every Sunday for lunch. Now all my childhood friends look on me as the one who made it. They ended up laborers and dustmen. They never got out. But I've never been knocked out by show business. I'm just not career-mad. I'm only happy when I have my old friends around me and don't have to act like an actress."

She hated studying. Peter Sellers told her the only way to learn was to watch other actors and she did. Then the British film industry entered its war-film phase and there was nothing left for girls to play but "dull, very stupid blondes in skin-tight dresses and bouffant hairdos in awful, second-feature films. I did four of those and all I did was wiggle across the screen, and then it hit me: what was I doing? I wasn't getting any satisfaction, so I quit."

Her boyfriend Terence Stamp introduced her to Lionel Bart, Bart introduced her to Michael King at a party, and three months later they were married. They lived in South Kensington near the West London Air Terminal and she gave up every hope for a career. "We moved back to Hammersmith, where I was born, and I did my clothes at the wishy-washy just like all the other mums, and was quite content to settle down. Everybody forgot all about Carol White and I was terribly, terribly happy."

Then, when the kids entered nursery school, she got bored. "I went to 20 auditions, just to occupy my mind, then I met Ken Loach, who was casting a TV play called *Up the Junction,* written by Nell Dunn, a rich heiress who gave up her posh town house in Chelsea and moved to a tiny flat in a slum near Battersea. She wrote up her experiences there and they wanted a girl to play it. So Ken gave me the script and said, 'Just improvise. Pretend you've just come out of a public house drunk and you see your husband across the street and he calls you a slut and a whore.' We ended up having a terrible fight and I screamed some dirty cockney words at him and he said, 'That's it, you've got the part.'"

The TV show caused a furor and Carol became a star in London. Now with *Poor Cow* she's an international star. "We couldn't get it distributed without someone who was already a name in America, though, so Terry said he'd do it. We all worked incredible hours living in a slum environment for 10 weeks without a single day off for practically no money. Everything was spontaneous, nothing was planned. We'd go around shooting people on the street and in pubs, but because of the unions we had to scrap most of the good stuff and use actors in all the speaking parts. But we sort of made up the scenes as we went along. The interview at the end was completely improvised. And the voyeur scene! I'd been dreading *that* from the first day. So Ken took me down to this club where I watched this hard French piece pulling off her clothes and I was so embarrassed I walked out. Ken said I could wear a negligee, but when I got into the scene something re-markable happened. I was so involved that I started ex-posing myself all over and I just didn't care. I peeled everything off and actually enjoyed it and every time I laughed out of embarrassment Ken would just leave in all the laughs and blushes. He shoots as much film as he's got in the camera, without ever stopping, and I knew if I just stood there and said, 'I can't do it,' he'd leave that in the film anyway, so I just did it. And I think we ended up with a comment on what it's like to be a young person with no social background and no chance. I've noticed it a lot among the young lower-class kids in Eng-land. They only want something to eat, someone to love them and a room to live in. They say 'What the hell?' to everything else because the only jobs offered to poor cock-ney kids anyway are in shops or as laborers. So they rebel. It's easier for the guys from the lower classes to go out and rob some old lady than walk into the Labor Exchange and get some 9-to-5 job that will drive them around the bend. Some of them are offered help, but they don't trust anyone. They've had their ears boxed so long they just don't care any more."

Carol has ears, pretty and soft as camellia petals. Nobody is boxing them. She has a five-film contract with Joe Janni, another contract with Universal, and just com-pleted a role in John Frankenheimer's new film, *The Fixer*. As the wife of Alan Bates, a Russian Jew imprisoned for the ritual murder of a child, she has to age from a girl of 17 to a tired, older woman. "I had to cry a lot, so I made myself think of a sad experience. It always works." Which one? "Well, we took the train from London and the Communists threw us off because Michael had no visa. We were then arrested by the Hungarian border police and all the time I kept saying 'We have to be in Budapest at 6 A.M. to make a movie. Mooo-vie. MGM. Understand?' And they kept saying 'MG-who?' and Michael would roar like the MGM lion and they thought we were loonies. They sent us all the way back to Vienna and we sat in the railroad station on top of our luggage in the rain and finally someone said, 'You can go back to the border by taxi and get a visa there.' So then we set out trying to explain in bad cockney French that we needed a taxi to take us 150 miles to Budapest and finally some journalists told us they'd take us in a Volkswagen, so we piled all our luggage on top of the Volkswagen and then they couldn't get *their* visas, so we hitched a ride with an old man who stopped every 20 miles and bought triple gins and then we hit a heavy fog and had to open all the doors to watch the white line down the center of the road just to see which direction we were heading, and finally we arrived at the hotel in Budapest at 3 A.M. and I had to shoot at six, so when you see all the tears just remember they were easy."

Carol blew her nose. "I don't see how you people breathe in New York. I think I'll just go to bed, and watch the telly. I don't like all this dressing up anyway. In London you can wear dirty blue jeans everywhere. Why, Michael can't even get into a restaurant here without a tie!"

Carol lives right across the Putney Bridge now, about 10 minutes from all the action on King's Road. She hangs out at all the in spots, like Alvaro's and Brown's Boutique, where nobody bothers her but the creeps. "A man followed me around last week for three hours and when I got back to me car the keys had been stolen. That frightens me."

"He probably thought you were Julie Christie, luv," said Michael.

Carol shook her fist. "Look. About Julie Christie. That doesn't worry me at all. In fact, I hear the only one worried is Julie Christie. I mean, imagine how awful it must be for her to go around hearing about me, hearing all this talk about a '*new* Julie Christie.' I mean, it must make her feel like the *old* Julie Christie." She sneezed, swallowed an aspirin, and blew her pretty pink nose into a pretty pink Kleenex. She looked glorious. Poor Julie Christie. She's going to be hearing a lot more.

Leonard Whiting and Olivia Hussey (Romeo and Juliet)

Once upon a time . . .

It was Saturday morning in London, one of those marble-gray, rainy-wet-cold-windless mornings in March when everybody sleeps late and traffic moves slowly in a soupy haze of muted headlights. But on this particular rainy morning there was excitement in the air. The Nazi Party was holding a rally in Trafalgar Square, 3,000 anti-Vietnam demonstrators were marching on the American Embassy, Her Majesty Queen Elizabeth was bickering with Rhodesia and over at the Savoy Hotel two teenagers were getting ready to play Romeo and Juliet.

They had been playing the star-crossed lovers for almost a year in front of the wide-screen Technicolor cameras of Italian super-colossal movie director, Franco Zeffirelli, and now they would play the parts once more for an even bigger audience. In three days their film would be paid the supreme tribute in England of being the one highly exalted film of 1968 chosen for the 22nd Royal Film Performance. This is the biggest movie event of the year in London. The Royal Family comes. And although past years have seen the unveiling of such all-time cinematic masterpieces as *Rob Roy* and *Move Over, Darling*, hopes were especially high this year, since one of England's all-time most cherished Shakespearean plays would be given the "Zeffirelli" treatment, making 1968 the second year in a row for such a phenomenon. (In 1967, the film was Zeffirelli's *Taming of the Shrew*.) What's more, Romeo and Juliet would really be played for the first time on screen by teenagers. What's more, they do a nude love scene. The press is flying in from all over the world to interview them (not necessarily because of the nude scene). Practically everybody has forgotten about the Nazi rally and the angry marchers at the American Embassy and Rhodesia have temporarily moved to page four of the *Daily Express* with a new page-one headline: QUEEN TO SEE NUDE JULIET! Sells papers.

They're *here!* The press agent leads the way to Juliet's suite and rings the bell, listening for lovely medieval madrigals played on a four-string lute. Instead, the walls jump with Otis Redding wailing funky soul music on a portable phonograph. "You're ringing the wrong bell, that's the bell for the maid," said the vision behind the door. Olivia Hussey, 17, is beautiful, like one of the milkmaids in 16th-century tapestries. Creamy porcelain skin, dark, voluminous avocado-colored eyes and a tiny turned-up nose stare out freshly scrubbed from long burnished brown hair. It looks like a carefully embroidered wig, but it's real. She is nervous and speaks in a husky womanly voice in a rush of childish giggles and half-sentences. She rushes about in a beige wool jumper and brown turtle-neck sweater from Wally's Boutique, nibbles on a pear, and constantly tugs at her hair, which hangs in a long droopy pony tail tied with a white shoe string. "Is this an interview? Shouldn't we wait for Romeo? Do you want to ask me any questions or anything? I hate interviews." She changes the record to Cream, the hottest new recording group in London, and begins dancing the Shing-a-ling all by herself. I could hardly wait to meet Romeo.

I didn't have to. He bounds into the room like a young colt. Leonard Whiting, 18, looks like a young Rimbaud. Deep sensitive eyes like pools of sea water, long hair twisting around his neck and ears like the unruly mane of some thoroughbred at Ascot. He's wearing a white turtle-neck ski sweater he paid 15 pounds for at Lord John in Carnaby Street. Together they are like new puppies, jumping, dancing, leaping, crawling across the floor to fight over a banana. "Franco saw about 200 girls and 200 boys before he chose us. We've been Romeo and Juliet for nine months," says Leonard, "now it's time to be ourselves." "Have you seen the movie?" asks Olivia. "I took my best friend Annabelle to see it last night and we both cried all the way through it." "Did you cry in the death scene?" asks Leonard. "Oh yes, Annabelle cried too."

"Shall we have tea?" asks Leonard. "Paramount is paying for everything for the whole weekend, then we have to go back home, so we might as well have tea."

Leonard is a London boy with a cockney accent that he worries about a lot (Romeo is not supposed to be common) who lives with his family in a suburb called Woodgreen. Olivia was born in Buenos Aires, the daughter of an Argentine opera singer who died when she was two and an English mother who works as a secretary and lives with Olivia in a tiny flat near the Tower of London. For this particular weekend, they are both on their own.

"This is a super room," says Olivia, biting the ends of her hair. We all look around at the suite, which looks like the inside of a ship, with portholes, Thirties chrome lamps and slipcovers right out of old Myrna Loy movies. "I hate mine," says Leonard, "it overlooks a brick wall. I'm going to ask Franco if I can get it changed to one of those suites that overlook the Thames." Both of them are typically British teenagers, the kind who throw Granny Smith apple cores at bobbies in Piccadilly Circus. Ten minutes with them and you know they aren't Romeo and Juliet.

Tea arrives, as Leonard lapses into a deep discussion with the photographer, who is trying to snap pictures as he leaps about the room like a cocker spaniel. "Is that a Nikon? Could I work it?" "I hate tea," says Olivia.

Up in Franco Zeffirelli's suite, the kids collapse on a Victorian sofa giggling over their press clippings. It is clear at once that both of them adore Zeffirelli, a cherubic-looking man with soft blond hair falling across his forehead who sits regally in a lavender rosewood chair in a room that looks like the inside of an Easter egg. "I saw 800 girls and 800 boys before I chose Olivia and Leonard. They had the exact qualities. She had to be strong and he had to be gentle. I created a chemistry in this pair. I didn't want stars. The screen needs new images and new idols, and they are total unknowns." (Well, not exactly. Leonard was the Artful Dodger for 15 months in the London production of *Oliver!* and appeared with Laurence Olivier for 13 months in *Love for Love*. Olivia appeared for two years with Vanessa Redgrave in *The Prime of Miss Jean Broadie*.) "I had to train them to have confidence. There were problems—" looking at them sternly—"but for every keyhole there's a key. This is basically a story of young people finding identity in a troubled era, just like today. The way they play it, it *is* like today. You believe it. The main problem was to make them feel natural in every scene. I didn't want actors who could pretend to be Romeo and Juliet, I wanted them to *be* Romeo and Juliet. It's amazing. I watched them change cells, change bones, grow in the process of tragedy. They started like babies and ended up mature, with the tenderness of young animals. They are so dear, like young virgins." Well, not exactly. Leonard has been out until 2:30 in the morning at the Bag of Nails, a popular London discothèque, and keeps complaining of a hangover. Zeffirelli shoots him shut-up looks as his assistant, a pretty English girl in a powder-blue suit, named Sheila Pickles, announces they must all break for a luncheon interview. "I feel sick," moans Olivia, as the door to the Easter egg closes.

At 2:45, I'm back at the Savoy waiting for the kids to be shuttled off to the BBC for a television interview.

Leonard appears in a new Edwardian suit of navy-blue corduroy with an Aunt Jemima bandana around his neck. Olivia wears a simple A-frame mini-dress. We pile into the limousine and head up the Strand, around the National Gallery and up toward Buckingham Palace. "Is the flag down? The Queen must be out of town." "She'll be there Monday night, won't she?" "I've never met the Queen. I'm scared to death."

Olivia sits silently, smoking Benson and Hedges, staring out the window in a mood. Leonard sings a pop song loudly. Zeffirelli says something shocking to Sheila Pickles in Italian and Leonard laughs. "You little bastard, you're not supposed to understand Italian!" Zeffirelli grins, "They picked it up in Rome."

After we arrive at the BBC, the kids are led off to the studio where the interview will take place and Sheila turns to me: "Olivia is very shy. She doesn't talk about herself. Leonard's all right, but she's very difficult. She did a radio interview the other day and the lady said, 'Here you are with a plum role thousands of girls would love to have, how does it feel?' and Olivia said, 'It's OK.' We've had a time with them in interviews. Everyone expects them to be Romeo and Juliet, but they're just ordinary, healthy, well-adjusted English teenagers and it's hard for them to be something they're not. We'll all be glad when it's all over."

From the control room we can see the announcer, Tony Bilbo, trying to warm them up over the color monitors. "I'll start with you, Mr. Zeffirelli, and then continue to Miss Hussey."

"Oh no!" cries Olivia, "I don't want to . . . you won't ask me very much, will you?"

Leonard is picking his nose. Olivia bites her fingernails. "Well," says Bilbo, "then I'll ask young Whiting here how he got started as the Artful Dodger." "I just went in and did my bit," says Leonard. We all wince. "Well," says Bilbo frantically, "what kind of TV do you watch?"

"I never watch TV." "Do you not like it or what?" "I can't afford to buy one." Miss Pickles moans audibly.

Crisis! Olivia needs some chewing gum. "Give her a chew of tobacco," quips one of the engineers, who receives a hard stare from Miss Pickles.

"Leonard's got a running nose, anybody got a tissue?" Leonard comes into the control room, blowing his nose.

"It reminds me of the time we did a telly in New York," says Miss Pickles gaily, trying to soothe everyone's jumbled nerves, "and it was very tense. Five-four-three-two-one . . . then the announcer said, 'Many good things come from Italy, one of the best is'—and Franco got up to be introduced—'spaghetti. Ronzoni Spaghetti.' We were all so embarrassed."

Out on the set, the announcer is trying to cheer Olivia. "Have you seen the new Bet Davis film?" (The British always mispronounce Bette as "Bet.") "It's very funny." No response. "They clamp a red eye-patch on her eye." Olivia frowns. "I didn't see it." Bilbo dashes into the control room. "She's warming up."

They're all warmed up now. Franco is cool, reading the paper. Leonard is humming. Olivia is tapping her foot. "Now, Olivia, the first thing we'll ask—" "Don't ask me anything. I get so muddled."

The show begins anyway. Olivia looks like Dresden china in color. She quickly stubs out her cigarette. (Juliet must not be seen smoking.) Five-four-three-two-one . . .

Mr. Zeffirelli, how many actors did you see for the roles of Romeo and Juliet? "It was about 80 each for the boy and girl." (It had been the third mention of the number that day—each time the number changed.)

Olivia Hussey, had you read the play? "No," she said, biting her fingernails.

Leonard, had you read the play? "No."

Do you agree with Mr. Zeffirelli that it is a contemporary drama? "Yes, acting in it you forget the age."

Do you think young people will go see it? (Pause.) *Well, yes or no?* "Yes, I think so."

There was a lot of publicity surrounding the making of the film in Italy. Were you polite to the journalists? "We just sat and listened. They didn't know what to ask."

What about the publicity, Olivia, involving the nude scene? Today's paper carried a headline that read QUEEN TO SEE NUDE JULIET. "It's all very boring, really."

How can you top Romeo and Juliet? Have you made any plans for the future? "No."

It was a total disaster. The control room went wild. "Do it again," said one engineer. "Lead them in a community sing," yelled another, beating his temples.

Miss Pickles poured into the studio to comfort Olivia. "Darling, you've got to relax!" Zeffirelli stared at the ceiling.

They started all over again with a new video tape. This time they began with Zeffirelli, who sounded off about the movie: "The way Shakespeare portrayed these kids, it is similar to kids today. This general breaking of the rules and patterns was revolutionary then, because if you think of them in the setup of a Renaissance society, they *were* quite revolutionary."

How many aspirants did you see? "About 5,000." (Miss Pickles covered her head in the control room. "The number gets bigger each time," she said.)

At least Leonard was talkative this time. "I find Shakespeare very boring, but in Franco's film there's a lot of action, so I don't think of it as poetry at all. The only time the photographers bothered us was during the hard scenes, then Franco would throw a big Italian fit and throw everybody off the set."

Zeffirelli stalks toward the limousine, smiling for photographers' flashbulbs. "I don't think people are going to understand what you were talking about," said Olivia. "Not everybody is as stupid as you are," snaps Zeffirelli. "Did I sound too cockney?" asks Leonard. The car speeds back to the hotel in hostile silence.

"Freedom at last," sighed Olivia, closing the door and kicking off her shoes. "I can't stand it when people talk all the time. I hate interviews. I just want to be with my friends." Olivia's best friend, Annabelle, came bounding into the room wearing penny loafers, slacks and a boy's crew-neck sweater, looking very American. "Americans expect all English girls to be dollies. We're not mod, we're just modern." Annabelle's mother had given her permission to move into the Savoy for the weekend, to share Olivia's excitement.

"We're too young to go to nightclubs in London, but we manage to get in somehow. There's always some boy who lies and gets us in." Their favorite clubs are the Revolution and the Speak Easy. They dig modern jazz, and own lots of Jimmy Smith, Ramsey Lewis and Oscar Peterson records. They also like Vanilla Fudge and what they call "fuzzbox music"—fuzzy electric guitar with a beat "played by anybody." Annabelle put on "Disraeli Gears" by Cream. Olivia began to dance about the room like a wood nymph. "We don't smoke hash just because our friends smoke. It makes you dizzy," she said

"Olivia has really matured since she went to Italy," said Annabelle.

"I was scared to death and homesick at first. We lived in Franco's villa for nine months and it was super, but they assigned this chaperon who was 75 years old and I had to be in bed every night at seven. I couldn't go out. Every time I wanted to go to the toilet I had to say, 'May I be excused, please?' Leonard didn't have a chaperon at all. I finally raised so much hell they got rid of her and got me one who was 25 and after that we went dancing every night at the Titan."

Olivia left the room to try on some of her new clothes and Annabelle kept talking. "Olivia is a super actress. She was Rossano Brazzi's daughter in *The Battle of the Villa Fiorita*. We just love movies. Did you see *Valley of the*

Dolls? I had to go into the ladies' and have a good blabber in that one."

Olivia came back into the room modeling a Marlon Brando motorcycle jacket purchased for $20 at the Chelsea Antique Market. She wears no makeup except mascara and washes her hair every day.

Was she nervous about playing Juliet? "No," she shouted over the stereo, "I just did it. But the nude scene bothered me. I had flesh-colored panties at first, but Franco made me take them off because they showed. Everybody left the set except the electricians and they turned their backs. I don't think they saw anything." Annabelle giggled. "If you want to be an actress, you gotta get used to that. I'll probably have to do it a lot before I'm old."

The door swung open and two Italians popped in fresh off the train from Rome. "They're two guys we met while we were making the film. They can't speak English. Listen, I've got to wash my hair now. I'm tired of talking about Juliet anyway. I think the first thing I'll do when all of this is over is get my appendix taken out."

Annabelle, who couldn't speak any Italian, went into a fast watusi with the two Italians, who couldn't speak any English. Olivia went into the bathroom and locked the door. Everyone seemed to be communicating just fine.

Sunday morning at 11:30 the autograph hounds lined up in front of London's massive Odeon Theatre in Leicester Square as the stars arrived for the dress rehearsal. You don't just say hello to the Queen. You have to rehearse. "We have a jolly nice ending for the two stars of the evening," said a merry little Charles Dickens character from the stage. "Take the lineup order from center position. Danny Kaye will be on Miss Hussey's left."

A full orchestra was lowered into the orchestra pit as Richard Attenborough introduced David Hemmings to the tune of "Camelot." Hemmings introduced Lynn Redgrave, who plodded onstage several months pregnant in a black miniskirt. One by one, they took their positions and practiced their bows: Karl Malden in a turtle-neck sweater, Joanna Pettet in a cowboy hat, Richard Chamberlain in long Shirley Temple hair (Even the Queen watches television) not looking too happy about being introduced as "a refugee from Blair Hospital" to the tune of "Hi-Lili-Hi-Lo," Joan Collins, Peter Ustinov, Tommy Steele, etc., etc. Leonard and Olivia huddled together in the empty theatre like startled robins imprisoned in a shoe box. "Nobody introduced us to anybody," whispered Leonard. "Which one is Carol White?" "Shh," said Olivia, punching him in the arm.

Three hours later, when the bows and curtsies were perfected, the doors opened to the press and the entire assemblage was thrown to the lions. "Is it true you had a romance in Italy?" one pushy British journalist kept yelling, following Olivia into the ladies' room.

• • •

By five o'clock, Romeo and Juliet had completed three more television shows and been interviewed by 25 people. Back at the hotel, I found Leonard in his new room overlooking the Thames, with a sweeping view that took in everything from the Old Vic up to Tower Bridge. "Super, don't you think?" he asked with his mouth full of toothpaste. "I never thought they'd leave me alone long enough to brush my teeth. God, it tastes good. Ever since I got into this movie my life has been lived in two parts. About 30 percent of it is very happy and the other 70 percent tells me I'm going buggy. Then I have to sit down and ask myself what's happening. The more success I get, the more insecure I become. I just talked to a friend on the telephone. Not an especially good friend, just someone I knew in school, but now I find I need him. Then I hung up the phone and looked in the mirror and said, 'You just played Romeo. Christ, who *are* you?' I'm a very ordinary person.

I live in an ordinary house with my parents. After all this is over Monday night I'll go back home. When I go home I can spill tea on the carpet and say, oh hell, and nobody cares, but when I'm around all these movie people I can't spill anything because everybody's watching me all the time. I feel like I'm losing touch with everything that is real. Do you want to order something? They told me I could order anything I wanted."

We ordered Cokes with lots of ice (You can't find ice in England unless you ask, not even at the Savoy) and he stretched out on the bed and told me about Leonard Whiting. "I live in a suburban neighborhood with two sisters. Very normal. Dad works in a store. He said, 'If they don't want you any more you can always come and work with me in the store.' I've been Romeo for a year now without stopping and I hate Shakespeare. I don't even know what I'm thinking anymore. In Italy we lived in Franco's villa. It was OK. My mum always made spaghetti Bolognese for Saturday afternoon treat, so I loved that part of it. But I couldn't drive—no license. So I couldn't go out much. I want to save my money and buy a car. A red car. I used to walk two miles to school everyday uphill and watch all the people drive by in cars and I made a vow I'd never walk anywhere when I got money. Now I've become suspicious of thinking phony thoughts and I don't know what I feel. I never had much money as a kid so it was a great feeling when I first started acting and I had pocket money. I had an uncle who was trying to get a pop group started and he used to make me sing at Jewish weddings. Then one day during one of his recording sessions one of his boy's voices broke and I tried singing his part and this guy heard me and said why didn't I go and try out for one of the boys in *Oliver!* and I got the part of the Artful Dodger. I made $35 a week and saved $25 of that and put it in the bank. When I had saved enough, I made a down payment on my family's house. I still don't have any money. Do you know what they paid us for making *Romeo and Juliet?* We got 1,500 pounds each (about $3,600)—enough to bring my parents to Rome for two weeks. They had never seen a movie set or met people like Jane Fonda before. They had a super time." He sucked on a piece of ice, then threw it in the bathtub. "Deep down inside I don't like change. I have a lot of growing up to do yet. I'm not vain. People have been telling me I'm pretty since I was a baby. But look, my nose turns up on one side." He went to the mirror to see if his nose was still turning up, hoping it would be. It looked fine. "Women always have to look good. Men don't. Look at that pimple."

I asked him what he expected from his future. "I don't know. Ambition frightens me. I don't want to be cruel and ruthless. I always lived in a clique neighborhood and I love just being around the kids I grew up with. Listen to me, already I'm beginning to sound like Michael Caine. Now suddenly I'm in a business I used to respect for its art and I'm doing a nude scene. I don't think they put that nude scene in the movie for any other reason but money and publicity, and that bothers me. So I don't know if I can become an actor like Orson Welles and Marlon Brando, because you have to do a lot of things you don't believe in to get anywhere. I don't want to be a star. I guess I'll get married, but the idea of forever terrifies me. The more one sees of life before marriage the more one learns. Once you're married, what can you learn? I don't want to get married until I'm at least 40. I'm not much of a conformist. Hey, you want to see what I'm wearing to meet the Queen?"

He brought out his suit (black Edwardian tails, shirt with a detachable stand-up collar and tapestried vest, rented from a theatrical costume company). He couldn't tie one of the three white ties the costume company had sent along, so I helped him. He had put the collar on backward and we had to take out the stays and collar buttons and start all over. "See what I mean?" he groaned. "I don't want to be a star."

But he *was*. Thousands of people fought for his autograph, three girls got trampled in the street and it took 25 policemen to keep the uninvited public behind the barricades when his limousine drove up on opening night. Not only did he meet Her Majesty the Queen and Prince Philip, Duke of Edinburgh, but Prince Charles showed up too, with a nod to his tutor for giving him the night off. It was a royal flush. The stars and movie magnates formed a circle while more than a thousand people sat in their expensive seats and watched the whole thing on closed-circuit television. Without my help, a last-minute crisis had arisen to get Leonard into his rented suit and it had taken three hours to get Olivia into the apricot-colored silk gown designed especially for the occasion by Zeffirelli himself, made in one week by Capucci and flown in from Florence. But they looked like the stars of the evening.

Prince Charles talked to them so long the Queen had to send Prince Philip to tell him to "Get a move on." "I think I'm being left behind," he said, bowing deeply to Juliet, who giggled. Then with the pomp and monstrous circumstance reserved only for crowns and legends, the orchestra played "God Save the Queen" and everyone bowed and curtsied once more and the stars were led backstage to be presented to the entire audience. Leonard was all fingers. "How does that music go again? Are we supposed to come out right after Danny Kaye or what?" "Don't be silly, I'll tell you," said Olivia, shoving him into the spotlight.

Although some sourpuss movie critics had a few harsh words to say in the next morning's newspapers (How dare an Italian tell the British how to jazz up Shakespeare?) it was a night when nobody cared about critics. It was Romeo and Juliet's night. Women cried, men patted them on the back, they shook about a million hands and at 2 A.M., when everybody else started turning into pumpkins, they stood in the middle of a lavish crystal ballroom at Claridge's holding the magic as long as they could. Dazzling under the chandeliers like uncut diamonds, Romeo pulled off his tie, tore off that damnable collar, and lit into his third *soufflé glacé grand marnier*, and Juliet kicked off her slippers, stepped all over the train of her Capucci grown, and thrashed away with Prince Charles, heir to the throne of England, in one last sweaty Funky Broadway.

. . . *and they all lived happily ever after.*

Patty Duke

Two P.M. on a Sunday afternoon. One of those glass cages overlooking the noise and smoke of midtown Manhattan the people at the Hilton call a hotel room. José Feliciano is playing quiet guitar clusters on the phonograph and Patty Duke, ex-child star, is smoking a cigarette and eating scrambled eggs in her bare feet. (Her name used to be Anna Marie Duke from Elmhurst, Queens, but when Patty McCormick, another ex-child star, made a splash in *The Bad Seed,* some bright, forgotten child-star manager cashed in on the name and changed it to Patty. Now nobody knows what happened to Patty McCormick, but it's been Patty Duke ever since.) She is 21 years old now, and no longer *feels* like a Patty, but they won't let her forget. She asks people to call her Pat, and when they slip she makes little frowns that turn her nose up like a half-nibbled gingersnap. She has been in New York for several months, starring in a movie called *Me, Natalie,* directed by Fred Coe, who produced her greatest triumph, *The Miracle Worker,* and the strain shows. Her mother is in the next room packing her things and in a few hours she'll be on a plane back to Hollywood. She is very blue and her eyes are red from crying.

She rests her feet on top of a child's Funny Mooners game and stares at the smoke ring her cigarette makes as it curls in the air. "I've had no sleep for four days. I'm black and blue from doing all my own stunts in the picture. I rode my own motorcycle and even jumped into the East River in one funny suicide attempt scene. They made me take a bath when I got out. I guess they were afraid I'd get the clap or something."

The words sound tough coming from the candy-box bow-ribbon mouth of a girl who still looks young enough to pay half-price at Radio City. But the girl in the pony tail is also a veteran of 15 years in show business, and the survivor of: a personal private life that reads like *Elsie Dinsmore,* a miscarriage, an unhappy marriage that is now ending after three years, and a career that has been a constant battle between a frightened young woman and a public which has always treated her like a midget with vitamins. One interviewer called her "Little Miss Sewer Mouth" and she cried for three days. She does come on like a pint-sized Jimmy Cagney, but stick around and you can hear the heartbeats. It's the only way people will listen. When she was a kid, all her interviews were conducted on sheets of mimeographed paper with stock answers. If anyone asked how it felt to be a child star, she would turn to Answer Number 40. Like that. But on this particular day, in this particular hotel room, Patty can take care of herself. "I've been knocked down before. I always get up again. All I want now is some peace and dignity in my life. I'm just not going to be hurt any more by what people write about me. Like my divorce. If they want to insinuate it was anything but incompatibility, then let them. I was looking for a father. I've been looking for a father all my life and now it's time I stood on my own two feet."

She means it. All her life she was coddled, pampered, told how talented she was. Her father was an elegant but sad man, a cab driver, who sought refuge from reality in a bottle. He left her mother when Patty was six, creating a void in her life that has never been filled. Patty was "discovered" at seven by the John Rosses, a husband-wife manager team with no children of their own, who dressed, fed and exploited her, and although she is not ungrateful for the star they pinned on her door, a certain bitterness creeps through when she talks about her childhood. While all the other kids were playing kick-the-can, Patty was walking up and down Madison Avenue looking for tooth-paste commercials. She can still feel the phony smiles she was forced to smile when her tight Mary Jane shoes bit into her feet and the way the starched organdy petticoats chapped her legs and thighs.

When she was nine, Walter Pidgeon bought her "my first good piece of jewelry—a little gold turtle in a gold clasp at Tiffany's." Before she was 12, she had already played opposite Kim Stanley, Helen Hayes and Laurence Olivier. By the time she got the role of Helen Keller in *The Miracle Worker*, she had already starred in more than 50 television shows. There was no time for hopscotch. Her days were filled with diction lessons, singing lessons, drama school, making the rounds of casting offices. While the other kids on her block learned arithmetic, Patty learned how to reach the last row in the balcony by crying real tears. Fifteen months before *Miracle Worker* was produced on Broadway, the Rosses taught her to *be* Helen Keller. She read books about her, she lay on the ground in Central Park with her eyes closed and felt the grass grow. She went to school with her eyes closed, bumping into walls. They taught her deafness "games" for hours on end. "Patty, would you like a Coke?" If she answered, she lost; if she showed no emotion, she won. She got the part and played it for two years, going to work every night on the subway and riding home in a taxi. She never got a vacation. Sometimes if she was good, she got to pack a steak and have a picnic under the George Washington Bridge. By the time the movie version was made, in an old house in Pleasantville, New Jersey, Pleasantville was the farthest she'd ever been from home.

Patty's father came to the matinees, but he stood in

the back of the theater and watched. She didn't know it at the time, but he had been forbidden by law to see her. All she knew was she had a father somewhere and she wanted him with her. One of the fan magazines ran a contest: "Patty Duke Cries Herself to Sleep Every Night! Find Patty Duke's Father!" They did. In the next issue, they published a photograph of his tombstone. "I could have helped him. There's so much I could have done, but I never knew he was there. I blamed myself and grew so insecure I took everything as a personal rejection. I would cry and cry because I thought I had failed these people who took care of me. Can you imagine what that's like to a child? It's a miracle I'm not in a nut house!"

And the world heaped praise on her tiny shoulders. Walter Kerr wrote that she was a "very great actress who only happens, at the moment, to also be a child." At 16, she won an Academy Award. Where does a child star go from there? Patty went into her own successful TV series, "The Patty Duke Show," which she hated. She was playing the all-American teenager, but inside her head terrible things were happening. "I wanted to grow up, function for myself. It was time my personal life caught up with my professional one. I was working like an adult, with none of the advantages. I couldn't go to any of the parties because nobody was supposed to see the little shrimp smoke or drink. I didn't have any friends, because I had never been to regular school except on the set. Most kids take stands, and fall on their tails. I had missed even that and I was eager to have some kind of life for myself, for *me*, Patty." Summoning all the strength in her mini-frame, she fired her managers and, knowing nothing of the world outside their protective wings, declared her Independence Day. "I heard Suzanne Pleshette mention a building in Hollywood where bachelor girls could live without fear of being raped, so I moved in there. I had wanted a garret, but I ended up paying $500 a month with a doorman. My plan kind of backfired."

Director Harry Falk had first met her when she was 8 years old. Years later, he showed up in California directing her on her own series at a time when she was going through an emotional crisis. She had learned the truth about her father and was no longer on close terms with her family. She was 18 and still fighting the battle of the eternal teenager. After living with her managers for 10 years, she had moved out on her own and was lonely. He was divorced and experienced. To the horror of her advisors, she married him and retired for a while. "I had decided to sink or swim and I was sinking. I felt emotionally unequipped to take care of a man. I had worked all my life as a kid actor, then suddenly I wasn't one anymore. I was married and a homemaker. It was what I chose, yet I didn't know how to be one. I didn't even know how to cook. I wasn't holding up my end of the bargain and I needed someone to talk to. So I went to a psychiatrist. That took guts, but I'm glad I went. It's nothing to be ashamed of. If you break a toe, you go to a doctor, right? So if you have something wrong in your head, you gotta get help or it gets worse. Analysis is a lot better than pills. I learned where my problems were coming from. As a kid, I had days when I did nothing but cry for nine hours straight. If I blew a line, I worried that people wouldn't like me. It was that fantastic drive to be liked because I was so insecure. Hell, I was just a child, for God's sake, and what do kids know? They just want to be accepted and liked by everybody. Analysis taught me to laugh. When I was a child I wasn't impressed by anybody. The only person I ever met who impressed me was John F. Kennedy. Now I have more compassion for people. I don't have such a high opinion of *me* anymore, because I have more important things to work out than the drive to succeed.

"I was very poor when I was little and if I hadn't become a child star I don't know what I would have been. I might have turned into a prostitute or something. But that one-track mind that used to demand attention isn't so important anymore. I don't need the love of everybody. Judy Garland doesn't have to worry about me. I'm not going to take over the Palace. I have learned that the public needs a dream, a fantasy idol to bring them out of their problems. You've gotta protect yourself, or you'll become a Frankenstein. That's why I did *Valley of the Dolls,* to change the image the public had of me as the little kid in pigtails. I changed my walk. I penciled red on the bottom of my eyelids until it ran into my eyes and they were bloodshot. I had to eat pills all through the movie. They were filled with powdered sugar and I washed them down with booze that was really Coke and watered-down tea. They were so fattening I gained 20 pounds. I went to bars and watched confused, tormented people full of self-pity and wondered how they got to be that way. I really thought it would work."

Somehow it didn't. *Valley of the Dolls* was an unmitigated disaster so total it almost destroyed her reputation as a quality actress and netted her some nasty publicity as well. When audiences saw little all-American Patty Duke playing a ravaged, alcoholic, drug-addicted Hollywood vampire pushing aside autograph hounds, sleeping with homosexuals, falling into ashcans, waking up with strangers in waterfront dives, washing down overdoses of pills with stale beer, and ending up in an asylum in a straitjacket, they roared. When she talks about it, her eyes fill with tears. "It was garbage. In spite of the publicity, all three of the girls liked each other, but we knew something was wrong. Our communication as friends was not allowed to continue on the set. We got no direction. An actor can't go out there alone and make a movie. I don't know any actor who doesn't need a director. We were flying blind, in a fog. We were never even told from one scene to the next how long it had been since the characters had even *seen* each other. I was miscast, I admit it. I thought I could play that girl, I really did. Not from my own experience, but from what I knew about life. I played Helen Keller too, but I was never deaf, dumb or blind. But they changed everything in the book. I had to go from 17 to 46, which was physically impossible. They made me look like Tugboat Annie and every time I complained, they said, 'It's funny. Just *do* it.' Well, it wasn't supposed to be funny. In fantasy you can do anything. Walt Disney got away with murder. But if you're going to make a movie about *people*, you've got to touch on reality. When I pulled Susan Hayward's wig off, that was supposed to be very sad. Jackie Susann never wrote it to be funny. When I saw it, there was the most marvelous roar of hysterical laughter I ever heard in my life and I wanted to die from embarrassment. I had just come out of the hospital after losing my baby, and I was very depressed, so Harry thought it would give me a lift to see the film. Everybody said I was so magnificent in it. Hah! Another trap. I believed them. That was Mistake Number 990,000-B. Next time, in my head, I'm going to say, '*I'll* be the judge of that.' I needed an air-sickbag to sit through that movie."

Me, Natalie, she says with pride, is the best movie she has ever made. "It's about me, really. A girl my age, an ugly duckling, who leaves Brooklyn and moves to the Village and falls in love. It taught me I have only scratched the surface of what I can do if I try. *Valley* was rotten, this is just the opposite. I don't care if nobody likes it, I know it's the best work I've ever done. I didn't have Harry or anyone to lean on. This was solo. After *Valley* I went into such a depression that the marriage just wasn't working at all, so I came to New York and moved into an apartment on East 67th Street next to the Cuban Embassy. I didn't even need an alarm clock to wake me up. A bomb went off every morning at four o'clock. I finally moved to this hotel to get some sleep, but I haven't had any. You know what I've been doing? I went to see my mother again and we've been staying up all night talking, trying to erase all the misunderstandings. I understand about my father now and why they kept him from seeing me. I've found my family again."

She brings out snapshots of her brother Ray and her sister Carol and a dozen smiling, healthy babies, including one of herself, naked as a jaybird on a fur rug. "This is me—little Anna Marie, before anyone ever heard of Patty Duke. And this is my mother's wedding dress, which I'm taking back to California. It fits me perfectly. And this is Old Friend, my doll I've had all my life." Old Friend's fingers had been chewed off by some longago child and Patty squeezed it so hard it would have yelled if it had not already lost its voice in some faraway backstage dressing room. "It's wrong to carry grudges against people for what your life has been. I refuse to say 'Mea culpa!' and blame things on Mama or Daddy or the Rosses. Annie Sullivan said, 'No pity! I won't have it!' I heard Anne Bancroft say it every night for two years straight in *The Miracle Worker* and I've never forgotten it. I may in my actions ask for pity, but I don't want it. At 21 pushing 22, I'm the same size I always was. My name is still Anna Marie Duke, I'm still trying to find the same answers to the same questions as everyone else in the world. If I was Anna Marie Duke the telephone operator, not written about in *The New York Times* or photographed with Helen Keller in *Life*, nobody could care less except the people directly involved. I don't regret being Patty Duke the actress. I'm only ashamed that so many people have been forced to share my problems with me. But the marvelous thing is they also got to share an experience with a 16-year-old girl winning an Academy Award. They got to share the highs, too."

She picks up the script from *Me, Natalie* and begins to read. "In the last scene, she leaves the boy she loves to go out and find her own life. She says, 'Maybe I'll be miserable, maybe tomorrow I'll be happy. But it'll be *my* miserable, *my* happy. Because I'm *me*, Natalie.' Fact-wise,

I only know two things—you're born and you die. What happens in-between is up to you. Nobody's there with you when you're born and nobody crawls into that box with you when they bury you. You can't fail unless you try. I've blown it many times, but my track record is pretty good. From now on, it's going to be *me, Patty,* and I'm going to live that in-between part to the fullest of my capabilities. Some people may call that a threat, but I call it a promise."

Her mother had finished packing and it was time to catch the plane back to—what? Her husband had moved away and her nine-room colonial house on the same street as "Pickfair" would be empty. But there was a life to work out, and Patty Duke was sure as hell going to find a way. The limousine was waiting, so she hugged her mother, who was crying in her mink stole, and still looking small and vulnerable for such a tough little girl, said goodbye. She was still holding her doll when the door closed.

Malibu

"Malibu," says one sage who has lived there for 18 years, "is the place where you lie on the sand and look at the stars—or vice versa."

It's not a city or a town or even a village, although it has a post office, a sheriff and a weekly newspaper published on green paper. You can't walk around the block in Malibu, because there isn't a block to walk around. There isn't even a movie house. Yet if you want to see movie stars, stay out of the Brown Derby. They're all at Malibu.

Picture a lazy dinosaur lying on its side in the noonday sun, and you get an idea of what it looks like on the map—a tiny slash of California coastline, 26 miles long and half a mile wide, spread like mayonnaise over 20,000 acres of sand, surf, canyons, rocks and rattlesnake dens, and stretched in Technicolor over a fabric of terrain being crowded out to sea by a sweaty, smoggy collage of hick towns connected by freeways called Los Angeles. At first glance, Malibu looks like a place to drive through fast. A tiny Vegas-like strip of liquor stores and tacoburger stands threatened daily with extinction by the violent mudslides which come crashing down from the Pacific Palisades every time it rains. For nine months of the year, this ugly little collection of motels and empty Coke bottles looks like any other boring retirement center marked by a bright flag on a Medicare map. Then comes June, when it all starts happening. The movie stars and jet-set buddhas pack up their sneakers, their cocoanut oil, their martini mixers, their poodles and the kids from all their previous marriages, and head for the sea, descending on Malibu like sand crabs in their blue jeans and their Yves St. Laurent chain belts. Then, for as long as the summer sun lasts, they get stoned on pot, barbecue everything but the delivery boys from Western Union, and work like hell to make their summer rent money pay off.

It's hard to figure out why. There's no entertainment (except what goes on in the homes, and considering some of the scenes I've seen staged in Malibu, I'd say all the Oscars are going to the wrong people). There isn't one good restaurant worth eating in. Unless you subscribe to a cable service, the barrier formed between Los Angeles and the oceanfront by the Pacific Palisades cliffs and the Malibu Canyon makes TV reception impossible. The water tastes like a combination of mineral oil and sulfuric acid. Every time you leave home there is the danger that when you return your beach house will either be buried under a rock slide, demolished by one of the several earthquakes which reliably occur each summer, or washed out to sea by the tide which rises higher each year, taking part of the beachfront back into the ocean with it.

And still they come. According to the Malibu sheriff's office, 14,000 strangers crowd into the place each summer like Ringling Brothers clowns in a two-seater Volkswagen, braving the elements and hardships for a whiff of air they can breathe without fear of lung collapse. None of them have anything in common, except that (1) they hate the smog of L.A., and (2) they love the sea. It's enough. Dentists go scuba diving with starving actors. Angela Lansbury's kids run up and down the beach drinking Fresca and digging for mussels with the kids of an Akron tire manufacturer. Surfniks and rock singers fry fish in a nest of water pilings while Warren Beatty and Julie Christie watch them, hand in hand, from the Malibu pier. Class barriers are down. Everybody's equal. Nobody says don't. All of them taking their bite out of this tranquilizer made of sand, for the price of a summer.

I was there, for three months, last year. I had writing to do—a weekly column, some film reviews, a screenplay which never materialized—and Malibu seemed like the place to do it quietly. New York's claustrophobia and heat were getting to me. I wanted a cool place, away from everything familiar, but not so far away that all the newspapers would be written in French. So I found a house on a slice of Malibu beach, a funny comic-strip house the color of lettuce, built Frank Lloyd Wright-style out of the bottom half of a London bus. The kitchen had a "No Smoking" sign and a series of hand straps along the ceiling, from which passengers held their balance years ago as they jogged along Piccadilly Circus. A winding metal staircase rose near the old conductor platform to a second-floor bedroom lined with wooden shutters; a collapsible door opened out onto a spacious brick terrace kissed with the scent of a labyrinth of cabbage roses and geraniums, beyond which the crashing surf splashed the cobalt blue sky as far as the eye could see. Anywhere else in the world, I would probably have felt like I was living in a double-decker house trailer, but in Malibu, where nothing much makes sense anyway, it seemed perfect.

The summer frittered away there, in an endless pattern of word pictures which, thinking back, now bounce off my mind like raindrops on glass. I remember the garbage collectors, hippies and wild men, with the sun and salt air in their eyes, picking up champagne bottles along the beach from the exclusive party where Nureyev taught Streisand how to dance the night before, then clanging off down the highway in their flower-power trucks painted with McCarthy stickers. Malibu must be the nicest place in the world to be a garbage collector. I remember the dregs of marijuana left by the cops who used to hide out under the Malibu Pier and turn on with the yippies from time to time. Pot is no big deal in Malibu. It's as much a part of life there as getting used to the sound of the waves breaking against the rocks when you go to sleep.

And, of course, I remember the parties. If Los Angeles has what Phyllis Diller calls "a cesspool of culture," it probably empties somewhere in the vicinity of Malibu. Afternoons, over at Jacqueline Bisset's house, soaking up gin in the orange Sunday sun while Mia Farrow played in the traffic. Or sitting on crude, whitewashed sailor chairs at writer John Hallowell's, listening to Melina Mercouri debate Paul Newman on American politics ("Hélas, le's have ze Nixon; then we have ze disaster much sooner and we can start all over again!"); or watching Natalie Wood sparkling like ginger ale under a pink straw hat. Dark coming on, and moving indoors where, on a slow, calculated glide through the candlelight you could catch Christopher Isherwood in a rare moment of candor, telling Patty Duke about pre-war Berlin and the *real* Sally Bowles; Vincente Minnelli describing how he filmed Judy Garland on that trolley; Angela Lansbury telling us all she'd remake *Harlow*, only this time *she'd* play Harlow. Or moving down the beach to the warm, hearthside glow of Barbara Rush's house, where Joanne Woodward confessed over homemade peach ice cream that she took her kids out of school the day she discovered Debbie Reynolds was head of the Girl Scouts. Or the afternoon playwright Jerome Lawrence, who has written almost all of his Broadway successes in Malibu, threw a party for Ingrid Bergman—50 and beautiful, without makeup, hair in an unstylish pony tail, wearing a two-piece bathing suit, she swam three times, clapped her hands, and joyously proclaimed, rising from the sudsy cold water, "Malibu? It's the only part of California that hasn't changed in 20 years. Smog and housing developments have taken over the rest."

Physically, Malibu seems as resistant to any claim on history as everything else in teeny-bopper-conscious Southern California. The minute something shows its age, the wrecking crew moves in. Yet Malibu does have a history, as offbeat and kooky as the people who live there. It was discovered on October 9, 1542, by Juan Rodriguez Cabrillo, the Christopher Columbus of the West Coast, who sailed into the bay accidentally, searching for fresh water. Inhabited only by naked Indians who lived on raw fish and called themselves the "Maliboux," the vast Malibu domain was claimed by Cabrillo in the name of the Spanish crown. A princely jawbone of shoreline, Malibu was composed of forbidding mountains, beaches, mesas and hidden valleys—a pristine land of mystery and romance which quickly became the Cornwall of America. At one time a dozen rum ships operated in the secretly guarded coves off Point Dume, which is now the hippie necking ground. Rum-runners drove officers to cover in constant gun battles off the Castle Rock coast. Horse thieves, smugglers and predatory bootleggers operated along the Malibu cliffs. There is one spot, near Carol Channing's house, called La Chusa ("the Owl") Canyon, named after a lady pirate who lived in a cave and terrorized the entire Malibu coast for years. There are so many tales of stolen treasure buried in the Malibu hills by "the Owl" and her band of cutthroats that even today the county of Los Angeles posts armed guards in the area to ward off treasure hunters.

The first recorded date of the original Malibu land grant is 1805, when the king of Spain turned it over to a man named Don José Tapia as a reward for military services. In 1824, Tapia's property passed into the hands of his go-getter son, Don Tiburcio, who, according to legend, buried several chests of hard cash in Malibu which have yet to be discovered. He died unexpectedly in 1845 and three years later the last of the Tapia descendants deeded Malibu to Leon Prudhomme, a Frenchman, for $400, half of which was paid in groceries and wine. Prudhomme sold it again in 1857 to Don Mateo Keller, a leader in the California wine industry, whose heirs sold the property for $10 an acre to Frederick Hastings Rindge and his wife May in 1892.

The real history of Malibu as it is known today begins with the Rindge family. It is a history as bloody as any movie Hollywood ever filmed. Whereas Malibu had always been ruled by wild and unruly Spaniards and pirates, Rindge was a Harvard man, raised in an atmosphere of Cambridge wealth. He was an unrelenting foe of Demon Rum, a devout leader in the Methodist Church and a close pal of Teddy Roosevelt's who was ruled by a mind bent on keeping the railroad out of Malibu. After his death in 1905 at the age of 42, his wife May took over his six-guns and became known as the "Queen of the Malibu." Her armed vaqueros patrolled the vast rancho, creating a barrier along the coastal route to San Francisco that cut off trade and aroused the fury of Los Angeles merchants. Stories abound in Malibu of the traders and railroad barons murdered in the Malibu canyons by the Queen's henchmen, hired to protect Malibu against the invasion of commerce and industry.

In the bitter end, the fight to barricade the wild Malibu frontier against the forces of progress brought financial ruin to the Rindge estate and feudalism crumbled as the courts established a right-of-way for the railroad through the Malibu territory under the law of eminent domain. Instead of the million dollars May Rindge asked from the government for damages, California gave her a drop in the bucket of little more than $100,000. Before the Depression, the Rindge estate in Malibu was worth $100 million. By 1938 it was bankrupt. But even this debacle didn't dampen May's spirit. She was a game girl. In her last days she constructed a magnificent castle on a hill behind the Malibu Creek, where she lived in seclusion until she died. Later it was sold to the Franciscan monks for $50,000 and now it is used as a monastic retreat for tired businessmen. It's a different world up there near the castle. On a clear day free of smog, you can even see a Basque shepherd tending his flocks, untouched by time or the Hollywood aura which has permeated the world below.

Under the revised bankruptcy laws of the 1930's, the Rindge fortunes showed promise of rebuilding. War industry helped real estate. The state of California acquired large sections of beach foreshore for parks. Crossroad settlements, business districts and private enterprises sprang up out of sand. Mansions and smaller, chic beach cottages are now scattered in profusion along the 26 miles of Malibu, resting indolently against indigo slopes. All the fears of the Rindge dynasty have finally come true, although they never lived to see the transformation of their wilderness into an oceanside panorama. In one respect, however, the Rindge ghosts have had the last laugh on progress. You still can't get a train to Malibu. Nothing stops there.

Nobody seems quite certain where Malibu begins. Some folks will tell you to drive out Sunset Boulevard until it runs right into the Pacific Ocean and that's the starting place. Others insist you can smell the difference when you pass Ted's Rancho, a glass restaurant overlooking the ocean near the official "Welcome to Malibu" sign. But no matter how you find the place, you will never find two people who will give you the same tour when you get there. Most of them say there's nothing to see anyway; I disagree.

My personally guided tour begins, if we cheat a little,

farther down the coast near the Santa Monica Pier. This is the best starting point to catch the Malibu montage in all of its flavors, all of its history, and all of its fickle moods. Here, witness a scene right out of *Inside Daisy Clover*. Roman Polanski and Sharon Tate are in The Boathouse picking at their lobster and grog. Girls red as sugar beets hang around outside Clara's Café smelling of Bain de Soleil, and eating 25-cent hot dogs on a stick. Doreena ("Psychic Clairvoyant— Tarot Cards and Palmistry!") leans against her awning peeling in the sun rays and munching boardwalk cotton candy in her gingham apron and Spanish coin earrings. Maria Ouspenskaya, Sixties style. Pass the shooting galleries, the only penny arcade in the world where you can still get an autographed picture of Fatty Arbuckle, push on past the Plush Ball 'n' Cue Billiard Parlor and the Cocky Moon Burrito Stand, and look out over the bodies crumpled on the dirty sand like broken potato chips, all the way up to the old red frame of Synanon, where the addicts insist on being called "dope fiends" and Jennifer Jones sells candy bars in the concession stand.

Memories begin. Drive up the coast toward Malibu proper, along the Palisades cliffs, and it is possible, on a night as blue and dark as a sailor's middy, to conjure up a nostalgia for what it used to be like. Along the beach the once-famous casinos and bawdy houses once stood, where Mickey Cohen and Bugsy Siegel and Good Time Charley Crawford played and gambled their lives away. The famous Hollywood roadhouses are all boarded up now; "the Gold Coast" they used to call it. Mae West still lives here, and Darryl F. Zanuck. Jennifer Jones has a Spanish style house with "No Parking" signs to keep away the surfers and beach bums.

The sumptuous $1,750,000 beach house William Randolph Hearst built for Marion Davies has been torn down and turned into a parking lot, but old-timers still talk about it: Grinling Gibbons, England's distinguished carver of decorative woods, executed the interiors. Special woods from India, carvings from the Metropolitan Museum in New York, original and hand-blocked wallpaper, and a 6½-month gold-leaf covering job taken from the bedroom of the Earl of Sussex in

1740 were just a few of the movie crowd's playtoys. There was also a banquet room, with $30,000 worth of paneled hardwood reassembled from the Georgian house of Eleanor, Duchess of Northumberland; a marble swimming pool; a Rathskellar from a 16th-century inn in Surrey; a $90,000 dining room; priceless mantels, Tudor paintings, Wedgewood medallions, and a tiled swimming pool crossed by a Venetian bridge of Vermont marble. Like most of the vulgar grandeur which typified Hollywood in the era when it was still unique enough to be amusing, the house has been torn down and washed into the sea, no more of a monument to the glory that once was Rome than the old Mocambo or Ciro's. The guest house at the northern end of the property is, however, still visible through white locked gates. Its shadowy rooms, where John Gilbert drank champagne from Clara Bow's shoes while the rest of the world went silently mad with ecstasy, have been turned into a private beach club. Hundreds of reputations remain secure forever; the ocean can't talk.

Not far away, a ghostly ruin stands hugging the cliffs like something out of an old Karloff film. This was the scene of one of Hollywood's famous unsolved mysteries, the 1935 murder of Thelma Todd. Thelma was the movies' angel-faced golden girl, and in private life the proprietress of a roadhouse called Thelma Todd's Sidewalk Cafe, on top of which she also shared an apartment with her partner, movie director Roland West. At the time of her death, Thelma had a year to go on a Hal Roach contract and no money worries. Yet she was found dead on a hilltop 270 steps from her house in her chocolate-colored Phaeton, wearing a $20,000 mink coat, diamonds on her throat and wrists, and a mauve and silver evening gown.

Thelma was divorced from a handsome Hollywood agent named Pat de Cicco. She had been expected to meet him at a party that Saturday night at the Trocadero, yet because post mortem investigation revealed she had eaten food not served at the Trocadero, it appeared she had eaten after arriving home Sunday morning. Her body was not found until Monday morning at 10:30. Nobody had noticed her absence all day Sunday, while she lay dead in the parked auto. She had not entered her own apartment after arriving home, so where had she eaten, and with whom? All the famous stars in Hollywood were dragged into the case. The police said she died from monoxide poisoning. The case seemed closed. Then suddenly Mrs. Wallace Ford, wife of the late actor, announced she had been awakened by a mysterious phone call from Thelma—12 hours *after* the time of death!

The case has never been solved and to this day the Sidewalk Café stands boarded up just the way Thelma left it. It is supposed to be haunted and if, on some midnight drive under a citrus moon, you look up at the broken windows overlooking the eerie rushing sound of the surf, you can almost swear ghostly figures from beyond the grave are moving about behind the dusty panes of forgotten glass.

After you pass the foot of Sunset Boulevard, start looking for a bizarre, Arthurian-looking castle spire, rising up above the cliffs like a sentinel, guarding the J. Paul Getty museum. Most tourists (and many residents) think this castle is the Getty mansion. Not true. A millionaire built the castle for his wife in 1929 as a surprise, but she died on the train to California. Then the stock market crashed. The millionaire committed suicide and the house lay dormant until Aly Khan married Rita Hayworth, reigning glamour goddess of the Forties, and found the white elephant for a beach retreat. By the time the prince was ready to move in, Gilda had already done a retreat of her own—in a different direction—and they never lived there. Now everyone calls this spooky remnant of Hollywood's ridiculous past "Rita's Back Aly."

Down below, hidden behind iron gates, is the eccentric J. Paul Getty's private museum, which goes unnoticed by the thousands of beachgoers who motor past it each day on their way to the Malibu sun. By appointment only, you can visit this curiosity on Wednesdays and Saturdays only at 2 P.M. After a burly guard right out of a prison-break movie checks off your name, you can park near a kennel housing two vicious, snarling watchdogs and proceed by foot into a courtyard with a sculptured fountain. A guide takes you through three major areas: classical sculpture (mostly Roman copies of Greek originals dating from the 5th century B.C.); French decorative arts of the 18th century; and Italian and Dutch paintings of the 15th to 17th centuries, both Renaissance and Baroque. The museum is housed in Mr. Getty's former home, but he has never seen it. "For the past 17 years, Mr. Getty has said that he was coming back next month. So far he hasn't," sighs the guard. Then, at 4 P.M., he rushes you past a Landsdowne Hercules from Hadrian's villa at Tivoli which looks suspiciously like a bust of Elvis Presley, and you have to leave the premises. Otherwise, you get locked in with the snarling watchdogs.

On up the beach, notice a peculiar white clapboard establishment right out of John Steinbeck, jutting out over the water which, to avoid trouble, I'll call the "Ancient Mariner." During the entire three months I lived in Malibu, nobody was ever able to tell me what went on inside this strange and awesome place, but half the residents think it is a bawdy house and the other half seem certain it's some kind of boarding house for beachboys. It is advertised as a restaurant, although nobody ever eats there and business is actually discouraged. (A hamburger costs $3.50.) There are never any cars parked in front of the place, yet it is crawling with blond, sun-licked, Man-Tanned Troy Donahue types. One night, out of a curiosity which was threatening to get out of hand, I drove up to the place and walked in. A rouged woman in her 70's (something like the part Jo Van Fleet played in *East of Eden*) stopped me at the door before I even got a foot inside. "We're closed, babe," she rasped, pushing me outside and turning off her neon sign. Later I learned she was the owner. One morning a week her purple Cadillac filled with beachboys drives into Los Angeles and drops them off on Wilshire Boulevard. The same Cadillac picks them up again at sundown. It's the talk of the beach.

Nearing the Malibu Pier, you'll pass a great cleft in the chin of the coastline near Louis (*The Count of Monte Crisco*) Hayward's house where Doris Day goes to meditate. It's called Meditation Point. A private road veers to the right, leading up to the Serra Retreat. One afternoon I talked Dave Diefenderfer into driving me up toward the monastery to view the remains of the old Rindge ranch. Dave runs a real estate office at Coral Beach and looks very much like a Salvation Army Santa Claus who is up to no good. Nobody knows how old he is (Some folks in Malibu claim he was around during the Gold Rush), but a sign hangs in his window overlooking the ocean which reads: "We Know the Malibu." Believe it.

Dave angled his old Packard off the coast highway and another world opened up before my eyes, the world of the original Spanish land grants. The lemony sun shines through the white, muscular branches of imported Australian eucalyptus trees. The old Rindge dairies lie dormant, overgrown with ripe bougainvillea vines, and the orchards go untended now—fortunes in lemon groves, avocados, apricots and oranges, lost to the cruel passing of time. A few private homes are visible through the underbrush, carved out of old carriage houses, adobe barns and horse corrals. Palm trees, almond trees, flowering jacarandas and meadows of lush, wild geraniums slope gently forward toward the hills where mountain lions, rattlesnakes and wild deer roam. Sections of the old railroad bed and some of the original steel rails can be seen through the sagging trees. Houses like little seven-dwarf gingerbread cottages remain hidden in jungles of rare strawberry guavas and Mexican *sapote* trees, and, up on the rise, holly, live oaks and matilija poppies form shelters for patches of banana squash, pumpkins and watermelons. The Franciscan monks up at the old Rindge ranch eat as well as the movie stars who pull up to the hippie fruit stands on the highway, park their Bentleys and haggle over fresh tomatoes trucked in from the valley.

Movie stars have always been drawn to Malibu, but they weren't always able to get in. When Vitagraph moved west and opened its studios in 1911, the movie industry was born. William S. Hart, Sessue Hayakawa, Ruth Roland, and Marie Dressler all got as close to the beach as they could, but they couldn't get through the barbed wire into Malibu, where the Rindge vaqueros in their Mexican hats and knee-length boots were still shooting at the trains which threatened to cross their private frontier. Hollywood became the production center, but the stars all wanted to live out by the sea. Malibu, with a climate governed by the Pacific as a giant thermostat, had the edge. (On the hottest day of the year the temperature seldom rises above 80 degrees, and in the winter it seldom drops below 54.)

Then, as Los Angeles' tide of automobiles and industry began to complicate atmospheric conditions, a new word appeared in the language: "smog." The sea breezes, which keep Malibu clear of warm, polluted air, provided a natural sanctuary from the discomfort. In 1927, the famous Malibu movie colony began when May Rindge leased some land to silent screen star Anna Q. Nilsson with the promise that no alcohol would be consumed on the premises. Soon she was joined by W. C. Fields, Bebe Daniels, Greta Garbo, Norma Shearer, Tyrone Power, Cary Grant, Barbara Stanwyck, Jean Arthur, and everybody who was anybody. Elzie Segar based his Popeye comic strip there. Thomas Mann wrote novels there. The early Mack Sennett comedies were shot there. Gloria Swanson cavorted in the waves, creating the first cheesecake.

Some stars went to greater lengths for privacy. In Azuma Canyon, there is a lush hidden jungle with seven waterfalls shrouding the remains of the old Lewis Stone estate. One day in 1947, Stone, who played Judge Hardy in the Andy Hardy pictures, drove out to see Dave Diefenderfer. He wanted complete seclusion, he said. Old Dave sold him some land so remote his guests had to be lowered down on ropes from the top of a cliff. A poison ivy jungle grew like trees in a rain forest and Mrs. Stone was once in the hospital for two weeks from being exposed to her own front yard. A road now leads to the Stone ranch, but the surrounding area is still an impenetrable wilderness, impossible to reach by car.

When May Rindge first leased her land to the movie stars who saw in Malibu a retreat from life and a clamoring public, it went for $75 an acre. Today, the half-mile strip known as the Malibu Colony recently replaced Newport Beach as the most expensive real estate in America. Property goes for about $2,000 per square foot. Adam *(Batman)* West just bought a postage stamp covered with vines for $97,000 from the producer of *Catch-22*. A beach house with one bath can run $200,000 and up. Most of the houses in the famous Colony are ugly and built so close together you can borrow a cup of sugar from your neighbor without ever leaving your own kitchen. (One day I was having a drink with Carol Burnett and we heard one of her kids fall into Lana Turner's swimming pool. It was that close.) Realtors ask anything from $2,500 to $5,000 a month in rentals, and get it. They'll take a run-down shack with lopsided windows and a fence running halfway down a hill, pass it off as a "boat effect," and get whatever they ask. Hollywood lawyer Greg Bautzer found a clever little place for "only $5,000 a month"—then he had to hire the maid along with it and give the owner of the house a free trip to Hawaii to close the deal.

Lon McCallister (remember him?) was one movie hero of the Forties who knew he wouldn't last forever as an all-American idol (smart boy). So, during the war, when the whole beach was blacked out and rumors of Japanese subs sent the beach-dwellers into panic, everyone sold out and moved away except McCallister, who bought a vast house for $18,000. Today the rental alone on that house supports the ex-star and is worth more than $250,000.

And still they come, because it's all they've got. To the film stars who rush to the sea like lemmings, Malibu is a place to get away from the cameras and, as my Southern belle mother used to say, "collect one's thoughts." In Malibu, nobody stares when they see Lana Turner in the Market Basket buying Tom Collins mix in a faded pair of levis. They just smile and say, "There goes Lana Turner buying Tom Collins mix in a faded pair of levis." Because the Pacific Coast Highway, Malibu's main street, is an extension of the Santa Monica Freeway leading into the coastal Highway One to San Francisco, they can also turn their Jags and XKE's south and be at MGM in 15 minutes, or as far away as Warners-Seven Arts in the San Fernando Valley in half an hour. It's one of the few sanctuaries in this crowded world where you can escape from the pressures of the workaday world and still be part of the action.

To the retired businessman from Pomona, Malibu is a respite overlooking the sea, where the crash of the waves tells the time of day because nobody has yet figured out a reason why any of the clocks should work there. And to the surfers, it's a place to ride the curls at Surfriders, near the pier, and smoke a little pot without getting busted. Serious California smokers avoid Hollywood, where the fuzz is always out trying to crack down on the hippies, and head for the private beaches where anything goes. A house-to-house survey of the swank beach houses along the Malibu coastline would probably yield enough foliage—from simple Mary Jane to exotic peyote—to start a national forest. One movie star told me she returned to her home in Malibu after wintering in Palm Springs to find her garden overgrown with the stuff. When she went into the kitchen to make some hollandaise sauce, her teenage kids even had the blender turned to "medium," grinding up the stalks. Ah, Malibu . . .

I remember it all. Carol Channing, munching organic frog's legs from a Mason jar and riding her private elevator down the side of a cliff to the lap of the sea. Ron Buck, owner of Hollywood's "in" hangout, The Factory, teaching his young children how to fish. An 87-year-old salesman for Singer sewing machines who has had five wives, sitting on the sand to wrap his racing forms in old newspapers. Paradise Cove, an isolated spot where they make nudie movies at night. The TV repairman who hands out glossy 8x10 photos of his surf-champ son, hoping each new customer will be somebody important enough to get his kid into the movies. Laurence Harvey out on the highway at high noon, just waking up from the night before, with the sea breeze whipping his silk Japanese kimono about his naked legs as he washes off the windshield of his English touring car. And a funny, floppy dog named Bilbo, who appeared to be a hybrid mixture of half New Zealand sheep dog and half wharf-rat. Bilbo had an amusing, inquisitive face and two ears that had been chewed on by battalions of larger dogs for more years than anyone could count. He didn't belong to anybody, but lived at all the houses on the beach, like a mascot, helping himself to whatever was cooking on everyone's barbecue grill and nipping at the girls in their Helen Rose bikinis. Actually, I think Bilbo was obviously smarter than anyone gave him credit for being.

Eventually, I said goodbye to all that. I got tired of being awakened at daybreak by the Hell's Angels roaring up the highway each morning in a nauseous film of gasoline and body odor, on their noisy way to God knows what unspeakable ritualistic horror up the road. I lost a taste for the car accidents outside my window, especially after the afternoon I dragged a bleeding high-school junior from a burning Porsche. I got tired of eating barbecue and buying bottled water every time I wanted a drink, and cleaning off the windshield every time I had to drive into town (The salt air from the ocean, mixed with the dust from the canyons and the highway, cover the windshields at Malibu with a never-ending slime which makes driving there a hazard and a visit to one of Los Angeles' 750 car washes a daily requirement). Somehow it dawned on me that I was spending all my time watching the pelicans and getting no work done, and I suppose that's when I made my decision to leave. Summer ended, and so did my affair with the creamy lethargy which, in Malibu, becomes an atmospheric condition.

But on nights like tonight, as I gaze from my window at the dirty snow dropping like fallout on Central Park in the middle of winter, I remember those evenings in August, when the moon rises early in Malibu, full and jolly like a pumpkin pie, and shares the sky with the sagging sun before it sinks into the sea. Side by side, the moon and the sun light the last bronze surfers of the day, riding the last hanger-on waves, lined up like lizards on their flat-stomached boards, being lifted and carried abreast into the silver curve of coastline that is Malibu at nightfall. And I know that Old Dave Diefenderfer was right. "Malibu," he said, "is not so much a place to live, as it is a way of life."

I loved it.

I hated it.

I'll be back . . .